Words and Arms:
A Dictionary of Security
and Defense Terms

Other Titles of Interest

About the Book and Authors

Words and Arms:
A Dictionary of Security and Defense Terms
With Supplementary Data
Wolfram F. Hanrieder and Larry V. Buel

This comprehensive dictionary of terms frequently used in discussions of national security and defense policy contains approximately 800 entries on weapons systems, strategy concepts, military organization, and related items. Part 2 presents a more extensive treatment of such concepts as strategic force doctrine and deployment, Soviet and U.S. policies regarding the employment of tactical nuclear weapons, guidelines for assessing the Soviet-U.S. military balance, and the structure and function of U.S. general purpose forces. Part 3 contains tables, charts, and statistics on the performance of U.S. and Soviet missiles and aircraft; quantifications of the Soviet-U.S. strategic balance; comparative statistics for U.S. and Soviet defense activities; and tables on arms control agreements and related items.

Wolfram F. Hanrieder is professor in the Department of Political Science at the University of California at Santa Barbara. He is currently visiting professor at the Johns Hopkins University School of Advanced International Studies in Bologna, Italy. Larry V. Buel is a UCLA Foundation Graduate Fellow.

Words and Arms: A Dictionary of Security and Defense Terms

With Supplementary Data

Wolfram F. Hanrieder
and Larry V. Buel

Westview Press / Boulder, Colorado

Copyright © 1979 by Westview Press, Inc.

Published in 1979 in the United States of America by
  Westview Press, Inc.
  5500 Central Avenue
  Boulder, Colorado 80301
  Frederick A. Praeger, Publisher

Library of Congress Cataloging in Publication Data
Hanrieder, Wolfram F.
  Words and arms.
  Bibliography: p.
1. Military art and science—Dictionaries. 2. Military policy—Dictionaries. 3. National security—Dictionaries. I. Buel, Larry V., joint author. II. Title
U24.H33   355'.003   79-147
ISBN 0-89158-383-1

Printed and bound in the United States of America

Contents

Part 1
Terms and Definitions 3

Part 2
Policy Concepts

1. Strategic Nuclear Forces 141

2. Counterforce Strategies 145

3. Force Requirements for Alternative Deterrent Postures ...149

4. NATO Theater Nuclear Forces: Purposes, Capabilities,
   and Employment Concepts 153

5. Soviet Theater Nuclear Capabilities and Doctrine 163

6. History of NATO/Warsaw Pact Balance Assessments 169

7. NATO/Warsaw Pact Military Balance: How To Make
   the Balance Look Good/Bad 173

8. NATO/Warsaw Pact Military Balance:
   Modes of Analysis 181

9. Planning the General Purpose Forces 189

10. Chronology of Arms Control and
    Disarmament Agreements 193

Part 3
Statistical Information

Table 1.   U.S. Strategic Nuclear Forces: Present Force 199

Table 2.   U.S. Strategic Nuclear Forces:
Mid-1980s Projections 200

Table 3.   Estimated Soviet Strategic Nuclear Forces, 1985 201

Table 4.   U.S. Strategic Ballistic Missiles 202

Table 5.   U.S. Non-Strategic Missiles 203

Table 6.   U.S. Strategic Bombers 208

Table 7.   U.S. Ballistic Missile Submarines 209

Table 8.   U.S. Aircraft 210

Table 9.   USSR Strategic Ballistic Missiles 224

Table 10. USSR Nonstrategic Missiles 226

Table 11. USSR Strategic Bombers 231

Table 12. USSR Nuclear-Powered Ballistic
Missile Submarines 232

Table 13. Soviet/Warsaw Pact Aircraft 233

Table 14. U.S. Foreign Military Sales Agreements and
Deliveries, 1950-77 244

Table 15. Status of Multilateral Arms Control Agreements
as of February 1978 246

Figure 1. Total U.S. and Soviet Defense Activities,
1966-1976 250

Figure 2. U.S. and Soviet Major Missions, 1966-1976 251

Figure 3. U.S. and Soviet Forces for
Strategic Offense, 1966-1976 252

Figure 4. U.S. and Soviet Investment and
Operating, 1966-1976 253

Figure 5. Relative Burden of Military Expenditures 254

Figure 6.   Military Expenditures—U.S., USSR, NATO,
            and Warsaw Pact 255

References

Primary Sources 259

Further Lexicographic and Conceptual Resources ..263

Words and Arms:
A Dictionary of Security
and Defense Terms

Part 1
Terms and Definitions

A

A-6: Navy and Marine Corps night or bad weather attack aircraft.

A-7: Navy and Air Force attack aircraft.

A-10: Air Force attack aircraft designed mainly for close air support.

ABM (Antiballistic Missile/Interceptor Missile): A defensive missile designed to intercept and destroy a strategic offensive ballistic missile or its payload. This term is used interchangeably with "ballistic missile defense interceptor missile." ABM interceptor missiles are generally divided into three classes: (1) those which attempt to destroy attacking missiles very early in their flight and before the attacking missiles deploy penetration aids; (2) those which attempt to destroy attacking ballistic missiles at relatively long range outside the atmosphere; and (3) those which attempt to destroy attacking missiles at relatively short range in the atmosphere (terminal interceptors). All Soviet ABM (Galosh) interceptor missiles employ nuclear warheads. However, all ABMs are not interceptors; some are area-type weapons.

The deactivated Safeguard ABM system utilized two types of interceptor missiles: Spartan and Sprint. Spartan was a long-range, 55-foot, three-stage missile launched from an underground silo and intended to destroy or disable attacking missiles beyond the atmosphere. Sprint was a shorter-range, 27-foot, two-stage missile launched from an underground silo and intended for terminal defense against reentry vehicles in the atmosphere.

Absolute Dud: A nuclear weapon that fails to explode when launched at or emplaced on a target.

Absolute Weapon: A weapons system of such theoretically total and final effect that it is likely to prevent any type of war.

Absorbed Dose: The amount of energy imparted by nuclear (or ionizing) radiation to unit mass of absorbing material. The unit is the rad.

Absorber: Neutron absorbers like boron and cadmium, which are used in control rods for reactors, that absorb the intensity of ionizing radiation.

Acceleration Error: An error caused by the deflection of the vertical reference as a result of any change in aircraft velocity.

Accidental Attack: An unintended attack that occurs without deliberate national design as a direct result of a random event such as a mechanical failure, a simple human error, or an unauthorized action by a subordinate.

Ace High System: The first modern military communications capability, established in the 1960s when SHAPE (Supreme Headquarters Allied Powers Europe) installed the Ace High Troopscatter System, providing high capacity microwave voice and telegraph circuits throughout the area of Allied Command Europe, from the northern tip of Norway through central Europe and the Mediterranean to the eastern part of Turkey.

Acheson-Lilienthal Report: See **Baruch Plan**.

Active Air Defense: Direct defensive action taken to destroy attacking enemy aircraft or missiles or to nullify or reduce the effectiveness of such attack. It includes such measures as the use of aircraft, interceptor missiles, air defense artillery, non–air defense weapons in an air defense role, and electronic countermeasures and counter-countermeasures.

Active Defense: The employment of limited offensive action and counterattacks to deny a contested area or position to the enemy.

Active Deterrence: Strategic threat designed to deter enemy aggression against the friends and allies of a nuclear power and the military forces of that power stationed abroad.

Active Electronic Countermeasures: Electronic countermeasures that involve active, detectable emissions; for example, jamming (the deliberate radiating or re-radiating of electronic signals to obliterate or obscure signals the enemy is attempting to receive) and deception (the deliberate radiating or re-radiating of electronic signals to mislead the enemy in his interpretation of signals received by his electronic equipment).

Active Material: Materials like plutonium and certain isotopes of uranium that are capable of supporting a fission chain reaction.

Advanced Base: A base located in or near a theater of operations whose primary mission is to support military operations.

Advanced Fleet Anchorage: A secure anchorage for a large number of naval vessels, mobile support units, and auxiliaries located in or near a theater of operation.

Aegis: A Navy air defense system that represents a major improvement in the intermediate or area defense element of the **defense-in-depth** system that protects aircraft carriers. It is geared to defend against saturation attacks of the kind that are likely to take place when U.S. naval forces enter areas near the Soviet Union in order to project U.S. power ashore.

Aegis is an integrated group of systems for tracking (SPY-1 radar), weapons direction (MK-12 system), launching (MK-99 launcher), and fire control and target illumination (MK-99 fire control system, MK-90/MK-91 radars). It utilizes the medium-range version of the Standard Missile 2 (SM2/ER), a semiactive missile that relies on a radar illuminator to track a target and uses the reflected signals for homing guidance. The system also includes devices that monitor operational readiness of the various units. Aegis has good jamming resistance capability and can track and target a number of antiship missiles or planes simultaneously. Its integrated computer-linked network allows it to respond quickly to detected targets and enables it to control the firing of Harpoon antiship missiles and antisubmarine rockets, as well as standard missiles.

Aerodynamic Missile: A missile that uses aerodynamic forces to maintain its flight path, generally employing propulsion guidance. See also **ballistic missile**.

Aerospace Defense: A term encompassing all measures used to intercept, destroy, or otherwise neutralize hostile aircraft, missiles, and space vehicles. See also **air defense; antiballistic missile defense**.

Afterburning: 1. The characteristic of some rocket motors to burn irregularly for sometime after the main burning and thrust has ceased. 2. The process of fuel injection and combustion in the exhaust jet of a turbojet engine (aft or to the rear of the turbine).

Aggression: The first use of armed force to satisfy political, economic, or social aims.

Ailleret Doctrine: Late in 1967, General Charles Ailleret enunciated an "all-points" (or all-horizons, all-azimuths) deterrence posture for France that he justified on the grounds that by fashioning a threat of nuclear retaliation against any target on the globe, France could avoid involvement in conflicts among nuclear superpowers and hence establish and maintain independence of action toward them. This posture, revised in the **Fourquet Plan**

of 1968, was to be implemented with a quantity of intercontinental ballistic missiles and an "omnidirectional" thermonuclear strategic force, capable of a link-up with a future military outer-space force.

Air Alert: The operational status of airborne aircraft that are ready for immediate accomplishment of a mission.

Air Attack: 1. Coordinated: A combination of two or more types of air attack (dive, glide, low-level) in one strike, using one or more types of aircraft. **2.** Deferred: A procedure in which attack groups rendezvous as a single unit; used when attack groups are launched from more than one station with their departure on the mission being delayed pending further orders. **3.** Divided: A method of delivering a coordinated air attack that consists of holding the units in close tactical concentration up to a point.

Airborne Early Warning: The detection of enemy air or surface units by radar or other equipment carried in an airborne vehicle and the transmission of a warning to friendly units.

Airborne Early Warning and Control: Air surveillance and control provided by airborne early warning vehicles that are equipped with search and height-finding radar and communications equipment for controlling weapons. See also **AWACS (Airborne Warning and Control System)**.

Airborne Forces, Operations: Ground combat and airlift forces designed primarily to conduct parachute or other type air assaults that open up new areas of operation; the employment of such forces in combat. See also **airmobile forces, operations**.

Air-breathing Missile: A missile with an engine requiring the intake of air for combustion of its fuel like a ramjet or turbojet. To be contrasted with the rocket missile, which carries its own oxidizer and operates beyond the atmosphere. See also **cruise missile**.

Airburst: 1. An explosion of a bomb or projectile above the surface as distinguished from an explosion on contact with the surface or after penetration. **2.** The explosion of a nuclear weapon in the air at a height greater than the maximum radius of the fireball.

Air Defense: Measures designed to nullify or reduce the effectiveness of an attack by aircraft or guided missiles after they are airborne.

Air Defense Action Area: An area and the airspace above it within which friendly aircraft or surface-to-air weapons are normally given precedence in operations except under specified conditions.

Air Defense Area: 1. Overseas: A specifically defined airspace for which air defense must be planned and provided. **2.** United States: Airspace of defined dimensions within which ready control of airborne vehicles is required in the interest of national security during an air defense emergency.

Air Defense Artillery (ADA): Weapons for engaging air targets from the ground, including guns and surface-to-air missiles and support equipment.

Airhead: 1. A designated area in a hostile or threatened territory that, when seized and held, ensures the continuous air landing of troops and materiel and provides the maneuver space necessary for projected operations. Normally it is the area seized in the assault phase of an airborne operation. 2. A designated location in an area of operations used as a base for supply and evacuation by air.

Air Interception: The visual or electronic contact of a friendly aircraft with another aircraft. Normally the air interception is conducted in the following five phases: (1) climb phase: airborne to cruising altitude; (2) maneuver phase: receipt of initial vector to target until beginning transition to attack speed and altitude; (3) transition phase: increase or decrease of speed and altitude required for the attack; (4) attack phase: turn to attack heading, acquisition of target, completion of attack and turn to breakaway heading; and (5) recovery phase: breakaway to landing. See also **close-controlled air interception.**

Air Interdiction: Air operations conducted to destroy, neutralize, or delay the enemy's military potential before it can be brought to bear effectively against friendly forces. These operations are conducted at such distance from friendly forces that integration of air missions with friendly forces is not required.

Air-launched Ballistic Missile (ALBM): Any ballistic missile transported by and launched from land, sea-based aircraft, or lighter-than-air conveyances, such as blimps, balloons, and dirigibles.

Air-launched Cruise Missile (ALCM): A cruise missile designed to be launched from an aircraft. ALCMs approximately 168 to 190 inches in length could be launched from a variety of platforms: Boeing 747s, Galaxy Transports (C5A), LTV Aerospace A-7, Navy S-3As and P3Cs, and from short-range attack missile rotary tracks and pylons of B-52 bombers. The ALCM is also compatible with short-range attack missile (SRAM) avionics and ground equipment. Range varies as a function of payload, speed, and fuel volume; hence cruise missile range can be made to vary from 600 km to 2000 km. The new ALCMs come in a wide variety of lengths; some are as short as six feet. See also **Tomahawk cruise missile.**

Airmobile Forces, Operations: Ground combat units using assigned or attached fixed- and rotary-wing aircraft under their control to maneuver rapidly within given areas of operation; the employment of such forces in combat. See also **airborne forces, operations**.

AIRS (Advanced Inertial Reference Sphere): A guidance system consisting of a 10.3-inch diameter sphere containing a cluster of inertial navigation instruments floating without gimbals in a neutrally buoyant state in a highly controlled thermal environment. Designed to reduce the gyroscopic drift that decreases missile accuracy. To be deployed on board the M-X ICBM. See **M-X**.

Air Strike: An attack with specific objectives by fighter, bomber, or attack aircraft on an offensive mission. May consist of several air organizations under a single command in the air.

Air Superiority: That degree of dominance in any particular air battle of one force over another that permits the conduct of operations by the former and its related land, sea, and air forces without prohibitive interference by the opposing force.

Air Supremacy: That degree of air superiority wherein the opposing air force is incapable of effective interference.

Air-to-Air Missile (AAM): A missile launched from an airborne carrier at a target above the surface.

Air-to-Surface Missile (ASM): A missile launched from an airborne carrier against a target on the earth's surface.

ALCM (Air-launched Cruise Missile): See **air-launched cruise missile (ALCM)**.

Alert: 1. Readiness for action, defense, or protection. 2. A warning signal of a real or threatened danger, such as an air attack. 3. The period of time during which troops stand by in response to an alarm. 4. To forewarn; to prepare for action. 5. A warning received by a unit or a headquarters that forewarns of an impending operational mission.

All-Horizons Deterrence: See **Ailleret Doctrine**.

Alliance or Regionally Oriented (Related) Systems: Nuclear systems, other than central systems, deployed by the U.S. and USSR to carry out responsibilities to their respective allies and to help maintain regional power balances. Used by the U.S. in preference to the Soviet term "forward-based systems (FBS)" to convey more accurately the notion that both the U.S. and USSR have deployed tactical nuclear-capable forces in support of their respective allies. See **non-central systems; forward-based systems**.

All-Purpose Hand-Held Weapon: A light-weight, hand-held small arms weapon capable of projecting munitions required to engage both area and point-type targets.

Amphibious Assault Ship: A ship designed to transport and land troops, equipment, and supplies by means of embarked helicopters. Designated as LPH.

Amphibious Command Ship: A naval ship from which a commander exercises control in amphibious operations.

Amphibious Force: 1. A naval force and a landing force, together with supporting forces that are trained, organized, and equipped for amphibious operations. **2.** In naval usage, the administrative title of the amphibious-type command of a fleet.

Amphibious Striking Forces: Forces capable of projecting military power from the sea upon adjacent land areas for initiating or conducting operations in the face of enemy opposition.

Antiair Warfare: A term used by the U.S. Navy and U.S. Marine Corps to indicate action required to destroy or lessen an enemy air and missile threat. It includes such measures as the use of interceptors, bombers, antiaircraft guns, surface-to-air and air-to-air missiles, electronic countermeasures, and the destruction of the aircraft or missile.

Antiballistic Missile Defense: All measures to intercept and destroy hostile ballistic missiles or otherwise neutralize them. Equipment includes weapons, target acquisition, tracking and guidance radars, plus ancillary installations.

Antiballistic Missile (ABM)/Interceptor Missile: See **ABM (antiballistic missile/interceptor missile)**.

Antiballistic Missile System: A system to counter strategic ballistic missiles or their elements in flight trajectory. The system currently consists of (1) *ABM interceptor missiles* constructed and deployed for an ABM role, or of a type tested in an ABM mode; (2) *ABM launchers* constructed for launching ABM interceptor missiles; and (3) *ABM radars* constructed and deployed for an ABM role, or of a type tested in an ABM mode. The Soviet Galosh site deployment around Moscow is the only ABM system currently activated. The U.S. Safeguard site at Grand Forks, North Dakota, established to protect ICBM silos has been deactivated. As a result of the 1972 ABM Treaty (SALT I), both the U.S. and the Soviet Union are limited to 100 ABM launchers and interceptors at one site. The treaty contains additional provisions that prohibit establishing a base for nationwide ABM defense and giving non-ABM systems (missiles, launchers, or radars) the capability to counter strategic ballistic missiles. Prior to the deactivation of the Grand Forks site, the two major types of radar in the U.S. Safeguard system were perimeter acquisition radars (PARs) for long-range detection and missile site radars (MSRs) for precise, close-in target data. Both were electronically steerable, phased-array radars as opposed to the older mechanically-steered type.

Antiradiation Missile: A missile that homes on a radiation source.

Antisubmarine Action: An operation by one or more antisubmarine ships or aircraft, or a combination of the two, against a particular enemy submarine beginning when contact has been gained by any ship or aircraft of the unit. Any number of antisubmarine attacks may be carried out as part of the action, which ends when the submarine has been destroyed or when contact has been lost and cannot be regained.

Antisubmarine Air Area Operations: Carrier-based and shore-based aircraft operated singly and in coordination with other aircraft, ships, or both, to conduct offensive operations. While the purpose of such operations differs fundamentally from that of operations in distant support, the search localization and attack tactics are similar to those used in antisubmarine air distant support.

Antisubmarine Air Escort and Close Support: The provision of air protection to a particular convoy or force threatened by imminent submarine attack. Aircraft provide increased defense-in-depth and are under the control of the officer in tactical command.

Antisubmarine Air Search Attack Unit: The designation given to one or more aircraft separately organized as a tactical unit to search for and destroy submarines.

Antisubmarine Barrier: The line formed by a series of static devices or mobile units arranged for the purpose of detecting, denying passage to, or destroying hostile submarines.

Antisubmarine Carrier Group: A formed group of ships consisting of one or more antisubmarine carriers and a number of escort vessels whose primary mission is to detect and destroy submarines. Such groups may be employed in convoy support or hunter-killer roles.

Antisubmarine Rocket (ASROC): A surface ship–launched, rocket-propelled nuclear depth charge or homing torpedo. Designated as RUR-5.

Antisubmarine Torpedo (ASTOR): A submarine-launched, long-range, high-speed, wire-guided, deep-diving, wakeless torpedo capable of carrying a nuclear warhead for use in antisubmarine and anti-surface ship operations.

Antisubmarine Warfare (ASW): Operations conducted with the intention of denying the enemy the effective use of his submarines. There are five basic steps in antisubmarine warfare: (1) *detection*: the ability to determine that a submarine actually exists in the area under observation; (2) *classification*: the ability to distinguish friendly from hostile submarines, real from false targets, and one type of hostile submarine from another; (3) *localization*: determining the accurate position of the detected hostile submarine; (4) *attack*: the use of weapons capable of reaching the submarine at varying depths; and (5) *destruction*: actually rendering the submarine inoperable. All five of these steps require a high degree of technical sophistication. At present, antisubmarine warfare capabilities lag behind the capabilities of submarines to counter them.

Antisubmarine Warfare Forces: Forces organized primarily for antisubmarine action comprised of surface ships, aircraft, submarines, or any combination of these and their supporting systems.

Apogee: The point at which a missile trajectory or a satellite orbit is farthest from the center of the gravitational field of the controlling body or bodies.

Area Bombing: Bombing of a target that is a general area rather than a small or pinpoint target.

Area Defense: Defense of a wide geographical area against missiles and aircraft.

Area Munitions: Bombs that break open and scatter individual bomblets over an area.

Area of Influence: The portion of an assigned zone and the area of operations wherein a commander is directly capable of influencing the progress or outcome of operations through use of ground forces or firepower normally under his command. The geographical size of the area depends upon the mission, organization, and equipment of the force involved.

Area of Militarily Significant Fallout: The area in which radioactive fallout affects the ability of military units to carry out their normal mission.

Area of Operations: That portion of an area of conflict necessary for military operations, either offensive or defensive, pursuant to an assigned mission, and for the administration incident to such military operations.

Area of War: That area of land, sea, and air that is or may become involved directly in the operations of war.

Area Target: A target whose dimensions encompass two or more geographic coordinates on operational maps, such as cities and military bases.

Armed Forces Security Agency: An agency created in 1949 to consolidate the cryptologic effort; predecessor of the National Security Agency (NSA).

Arms Control: Explicit or implicit international agreements that govern the numbers, types, characteristics, deployment, and use of armed forces and armaments.

Arms Control Agreement Verification: A procedure that entails the collecting, processing, and reporting of data indicating testing or employment of proscribed weapons systems, including country of origin and location, weapon and payload identification, and event type.

Arms Control and Disarmament Agency (ACDA) Director: The ACDA was created in 1961. The director is the principal adviser to the president and the secretary of state on arms control and disarmament matters, and under the direction of the secretary of state has primary responsibility within the government for such matters. He is responsible for the executive direction and coordination of all activities of the agency and of its liaison relationships with other government agencies and the Congress.

Arms Limitation: An agreement to restrict quantitative holdings of or qualitative improvements in specific armaments or weapons systems.

Arms Race: A competitive relationship between two or more nations that results in weapons proliferation, an increase in the virulence of weapon systems, and a quantitative and qualitative growth in the armed forces of those nations.

Arms Stability: A strategic force relationship in which neither side perceives the necessity for undertaking major new arms programs in order to avoid being placed at a disadvantage.

Army Security Agency: One of the service cryptologic agencies. Its collection activities are under the authority of the director of the National Security Agency (NSA) in his dual role as the chief of the Central Security Service (CSS).

Artillery: Complete projectile-firing weapons consisting of cannon or missile launchers on suitable carriages or mounts. Field artillery cannons are classified according to caliber as: light—120 mm and less; medium—121-160 mm; heavy—161-210 mm; very heavy—greater than 210 mm.

Artillery-Fired Atomic Projectiles (AFAP): An artillery shell that produces a nuclear explosion.

Assault: 1. The climax of an attack; closing with the enemy in hand-to-hand fighting. 2. In an amphibious operation, the period of time between the arrival of the major assault forces of the amphibious task force in the objective area and the accomplishment of the amphibious task force mission. 3. To make a short, violent, but well-ordered attack against a local objective, such as a gun emplacement, a fort, or a machine gun nest. 4. A phase of an airborne operation beginning with delivery by air of the assault echelon of the force into the objective area and extending through attack of assault objectives and consolidation of the initial airhead. See also **landing attack.**

Assessment: Part of the intelligence process whereby an analyst determines the reliability or validity of a piece of information. An assessment could also be a statement resulting from this process.

Assumption: A supposition concerning a current situation or any future events, presumed to be true in the absence of positive proof to the contrary. Used for planning and decision-making purposes.

Assured Destruction: A highly reliable ability to inflict unacceptable damage on any aggressor or combination of aggressors at any time during the course of a nuclear exchange, even after absorbing a surprise first strike.

Atomic Bomb: A bomb whose energy comes from the fission of heavy elements like uranium and plutonium. See **hydrogen bomb.**

Atomic Demolition Munition (ADM): A nuclear device designed to be detonated on or below the ground surface or under water as a demolition munition against materiel-type targets to block, deny, or canalize the enemy.

Atoms-for-Peace Plan: The Eisenhower proposal of 1957 calling for cooperation among the nuclear states and other nations to develop peaceful uses of atomic energy. The Atoms-for-Peace Plan called for the establishment of an international agency to promote atomic cooperation and called on nuclear states to contribute to peaceful nuclear research by diverting fissionable material from their weapons stockpiles. See **International Atomic Energy Agency.**

Attack Aircraft: Tactical aircraft used primarily for interdiction and close air support purposes. See also **fighter aircraft.**

Attack Cargo Ship: A naval ship designed or coverted to transport combat-loaded cargo in an assault landing. Capabilities for carrying landing craft, and for speed, armament, and size of hatches and booms are greater than those of comparable cargo ship types. Designated as AKA.

Attack Carrier: An aircraft carrier designed to accommodate high-performance fighter or attack aircraft; primary purpose is to protect offensive striking power against targets ashore and afloat.

Attack Carrier Striking Forces: Naval forces with carrier-based aircraft as the primary offensive weapon. Ships, other than carriers, act first to support and screen against submarine and air threat, and second to defend against surface threat.

Attack Group: A subordinate task organization of the Navy forces of an amphibious task force. It is composed of assault shipping and supporting naval units designated to transport, protect, land, and initially support a landing group.

Attack Submarine: A submarine designed primarily to destroy enemy merchant shipping and naval vessels, including other submarines. See also **submarine**.

AWACS (Airborne Warning and Control System): A system comprised of a look-down radar and flying command post for directing manned interceptors. The aircraft will carry long-range surveillance radar to provide two hundred mile over-the-horizon coverage, including the detection of low-flying aircraft.

Axis of Advance: A line of advance assigned for purposes of control; often a road or a group of roads, or a designated series of locations, extending in the direction of the enemy.

B

B-52: The mainstay of the U.S. strategic bomber force since the 1950s. About 250 late-model G and H aircraft and 75 rewinged D bombers are expected to remain in the inventory until the early 1990s. Many of these will be equipped with cruise missiles in the early 1980s, while others will continue to carry gravity bombs and short-range attack missiles.

Backfit: To modify or convert an older system in order to make it compatible with new armament or hardware to be installed.

Background Radiation: The radiation in man's natural environment, including cosmic rays and radiation from the naturally radioactive elements both outside and inside the bodies of men and animals. It is also called natural radiation.

Balance: As applied to arms control: 1. Adjustments of armed forces and armaments in such a manner that one state does not obtain military advantage vis-à-vis other states agreeing to the measure; 2. Internal adjustments by one state of its forces in such a manner as to enable it to cope with all aspects of remaining threats to its security in post arms control agreement era.

Balanced Collective Force: The requirement for "balance" in any military force stems from the consideration that all elements of a force should be complementary to each other. A force should function as a combined arms team, and the term "balance" implies that the ratio of the various elements of this team is ideal for executing its assigned mission effectively and efficiently. Applied multinationally, the term "balanced collective force" may be defined as a force comprised of one or more services furnished by more than one nation, the total strength and composition of which is ideal for fulfilling the specific mission for which it is designed.

Balance of Terror: A state of mutual deterrence between the super-powers based on their possession of weapons that permit either side to deliver a devastating blow to the other.

Ballistic Missile: A pilotless projectile propelled into space by one or more rocket boosters. Thrust is terminated at some early stage, after which reentry vehicles follow trajectories that are governed mainly by gravity and aerodynamic drag. Midcourse corrections and terminal guidance permit only minor modifications to the flight path.

Ballistic Missile Defense (BMD): All measures that intercept and destroy hostile ballistic missiles or otherwise neutralize them. Equipment includes weapons, target acquisition, tracking and guidance radars, and ancillary installations.

Ballistic Missile Defense System (BMDS): A system designed to destroy offensive strategic ballistic missiles or their warheads before they reach their targets.

Ballistic Missile Early Warning System (BMEWS): An electronic system for providing detection and early warning of attack by enemy intercontinental ballistic missiles. The BMEWS in operation since 1962 is comprised of a small chain of very large radars at three operational sites: Sites I in Thule, Greenland; Site II in Clear, Alaska; and Site III on Fylingdales Moor, England.

Ballistic Missile Reentry Vehicles:

MK-4: Reentry vehicle under development for the Trident C-5 incorporating a W-76 warhead with a kiloton yield.

MK-5: Single-warhead reentry vehicle with a single-target capability and a one megaton yield. No penetration aids incorporated.

MK-6: Large reentry vehicle with a single multimegaton warhead and a three-target selection capability. Incorporates penetration aids.

MK-11: Single-warhead reentry vehicle with a two-target capability and a one megaton yield. No penetration aids incorporated.

MK-11A: Single-warhead reentry vehicle similar to the MK-11 but warhead yield may be different.

MK-11B: Single-warhead reentry vehicle with a one to two megaton warhead yield and an eight-target selection capability. Incorporates penetration aids.

MK-11C: Single-warhead reentry vehicle similar to the MK-11B but improved and hardened against nuclear weapons effects. Successor to the MK-11B.

MK-12: Three-warhead MIRV with a yield of two hundred kilotons for each warhead. Incorporates penetration aids.

MK-12A: See MK-12.

MK-17: Large multimegaton reentry vehicle originally planned for the Poseidon and Minuteman III but cancelled.

MK-18: Reentry vehicle with multiple unguided reentry vehicles for high saturation but cancelled.

MK-19: High-yield and high-accuracy system that could provide a hard-target kill capability.

MK-20: High-yield warhead to ultimately replace the MK-12 and MK-12A warheads.

MK-80: Nuclear warhead being developed for use with the M-X Advanced ICBM, Trident II, and possibly the Minuteman III.

MK-81: Alternative system to the MK-80 but less desirable because of its greater weight due to a limited use of the metal or alloy.

MK-100: Reentry vehicle for the Polaris A-1 and A-2. The single warhead is thermonuclear and has a yield of 800 kilotons.

MK-200: Reentry vehicle for the Polaris A-3 missile. It incorporates three 200-kiloton multiple reentry vehicle (MRV) nuclear warheads.

MK-300: Reentry vehicle for the Poseidon missile. Missile capacity for fourteen reentry vehicles with or without warheads. System currently incorporates ten MIRV fifty kiloton warheads plus penetration aids.

MK-400: Ballistic reentry vehicle developed for the MIRV system of the Trident missile.

MK-500: Reentry vehicle (MARV) capable of evasive maneuvers during the atmospheric phase of reentry.

Ballistics: The science or art that deals with the motion, behavior, appearance, or modification of missiles or other vehicles acted upon by propellants, wind, gravity, temperature, or any other modifying substance, condition, or force.

Ballistic Trajectory: The trajectory traced after the propulsive force is terminated and the body is acted upon only by gravity and aerodynamic drag.

Ballistic Wind: That constant wind that would have the same effect upon the trajectory of a bomb or projectile as the wind encountered in flight.

Bare-Base Kits: A complete prepackaged set of equipment designed to convert an air strip into a base capable of supporting combat operations.

Bargaining Chip: Any military force, weapons system, or other resource, present or projected, a country expresses willingness to downgrade or discard in return for concessions.

Barrage: 1. A prearranged barrier of fire delivered by small arms and designed to protect friendly troops and installations by impeding enemy movements across defensive lines or areas. 2. A protective screen of balloons that are moored to the ground and kept at given heights to prevent or hinder operations by enemy aircraft (balloon barrage). 3. A type of electronic countermeasure intended for simultaneous jamming over a wide spectrum of frequencies. See also **electronic warfare**.

Barrage Rocket: A combined blast and fragmentation weapon designed for firing from ship to shore in amphibious attack.

Barrier Forces: Air, surface, and submarine units with their supporting systems positioned across the likely courses of expected enemy transit for early detection and provision of rapid warning, blocking, and destruction of the enemy.

Baruch Plan: A U.S. proposal of June 1946 named after Bernard Baruch, for an international authority to own and manage all atomic materials. The proposal was based on the so-called "Acheson-Lilienthal Report" (named after Dean Acheson, then under secretary of state, and David Lilienthal, chairman of the Tennessee Valley Authority) that proposed that atomic energy should be used solely for peaceful purposes and that global atomic resources be placed under the ownership and control of an independent international authority.

Base Hardening: Improving the resistance of bases to air attack through concrete aircraft shelters, bunkered command posts, and other facilities.

Base Surge: A cloud that rolls out from the bottom of the column produced by a subsurface burst of a nuclear weapon. With underwater bursts the surge is a cloud of liquid droplets that has the property of flowing almost as if it were a homogeneous fluid. With subsurface land bursts, the surge is made up of small solid particles but still behaves like a fluid.

Basic Load: That quantity of nonnuclear ammunition authorized and required to be on hand within a military unit or formation at all times.

Battery: 1. Tactical and administrative artillery unit or subunit corresponding to a company or similar unit in other branches of the army. **2.** All guns, torpedo tubes, searchlights, and missile launchers of the same size, caliber, or used for the same purpose, either installed in one ship or otherwise operating as an entity.

Battle Control: The control of specific offensive and defensive forces, both friendly and enemy, during hostilities through the analysis of data provided.

Battlefield Interdiction: Air attacks on enemy forces in the second echelon that are moving up to the battle area.

Beaten Zone: The area on the ground upon which the cone of fire falls.

Biad: Any group of two military elements with separate characteristics but common basic missions; for example, land-based intercontinental ballistic missiles and ballistic-missile submarines.

Bilateral Infrastructure: Infrastructure that concerns only two NATO/SEATO members and is financed by mutual agreement between them; e.g., facilities required for the use of forces of one NATO/SEATO member in the territory of another.

Biological Defense: The methods, plans, and procedures involved in establishing and executing defensive measures against attack utilizing biological agents.

Biological Half-Life: The time required for a biological system, such as a man or an animal, to eliminate by natural processes half the amount of a substance that has entered it like a radioactive material.

Biological Warfare: Employment of living organisms, toxic biological products, and plant growth regulators to produce death or casualties in man, animals, or plants; defense against such action.

Biological Weapon: An item of materiel that projects, disperses, or disseminates a biological agent.

"Black Boxes": Automatic seismic stations usable as an adjunct to manned detection stations or on-site inspections for purposes of verifying arms control agreements.

Black Propaganda: Propaganda that purports to emanate from a source other than the true one.

Blanket: A layer of fertile material like uranium 238 or thorium 232 placed around the fissionable material in a reactor.

Blast: The brief and rapid movement of air vapor or fluid away from a center of outward pressure, as in an explosion or in the combustion of rocket fuel; the pressure accompanying this movement. This term is commonly used for "explosion," but the two terms may be distinguished.

Blast Shelter: Natural or man-made structures that afford protection against overpressures caused by nuclear blasts. Shelter effectiveness is a function of weapons-yield, proximity to ground-zero, and shelter construction.

Blitzkrieg: A fast-moving war waged for the purpose of gaining victory over the enemy in the shortest possible time; measured in days and weeks.

Blockade: 1. An action designed to prevent troops and supplies from reaching their destination. 2. A pacific blockade is a naval operation levied by one state against another during peacetime to deny the latter's ships (but not the vessels of other nations) entry into the blockaded nation's ports.

"Blue Book": The International Atomic Energy Agency's document, entitled "The Structure and Content of Agreements between the Agency and States Required in Connection with the Treaty on the Nonproliferation of Nuclear Weapons," in which appear the agency's safeguards system under the nonproliferation treaty, adopted in 1971.

Boat Lanes: Lanes for amphibious assault landing craft that extend seaward from the landing beaches to the line of departure. The width of the boat lanes is determined by the length of the corresponding beach.

Bomb: A weapon dropped from a manned aircraft of any sort. Gravity is the primary force, but "smart" bombs can be guided electronically.

Bomber: Military aircraft designed to deliver nuclear or nonnuclear weapons against targets on the ground. Generally, bombers such as the Soviet Bison and Bear and the U.S. B-52 have been considered heavy bombers; Soviet Badgers, Blinders, and the U.S.

FB-111 have been considered medium bombers; and Soviet Beagles and Brewers have been considered light bombers.

Bombing Errors: 1. *Fifty percent circular error*: The radius of a circle, with its center at the desired mean point of impact, that contains half the missiles independently aimed to hit the desired mean point of impact. 2. *Fifty percent deflection error*: Half the distance between two lines, drawn parallel to the aircraft's tract and equidistant from the desired mean point of impact, that contains half the missiles independently aimed to hit the desired mean point of impact. 3. *Fifty percent range error*: Half the distance between two lines, drawn perpendicular to the aircraft's track equidistant from the desired mean point of impact, that contains half the missiles independently aimed to hit the desired mean point of impact. (*Note*: These errors imply overall errors unless found otherwise stipulated by inclusion of the adjective "random" or "systematic.")

Bombing Height: Distance above a target at the moment of bomb release, measured vertically from the target to the level of the bombing aircraft.

Booster: 1. A high-explosive element sufficiently sensitive to be actuated by small explosive elements in a fuze or primer and powerful enough to cause detonation of the main explosive filling. 2. An auxiliary or initial propulsion system that travels with a missile or aircraft and that may or may not separate from the parent craft when its impulse has been delivered. A booster system may contain or consist of one or more units.

Boost Phase: That portion of the flight of a ballistic missile or space vehicle during which the booster and sustainer engines operate.

Breeder Reactor: A reactor that produces more nuclear fuel than it consumes during power generation. Fuel breeding in a reactor occurs when more free neutrons are being absorbed in U-238 than required to sustain nuclear fission. A breeder reactor discharges many times more plutonium than a light-water reactor of comparable power capacity.

Brigade: A unit, usually smaller than a division, to which are attached groups, battalions, and smaller units tailored to meet anticipated requirements.

Brinkmanship: Demonstrated willingness on the part of an adversary to approach the brink of disaster.

Broken-Back War: The war that would continue between the remaining forces of two adversaries after nuclear weapons had been employed by the powers to inflict unacceptable damage on each other.

Brushfire War: A local war that flares up without warning and either ceases prior to great power intervention or escalates to greater magnitude before great powers have a chance to stop the conflict.

Burnout: That point in time or in a missile trajectory when combustion of fuels in the rocket engine is terminated by other than programmed cutoff.

Bus: The part of a MIRVed missile's payload that carries the reentry vehicles (RVs) and has a guidance package, fuel, and thrust devices for altering the ballistic flight path so that the RVs can be dispensed sequentially toward different targets.

C

Calculated Risk: The deliberate acceptance of gaps between ends and means in accordance with estimates that indicate the enemy is unlikely to initiate actions that will interfere unacceptably with friendly forces.

Candu Reactor: Developed by Canada, this reactor is fueled by natural uranium and produces spent fuel of plutonium that (after processing) is usable in the production of nuclear explosives.

Capability: The ability of a country or coalition of countries to execute specific courses of action. Capabilities are conditioned by many variables, including the balance of military forces, time, space, terrain, and weather. See also **intention**.

Capsule: 1. A sealed, pressurized cabin for extremely high altitude or space flight which provides an acceptable environment for man, animal, or equipment. 2. In naval usage, an ejectable sealed cabin having automatic devices for safe return of the occupants to the surface of the water.

Carpet Bombing: The progressive distribution of a mass bomb load upon an area defined by designated boundaries in such manner as to inflict damage to all portions.

Carrier Air Group: Two or more aircraft squadrons formed under one command for administrative and tactical control of operations from a carrier.

Carrier Striking Force: A naval task force composed of aircraft carriers and supporting combatant ships capable of conducting strike operations.

Carrier Task Force: A group of naval warships usually comprised of an aircraft carrier, cruisers, and several additional destroyers. The cruisers and destroyers contribute to the defense of the carrier primarily by means of their area defense systems and antiship and antisubmarine weapon systems.

Catalytic Attack: An attack designed to bring about a war between major powers through the disguised machinations of a third power.

Catapult: A structure that provides an auxiliary source of thrust to a missile or aircraft and combines the functions of directing and accelerating the missile during its travel on the catapult; serves the same function for a missile as does a gun tube for a shell.

Categorization of Soviet Divisional Readiness: *Category I*: Fully equipped, three-quarters to full strength; *Category II*: Full combat vehicle deployment, one-half to three-quarters strength; *Category III*: Possible full combat vehicle deployment, one-third strength.

C-Day: The unnamed day on which a deployment operation commences or is supposed to commence. The deployment may be a movement of troops, cargo, weapon systems, or a combination of these elements utilizing any or all types of transport.

Central Systems: Offensive strategic nuclear weapons systems (currently consisting of ICBMs, SLBMs, and heavy bombers) the United States considers central to the strategic nuclear relationship between the United States and the Soviet Union.

The 1972 Interim Agreement on offensive weapons (SALT I) only limited until 1977 the number of ICBM and SLBM launchers on each side; the number of heavy bombers was not limited. In November 1974 at Vladivostok basic provisions for a new agreement limiting the central systems were agreed upon by the United States and the Soviet Union. See **SALT (Strategic Arms Limitation Talks); Triad.**

Chaff: Electronic countermeasure (ECM) aid dropped by aircraft or drones consisting of tinsellike bits of metal or synthetic material cut to block specific radar frequencies. See also **electronic counter measure**.

Chain Reaction: A reaction that stimulates its own repetition. In a fission chain reaction a fissionable nucleus absorbs a neutron and fissions, releasing additional neutrons. These in turn can be absorbed by other fissionable nuclei, releasing still more neutrons. A fission chain reaction is self-sustaining when the number of neutrons released in a given time equals or exceeds the number of neutrons lost by absorption in nonfissioning material or by escape from the system.

Chemical, Biological, and Radiological Operations: Used only when referring to the three areas of chemical operations, biological operations, and radiological operations in the collective sense.

Chemical Defense: The methods, plans, and procedures involved in establishing and executing defensive measures against attack by chemical agents.

Chemical Mine: A mine containing a chemical agent designed to kill, injure, or incapacitate personnel or to contaminate material or terrain.

Chemical Operations: Employment of chemical agents (excluding riot agents) to kill, or incapacitate humans or animals for a significant period of time, or to deny or hinder the use of areas, facilities, or materiels.

Circular Error Probability (CEP): A measure of the delivery accuracy of a weapon system used as a factor in determining probable damage to targets. The radius of a circle around the target at which a missile is aimed and within which the warhead has a .5 probability of falling. See also **bombing errors.**

Civil Defense: System of measures designed to protect human lives, natural resources, means of production, and the organizational fabric of human society from the effects of enemy action.

Civil-Military Cooperation: All actions and measures undertaken between NATO commanders and national authorities, military or civil, in peace or war, that concern the relationship between allied armed forces and the government, civil population, or agencies in the areas where such armed forces are stationed, supported, or employed.

Civil Nuclear Power: A nation that has the potential to employ nuclear technology for the development of nuclear weapons but has deliberately decided against doing so.

Civil Reserve Air Fleet: U.S. commercial aircraft and crews in international and domestic service allocated in emergency for exclusive military use.

Clandestine Intelligence: Intelligence information collected by clandestine sources.

Clandestine Operations: Intelligence, counterintelligence, or other information collection activities and covert political, economic, propaganda, and paramilitary activities, conducted so as to assure the secrecy of an operation.

Clean Bomb: 1. A nuclear bomb that produces relatively little radioactive fallout. 2. A fusion bomb.

Clean Weapon: A nuclear weapon for which measures have been taken to reduce the amount of residual radioactivity relative to a "normal" weapon of the same energy yield.

Close Air Support: Air strikes against targets close enough to ground combat units that detailed coordination between participating air and ground elements is required.

Close-controlled Air Interception: An interception in which the interceptor is continuously guided into a position from which the target is visible or in radar contact.

Close Supporting Fire: Fire placed on enemy troops, weapons, or positions that, because of their proximity, present the most immediate and serious threat to the supported unit.

Cluster Bomb Unit (CBU): Usually spherical metal bomblets of baseball size that fragment like a hand grenade and are dispersed in large numbers from aircraft-delivered cannisters.

Coastal Frontier Defense: The organization of the forces and materiel of the armed forces assigned to provide security for the coastal frontiers of the continental United States and its overseas possessions.

Cobalt Bomb: If a nuclear weapon is encased in cobalt, large amounts of radioactive cobalt 60 are produced upon detonation. With such a weapon one must consider not only the explosive force of the bomb but also the danger of highly penetrating and long-lasting gamma radiation emitted by cobalt 60.

Cold Launch: The technique of ejecting a missile from a silo before full ignition of the main engine, sometimes called "pop-up." All current U.S. submarine-launched ballistic missiles (SLBMs) are ejected in this manner. The Soviet Union has been testing ICBM launchers using the cold launch technique. Since full ignition of the main engine occurs only after the missile has cleared the silo, the requirement for extensive shielding of the missile from its own exhaust gases in the silo at launch is reduced thereby leaving more room in the silo for a larger missile. The cold launch technique leaves the missile silo essentially undamaged and available for reloading.

Cold War: A state of international tension wherein political, economic, technological, sociological, psychological, paramilitary, and military measures (short of overt armed conflict) are employed to achieve national objectives.

Collateral Damage: Damage to surrounding human and nonhuman resources, either military or nonmilitary, as the result of action or strikes directed specifically against enemy forces or military facilities.

Collocation: The physical placement of two or more detachments, units, organizations, or facilities at a specifically defined location.

Combat Air Patrol (CAP): An airborne force ready to achieve air superiority or fleet air defense.

Combat Load: The total warlike stores carried by an aircraft.

Combat Power: A compilation of capabilities related to a specific military balance between countries or coalitions. Ingredients include numbers and types of forces; technological attributes of weapons and equipment; discipline; morale; pride; confidence; hardiness; élan; loyalty; training; combat experience; command or control arrangements; staying power; and leadership.

Combat Service Support: Assistance given to operating forces by way of administrative services, chaplain services, civil affairs support, financial and legal services, health services, military police, supply, maintenance, transportation, construction, troop construction, acquisition and disposal of real property, facilities engineering, topographic and geodetic engineering, food service, graves registration, laundry, dry cleaning, bath, property disposal, and other logistic services.

Combat Support Troops: Those units or organizations whose primary mission is to furnish operational assistance for the combat elements.

Combined Operation: An operation conducted by forces of two or more allied nations acting together for the accomplishment of a single mission.

Command and Control: An arrangement of facilities, equipment, personnel, and procedures used to acquire, process, and disseminate data needed by decision makers to plan, direct, and control operations.

Commitment: An obligation or pledge to carry out or support a given national policy. See also **national security policies**.

Commonality: 1. A quality of materiel or systems that share interchangeable characteristics that allow personnel trained on one type of equipment to utilize, operate, and maintain other types of similar equipment without additional training. 2. A quality of equipment that is designed to use interchangeable repair parts or components. 3. A quality of consumable items that can be used interchangeably without adjustment.

Common Infrastructure: The essential infrastructure for training NATO forces and implementing NATO operational plans; owing to its mutual use and its compliance with criteria laid down from time to time by the North Atlantic Council, this infrastructure is commonly financed by NATO members.

Communications Intelligence (COMINT): Technical and intelligence information derived from foreign communications by someone other than the intended recipient. It does not include foreign press, propaganda, or public broadcasts. The term is sometimes used interchangeably with signals intelligence (SIGINT).

Communications Satellite: An orbiting vehicle that relays signals between communications stations. Satellites are of two types: (1) active communications satellites, which receive, regenerate, and retransmit signals between stations; and (2) passive communications satellites, which reflect communications signals between stations.

Communications Security (COMSEC): The protection of U.S. telecommunications and other communications from exploitation by foreign intelligence services and from unauthorized disclosure. COMSEC is one of the mission responsibilities of the National Security Agency. It includes cryptosecurity, transmission security, emission security, and physical security of classified equipment, material, and documents.

Compatibility: A characteristic of two or more items or components of equipment or material that can exist or function in the same system or environment without mutual interference. See also **interchangeability**.

Compellence: The process of influencing an adversary through a variety of positive means to cease hostile action or an undesirable activity. Contrast with **deterrence**, which is negative in nature.

Complete Round: Applied to an assemblage of explosive and non-explosive components designed to perform a specific function at the time and under the conditions desired. Examples of complete rounds of ammunition are: (1) *separate loading*: consisting of a primer, propelling charge, a projectile (or blank ammunition), and a fuse; (2) *fixed or semifixed*: consisting of a primer, propelling charge, cartridge case, a projectile, and a fuse (except when solid projectiles are used); (3) *bomb*: consisting of all component parts required to drop and function the bomb once; (4) *missile*: consisting of a complete warhead section and a missile body with its associated components and propellants; and (5) *rocket*: consisting of all components necessary for the rocket to function.

Composite Air Strike Force: A group of selected U.S. Air Force units composed of appropriate elements of tactical air power (tactical fighters, tactical reconnaissance, tankers, airlift, and command and control elements) capable of employing a spectrum of nuclear and nonnuclear weapons. Composite Air Strike Forces are held in readiness for immediate deployment from the continental United States to all areas of the world to meet national emergency contingency plans.

Condensation Cloud: A mist or fog of minute water droplets that temporarily surrounds the fireball following a nuclear (or atomic) detonation in a comparatively humid atmosphere. The expansion of the air in the negative phase of the blast wave from the explosion results in a lowering of the temperature, so that condensation of water vapor present in the air occurs and a cloud forms. The cloud is soon dispelled when the pressure returns to normal and the air warms up again. The phenomenon is similar to that used by physicists in the Wilson cloud chamber and is sometimes called the "cloud chamber effect."

Confidence-building Measures (CBM): The military-security aspect of Basket I of the Helsinki (CSCE) accord. CBMs include prior notification of NATO/Warsaw Pact military maneuvers and the exchange of observers at those maneuvers. The object of CBMs is to build faith in the political intention of the other side as a prelude to the concrete reduction of forces to take place in the context of MBFR (Mutual and Balanced Force Reductions) negotiations. CBMs became an important element in NATO Europe's expressions of solidarity. Specific confidence-building measures include the following: (1) notification of military maneuvers exceeding a total of 25,000 troops; (2) notification required for force movements within 250 kilometers of a participating state's border; and (3) notification to be given twenty-one days in advance of the start of the maneuver or as soon as possible in light of emergency maneuvers.

Conflict Spectrum: A continuum of hostilities that ranges from sub-crisis maneuvering in Cold War situations to the most violent form of general war.

Consolidation: The combining or merging of elements to perform a common or related function.

Contact Burst Preclusion: A fusing arrangement that prevents an unwanted surface burst when an air burst fuse fails to function.

Containment: Measures to discourage or prevent the expansion of enemy territorial holdings or influence. Specifically, a U.S. policy directed against communist expansion.

Contamination: The deposit or absorption of radioactive material or biological and chemical agents on and by structures, areas, personnel, or objects.

Continental United States (CONUS): Refers to U.S. territory, including adjacent territorial waters, located within the North American continent between Canada and Mexico.

Contingency Plans and Operations: Preparation for major events that can reasonably be anticipated and that probably would have a detrimental effect on national security, and actions in case such events occur.

Contingent Effects: The effects, both desirable and undesirable, that occur in addition to the primary effects associated with a nuclear detonation.

Control: To restrain or direct influence; to dominate, regulate, and hence to hold from action; to curb, to inspect, and to supervise.

Controlled Counterforce War: A war in which one or both sides concentrate on reducing enemy strategic retaliatory forces in a bargaining situation and take special precautions to minimize collateral casualties and damage. See also **controlled war**.

Controlled Effects Nuclear Weapons: Nuclear weapons designed to achieve variation in the intensity of specific effects other than normal blast effect.

Controlled Response: Responding to a military attack with military action that is deliberately kept within certain definable limits for the purpose of avoiding all-out nuclear war.

Controlled War: A war waged in response to the continuous receipt and evaluation of information concerning changes in the war situation, combined with the competence to adjust accordingly.

Control Rod: A rod, plate, or tube containing a material that readily absorbs neutrons; used to control the power of a nuclear reactor. By absorbing neutrons, a control rod prevents the neutrons from causing further fission.

Conventional Pause: A time period following an attack on Western Europe during which NATO would respond with conventional forces rather than nuclear weapons in order to assess the attacker's intentions and to consult among the Western allies. See also **flexible response**.

Conventional War: Armed conflict in which nuclear weapons are not employed.

Conventional Weapons: Nonnuclear weapons. Excludes all biological weapons and generally excludes chemical weapons except for existing smoke and incendiary agents, and agents of the riot-control type.

Converter Reactor: A reactor that produces less fissionable material than it consumes; in some usages, a reactor that produces a fissionable material different than the fuel burned, regardless of the ratio.

Coordinated Attack: A carefully planned and executed offensive action in which the various elements of a command are employed so as to utilize their powers to the greatest advantage for the command as a whole.

Core: The central portion of a nuclear reactor, containing the fuel elements and usually the moderator.

Corps: A tactical unit consisting of two or more divisions, auxiliary arms, and services.

Correlation Guidance: Map-matching devices useful for long-range guidance against known targets that either cannot be easily designated or do not have a strong enough signature for homing systems. Using optical, radar, infrared, or microwave sensors, correlation systems compare sensed pictures of a target area with stored reference pictures to generate course corrections.

Correlation of World Forces: A Soviet concept that rests on the following broad categories: (1) *economic*: levels of per-capita GNP, national income, labor productivity, industrial production developments in the applied sciences, and research and development; (2) *military*: levels of armament deployments (both quantitative and qualitative), proficiency and morale of troops, combat experience of troops, and the scope and nature of military doctrines; (3) *political*: organization of government, popular support for domestic and foreign policies, and the ability of government to render decisions as final; (4) *international movements*: role in the political life of the masses, size of movements, and their influence on state activities.

The correlation of world forces is calculated on two levels, global and regional. Quantification of elements is difficult, injecting uncertainty into the global calculation. The Soviets do not view the military component of the overall correlation of world forces as the dominant consideration and argue that military-strategic parity between the United States and the Soviet Union has shifted competition to the economic and political spheres.

Cost-Effectiveness: A condition that matches ends with means in ways that create maximum capabilities at minimum expense.

Counterair: A U.S. Air Force term for air operations conducted to attain and maintain a desired degree of air superiority by the destruction or neutralization of enemy forces. Both air offensive and air defensive actions are involved. The former range throughout enemy territory and are generally conducted at the initiative of friendly forces. The latter are conducted near to or over friendly territory and are generally responsive to the initiative of the enemy air forces. See also **antiair warfare.**

Counterattack: Attack by part or all of a defending force against an enemy attacking force, for specific purposes, such as regaining lost ground or cutting off and destroying enemy advance units.

The general objective is to deny the enemy its purpose in attacking. In sustained defensive operations the purpose is to restore the battle position and the attacks are directed at limited objectives.

Countercity Strategy: A strategy of nuclear warfare in which the attacker implies that he will strike at the enemy's population and industrial centers.

Countercity Strike: A nuclear strike directed against the population and industrial centers of an enemy with the objective of causing the greatest possible destruction to the fabric of the enemy society.

Counterdeterrence: A nuclear threat raised to nullify or weaken another power's threat to employ nuclear retaliation against limited aggression.

Counterforce: The employment of strategic air and missile forces to destroy or render impotent the military capabilities of an enemy force. Bombers and their bases, ballistic missile submarines, ICBM silos, ABM and air defense installations, command and control centers, and nuclear stockpiles are typical counterforce targets.

Counterforce Strategy: Strategy specifying the targeting of enemy forces, particularly those that it could use in retaliation. At Ann Arbor in 1962, Secretary of Defense McNamara stated that, in the event of a nuclear war, the principal military objective should be the destruction of enemy military forces, not his civilian population.

Counterguerrilla War: Operations and activities conducted by armed forces, paramilitary forces, or non-military agencies of a government against guerrillas.

Counterinsurgency War: Military, paramilitary, political, economic, psychological, and civic actions taken by a government to defeat subversive insurgency within a country.

Counterintelligence: Activities conducted to destroy the effectiveness of foreign intelligence operations and to protect information against espionage, individuals against subversion, and installations against sabotage. The term also refers to information developed by or used in counterintelligence operations.

Countervalue: The concepts, plans, weapons, and actions used to destroy or neutralize selected enemy population centers, industries, resources, or institutions. See also **counterforce**.

Countervalue Strike: An attack aimed at an opponent's cities or industries.

Counting Rules: Devices designed to permit U.S. verification of Soviet compliance with the numerical provisions of the strategic arms limitation agreements. These rules require: (1) that any missile tested with MIRVs must be counted as a MIRVed missile, and (2) that any launcher that has ever launched a MIRVed missile must count as a MIRV launcher. New launchers, not to be counted as MIRVed launchers, must be different from those tested launching MIRVed missiles. See also **multiple independently targetable reentry vehicle (MIRV); SALT (Strategic Arms Limitation Talks)**.

Covering Fire: 1. Fire used to protect troops when they are within range of enemy small arms. 2. In amphibious usage, fire delivered prior to the landing to cover preparatory operations such as underwater demolitions or minesweeping.

Credibility: Factors associated with a threat or a promise that create the expectation in the minds of others that it will be carried out if ever the relevant circumstances should arise.

Credible First-Strike Capability: Strategic nuclear weapons sufficiently strong and so deployed that the adversary believes the opposing power has a first-strike capability and is deterred by it.

Crisis Management: Institutional arrangements and procedures for dealing with an international crisis so as to keep it under control and to resolve it with the least possible damage.

Crisis Stability: A strategic force relationship in which neither side has any incentive to initiate the use of strategic nuclear forces in a crisis situation.

Critical Altitude: The altitude beyond which an aircraft or air-breathing guided missile ceases to perform satisfactorily.

Critical Intelligence: Information or intelligence of such urgent importance to the security of the United States that it is transmitted with the highest priority to the president and other national decision-making officials before passing through regular evaluative channels.

Critical Mass: The smallest mass of fissionable material that will support a self-sustaining chain reaction under stated conditions.

Criticality: The state of a nuclear reactor when it is sustaining a chain reaction.

Cross-targeting: Attack planning that assigns a target to warheads carried by different delivery vehicles.

Cruise Missile: A pilotless aircraft propelled by an air-breathing engine that operates entirely within the earth's atmosphere maintaining thrust throughout its flight. In-flight guidance and control can be accomplished remotely or by onboard equipment; conventional and nuclear warheads are available.

While both the United States and the Soviet Union deploy cruise missiles, technological asymmetries separate the cruise missile systems of the two powers. In contrast to the American system described above, the Soviet SS-N-3 Shaddock (deployed on cruise missile carriers and Echo-class submarines) is a relatively inaccurate missile, propelled by an inefficient turbojet engine over a range not exceeding 550 nautical miles. The SS-N-12, the follow-on system to the Shaddock measures, like the Shaddock, forty feet in length and six feet in diameter. It is reportedly capable of ranges approaching 2000 nautical miles. See also **Tomahawk cruise missile**; **air-launched cruise missile (ALCM)**.

Cruise Missile Carrier: An aircraft capable of delivering cruise missiles within range of their targets. Current plans call for the use of B-52 bombers in this role. In the mid-1980s, wide-bodied commercial aircraft may be procured to supplement, and eventually replace the B-52 force.

Cruiser: A large, long-endurance surface warship armed for independent offensive operations against surface ships and land targets. Also acts as an escort to protect aircraft carriers, merchantmen, and other ships against surface or air attack; may have an anti-submarine capability. Its own aircraft-handling capability is restricted to one or two float planes, helicopters, or other short takeoff and landing types.

Cryptanalysis: The breaking of codes and ciphers into plain text without initial knowledge of the key employed in the encryption.

Cryptography: The enciphering of plain text so that it will be unintelligible to an unauthorized recipient.

Cryptology: The science that includes cryptanalysis and cryptography and embraces communications intelligence and communications security.

CSCE (Conference on Security and Cooperation in Europe): The 1975 Conference on Security and Cooperation in Europe (held at Helsinki, Finland) in which the thirty-five nations that participated produced agreements in three areas (sometimes referred to as the Helsinki accord).

Basket I embodied a ten-point "Declaration of Principles" governing relations between participating states; from the Eastern perspective, it embodied the primary concern of the conference, which was security. While the Western states participating placed no particular emphasis on any of the "baskets," this section of the agreement did codify the post-war European status quo (in the absence of a post-war peace treaty) through the following principles: the inviolability of frontiers, territorial integrity, non-intervention in internal affairs (of participating states), and the sovereign equality of states. The inclusion of confidence-building measures (CBMs) in Basket I represents a significant contribution towards the lessening of politico-military tension in central Europe. See also **confidence-building measures.**

Basket II provided for cooperation in the field of economics, science, technology, and environment and was designed to bring material benefits to both East and West through increased trade and commercial exchanges.

The provisions of *Basket III* represented the extension of improved East-West governmental relations into the following areas of interstate activity: human contacts, free information flow, increased cultural exchange, and educational cooperation.

D

Damage Control: In naval usage, measures necessary aboard ship to preserve and reestablish watertight integrity, stability, maneuverability, and offensive power: (1) to control list and trim; (2) to effect rapid repairs of materiel; (3) to limit the spread of and provide adequate protection from fire; (4) to limit the spread of, remove the contamination by, and provide adequate protection from toxic agents; and (5) to provide for care of wounded personnel.

Damage Limitation: Active or passive efforts to restrict the level or geographic extent of devastation during war. Includes counterforce actions of all kinds as well as civil defense measures. See also **active defense; civil defense; counterforce; passive defense.**

Danger Space: That space between the weapon and the target where the trajectory does not rise 1.8 meters (the average height of a standing man). This includes the area encompassed by the beaten zone. See also **beaten zone.**

Day Fighter: A fighter aircraft designed for air interception purposes primarily in visual meteorological conditions. It may or may not carry electronic devices to assist in interception and in aiming its weapons.

D-Day: The unnamed day on which a particular operation commences or is to commence. An operation may be (1) the commencement of hostilities; (2) the date of a major military effort; (3) the execution date of an operation (as distinguished from the date the order to execute is issued); or (4) the date the operations phase is implemented, either by land assault, air strike, naval bombardment, parachute assault, or amphibious assault. The highest command headquarters responsible for coordinating the planning will specify the exact meaning of D-day within the aforementioned definition. See also **C-day**; **H-hour**; **K-day**; **M-day**.

Decontamination: The process of making any person, object, or area safe by absorbing, destroying, neutralizing, making harmless, or removing chemical or biological agents, or by removing radioactive material clinging to or around it.

Decoy: A device that accompanies the nuclear weapon delivery vehicle in order to mislead enemy defensive systems and thus to increase the probability of penetration and weapon delivery. The device may be designed to simulate an aircraft or ballistic missile warhead with the purpose of diverting defensive antiaircraft or antimissile fire. A relatively small decoy can be made to appear as large as a bomber on radar screens by electromagnetic techniques. ICBM decoys generally must simulate the radar signature of the actual warhead.

Decoy Ships: Warships or other ships camouflaged as merchantmen or converted commerce raiders with their armament and other fighting equipment hidden and with special provisions for unmasking their weapons quickly.

Deep Fording: The ability of a self-propelled gun or ground vehicle equipped with built-in waterproofing or a special waterproofing kit to negotiate a water obstacle with its wheels or tracks in contact with the ground.

Deep Interdiction: Air attacks on lines of communication, reserve forces, factories, etc., farther back in enemy territory than the area near the battleline.

Defense: Measures taken by a country or coalition of countries to resist political, military, economic, social, psychological, or technological attacks. Defensive capabilities reinforce deterrence and vice versa.

Defense Emergency: An emergency condition existing when: 1. A major attack is made upon U.S. forces overseas or on allied forces in any theater and is confirmed either by the commander of a command established by the secretary of defense or by a higher authority. 2. An overt attack of any type is made upon the United States and is confirmed either by the commander of a command established by the secretary of defense or by a higher authority.

Defense-in-Depth: 1. The siting of mutually supporting defense positions designed to absorb and progressively weaken attack, to prevent initial observations of the whole position by the enemy, and to allow the commander to maneuver his reserve. **2.** In naval usage, a concept of concentric carrier defenses compromising: (1) *airborne defenses*: interceptors that attack incoming raids hundreds of miles from the carrier; (2) *area defenses*: shipborne missile-firing systems that target missiles and planes that survive interceptor attacks; and (3) *close-in defenses*: rapid firing guns or short-range missiles fired at all residual attacking units.

Defense Intelligence Agency (DIA): Department of Defense agency for producing military intelligence, created by directive of the secretary of defense in 1961.

Defense Intelligence Objectives and Priorities (DIOP): A single statement of intelligence requirements compiled by the Defense Intelligence Agency for use by all Department of Defense intelligence components.

Defensive Sea Area: An area (usually including the approaches to and the waters of important ports, harbors, bays, or sounds) set aside as vital to the control and protection of shipping, to the safeguarding of defense installations bordering on waters of the areas, and to providing other security measures within the specified areas. The area does not extend seaward beyond U.S. territorial waters.

Defensive Weapons: Weapons systems deployed for the purpose of stopping and repelling an enemy attack, such as a weapon system designed to intercept and destroy enemy strategic delivery vehicles. Drawing a distinction between defensive and offensive weapons is difficult because one nation's defensive weapons may be considered offensive by another power.

Defoliant Operations: The employment of defoliating agents on vegetated areas in support of military operations.

Defoliating Agent: A chemical that causes trees, shrubs, and other plants to shed their leaves prematurely.

Degree of Risk: As specified by a commander, the risk to which friendly forces may be subjected after the detonation of a nuclear weapon used in the attack of a close-in enemy target; acceptable degrees of risk under differing tactical conditions are emergency, moderate, and negligible.

Deliberate Defense: A defense normally organized when out of contact with the enemy or when contact with the enemy is not imminent and time for organization is available. It normally includes an extensive fortified zone incorporating pillboxes, forts, and communications systems.

Delivery Error: The inaccuracy associated with a given weapon system resulting in a dispersion of shots about the aiming point. See also **bombing error; circular error probability; dispersion error.**

Delivery System: Includes the basic weapon (such as a missile or gravity bomb), the means of propulsion (such as a missile launcher or aircraft), and associated mechanisms and other equipment needed to complete the operational package. Components may be widely separated as in the case of missile launchers and radars.

Demilitarized Zone (DMZ): A defined area in which the stationing or concentrating of military forces or the retention or establishment of military installations of any type is prohibited.

Demolition: The destruction of structures, facilities, or materiel by use of fire, water, explosives, mechanical devices, or other means.

Demolition Belt: A selected land area sown with explosive charges, mines, and other available obstacles to deny use of the land to enemy operations and to protect friendly troops.

Deployed Nuclear Weapons: 1. When used in connection with the transfer of weapons between the Atomic Energy Commission and the Department of Defense, this term describes those weapons transferred to and in the custody of the Department of Defense. 2. Those nuclear weapons specifically authorized by the Joint Chiefs of Staff to be transferred to the custody of storage facilities or carrying and delivery units of the armed forces.

Deployment: 1. Act of extending battalions and smaller units in width, in depth, or in both width and depth to increase their readiness for contemplated action. 2. In naval usage, the change from a cruising approach or contact disposition to a disposition for battle. 3. In a strategic sense, the relocation of forces to desired areas of operation. 4. The designated location of troops and troop units as indicated in a troop schedule. 5. The series of functions that transpire from the time a packed parachute is placed in operation until it is fully opened and is supporting its load.

Depressed Trajectory: The trajectory of a ballistic missile fired at an angle to the ground significantly lower than the angle of a minimum energy trajectory. Such a missile rises above the line-of-sight radar horizon at a later state of flight and has a shorter time of flight, thus making detection and tracking more difficult and reducing warning time.

Desired Effects: The damage or casualties to enemy troops or materiel a commander desires to achieve from a nuclear weapon detonation. Damage effects on materiel are classified as light, moderate, or severe. Casualty effects on personnel may be immediate, prompt, or delayed.

Destroyer: A high-speed warship designed to operate offensively with strike forces, with hunter-killer groups, and in support of amphibious assault operations. Destroyers also operate defensively to screen support forces and convoys against submarine, air, and surface threats. Normal armament consists of three- and five-inch dual-purpose guns and various antisubmarine warfare weapons.

Destroyer Minelayer: Converted destroyers designed to conduct high-speed mine laying operations. Average load is eighty mines laid from two stern racks. Designated as DM.

Détente: Lessening of tensions in international relations, achieved formally or informally.

Deterrence: Steps taken to prevent opponents from initiating armed actions and to inhibit escalation if combat occurs. Threats of force predominate.

> *Type I Deterrence*: deterrent power inhibiting a direct attack against the United States; *Type II Deterrence*: deterrent power inhibiting serious infractions short of attacks against the United States, such as aggression against friends and allies; and *Type III Deterrence*: deterrent power inhibiting aggression by making limited provocations unprofitable.

Deterrence by Denial: The Soviet conceptualization of deterrence is conceived on a denial basis. The Soviet Union deters another power (by deploying a disarming and damage-limiting capability) from a first strike by convincing the opponent that no military gain could accrue by striking first. Essentially a counterforce posture.

Deterrence by Punishment: The American conception of nuclear deterrence is based on a capacity to survive a nuclear first strike and to inflict unacceptable damage on the aggressor in a retaliatory (second) strike. While military advantages accrue to the nation who strikes first, it is deterred from such action by the knowledge of the unacceptable damage it would suffer in a retaliatory blow.

Deterrent: The sum total of those policies and capabilities that deter the opponent from military aggression because of the threat of unacceptable damage.

Development: A three-phase process: *Phase I (concepts)*: Identifies options, sets priorities, and defines the project. Exploration and experimentation take place. *Phase II (validation)*: Produces "brass board" models used to establish program characteristics, including technical problems, costs, and schedules. *Phase III, (engineering)*: Terminates with "hardware" models (prototypes) ready for test and evaluation.

Differential Ballistic Wind: In bombing, a hypothetical wind equal to the difference in velocity between the ballistic wind and the actual wind at a release altitude.

Direction of Attack: A specific direction or route that the main attack or center of mass of the unit will follow. The unit is restricted and required to attack as indicated and is not normally allowed to bypass the enemy. The direction of attack is used primarily in counterattacks or to ensure that supporting attacks make maximum contribution to the main attack.

Direct Strategy: The existence of, or the application of, military force in conflict situations that relies on physical coercion rather than deterrence or indirect means of influence. See also **indirect strategy**.

Director of Central Intelligence Directive (DCID): A directive issued by the director of Central Intelligence that outlines general policies and procedures to be followed by intelligence agencies under the director's control.

Dirty Bomb: A fission bomb or any other weapon that would distribute relatively large amounts of radioactivity upon explosion as distinguished from a fusion weapon.

Disarmament: The reduction of armed forces and armaments as a result of unilateral initiatives or international agreement. See also **arms control; arms limitation**.

Disengagement: In arms control, generally proposals that would result in the geographic separation of opposing nonindigenous forces without directly affecting indigenous military forces.

Dispersal: Relocation of forces for the purpose of increasing survivability.

Dispersion: 1. A scattered pattern of hits by bombs dropped under identical conditions or by projectiles fired from the same gun or group of guns with the same firing data. 2. In antiaircraft gunnery, the scattering of shots in range and deflection about the mean point of impact. As used in flak analysis, includes scattering due to all causes; the mean point of impact is assumed to be the target. 3. The spreading or separating of troops, materiel, establishments, or activities that are usually concentrated in limited areas to reduce vulnerability to enemy action. **4.** In chemical warfare, the dissemination of agents in liquid or aerosol form from bombs and spray tanks. See also **bombing error; circular error probability; delivery error; dispersion error.**

Dispersion Error: The distance from the point of impact or burst of a round to the mean point of impact or burst.

Distant Early Warning System (DEWS): An array of thirty-one radars that stretch in a line across the northern areas of North America from Alaska to Greenland. Information received from these radars is transmitted to the Combat Operations Center of the North American Air Defense Command.

Diversionary Attack: An attack wherein a force attacks, or threatens to attack, a target other than the main target for the purpose of drawing enemy defenses away from the main effort.

Division: 1. A tactical unit or formation as follows: (a) a major administrative and tactical unit or formation; larger than a regiment or brigade and smaller than a corps, that combines in itself the necessary arms and services required for sustained combat; (b) a number of naval ships of a smaller type grouped together for operational and administrative command, or a tactical unit of a naval aircraft squadron, consisting of two or more sections; (c) an air combat organization normally consisting of two or more wings with appropriate service units. **2.** An organizational part of a headquarters that handles military matters of a particular nature, such as personnel, intelligence, plans and training, or supply and evacuation. **3.** A number of personnel of a ship's complement grouped together for operational and administrative command.

Division Artillery: Artillery that is permanently an integral part of a division; for tactical purposes, all artillery placed under the command of a division commander.

Division Equivalent: Separate brigades, regiments, and comparable combat forces whose aggregate capabilities approximate those of a division, except for staying power. See also **division.**

Division Force Equivalent: The average number of troops required to man a typical Army division and its supporting units in sustained combat.

Doctrine: Fundamental principles by which the military forces or elements thereof guide their actions in support of national objectives. It is authoritative but requires judgment in application. See also **national objectives; principles of war.**

Dosimetry: The measurement of radiation doses; applies to both the devices used (dosimeters) and the techniques employed.

Drift: In ballistics, a shift in projectile direction due to gyroscopic action that results from gravitational and atmospherically induced torques on the spinning projectile.

Drone: An unmanned airborne vehicle that flies a preprogrammed pattern of courses and heights.

Dual-capable Systems: Those systems capable of delivering either conventional or nuclear weapons. Certain artillery pieces, short-range missiles, and tactical aircraft are dual-capable delivery systems (e.g., NATO 155 mm howitzer, NATO Honest John missile, Warsaw Pact SCUD missile, NATO F-4 fighter, and Warsaw Pact SU-7 fighter).

Dwarf Dud: A nuclear weapon that, when launched at or emplaced on a target, fails to provide a yield within a reasonable range of what could be anticipated with normal operation of the weapon. This constitutes a dud only in the relative sense.

Dyad: A strategic force structure with two components: submarine-launched ballistic missiles (SLBMs) and "air-breathing elements" (cruise missiles and intercontinental bombers).

E

E-2C: Navy early warning aircraft.

E-3A: See **AWACS (Airborne Warning and Control System)**.

EA-6B: Navy and Marine Corps electronic countermeasures aircraft.

EF-111: Air Force F-111 modified as electronic countermeasure (ECM)—radar jamming—aircraft; program currently in development; none procured. See also **electronic countermeasure**.

Earmarked for Assignment on Mobilization: Forces specifically designated by nations for assignment to a NATO commander in the event of mobilization or war. In designating such forces, nations must specify when these forces will be available in the terms agreed to in the echelon system.

Earth Penetrator (EP): A device that mechanically buries a nuclear warhead in the ground before detonation. Can be used to create physical barriers to enemy military operations, to destroy hardened enemy targets, or to conduct nuclear strikes that require the confinement of nuclear effects to the ground.

Echelon: 1. A subdivision of a headquarters, such as forward echelon, rear echelon. 2. Separate level of command. For example, as compared to a regiment, a division is a higher echelon while a batallion is a lower echelon. 3. A fraction of a command in the direction of depth to which a principal combat mission is assigned, such as attack echelon, support echelon, reserve echelon. **4.** A formation in which the subdivisions are placed one behind another, extending beyond and unmasking one another wholly or in part.

Economic Action: The planned use of economic measures designed to influence the policies or actions of another state; e.g., to impair the war-making potential of a hostile power, or to generate economic stability within a friendly power.

Economic Mobilization: The process of preparing for and carrying out such changes in the organization and functioning of the national economy as are necessary to provide for the most effective use of resources in a national emergency.

Economic Potential for War: That share of the total economic capacity of a nation that can be used for the purposes of war.

Economic Warfare: The offensive or defensive use of trade, foreign aid programs, financial transactions, and other matters that influence the production, distribution, and consumption of goods and services. Seeks to achieve national security objectives by augmenting friendly capabilities and diminishing or neutralizing enemy capabilities and potential.

Effective Damage: That damage necessary to render a target element inoperative, unserviceable, nonproductive, or uninhabitable.

Effective Range: The maximum distance within which a weapon may be expected to fire accurately to inflict casualties or damage.

Electromagnetic Pulse (EMP): A nuclear weapon effect that can destroy or impair the performance of electronic equipment and wipe clean computer memories by creation of electrical and magnetic fields.

Electronic Counter-countermeasure: A form of electronic warfare taken to insure effective use of the electromagnetic spectrum despite enemy's electronic countermeasure efforts.

Electronic Countermeasure (ECM): Electronic warfare (EW) involving actions taken to prevent or reduce an enemy's effective use of equipment and tactics employed or affected by electromagnetic radiations; to exploit the enemy's use of such radiations.

Electronic Intelligence (ELINT): Technical and intelligence information derived from the collection (or interception) and processing of foreign electromagnetic radiations (noncommunication) emanating from sources such as radar. ELINT is part of the National Security Agency/Central Security Service signals intelligence mission.

Electronic Warfare: The military use of electronics involving actions taken to prevent or reduce an enemy's effective use of radiated electromagnetic energy, and actions taken to insure our own effective use of radiated electromagnetic energy.

Electronic Warfare Support Measures: Electronic warfare involving actions taken to search for, intercept, locate, record, and analyze radiated electromagnetic energy for the purpose of exploiting such radiations in support of military operations. Thus, electronic warfare support measures provide a source of electronic warfare information required to conduct electronic countermeasures, electronic counter-countermeasures, threat detection, warning, avoidance, target acquisition, and homing.

Elements of National Power: All the means that are available for employment in the pursuit of national objectives.

Elicitation: The acquisition of intelligence from a person or group while not disclosing the intent of the interview or conversation. This is a HUMINT (human intelligence) collection technique, generally of an overt nature, unless the collector is other than what he or she purports to be.

Emission Security: That component of communications security resulting from all measures taken to deny unauthorized persons any information of value that might be derived from the interception and analysis of compromising emanations from crypto-equipment or telecommunications systems.

Endoatmosphere: From sea level to about forty nautical miles altitude.

Ends: National security interests, objectives, and commitments along with military roles and missions that establish aims to be accomplished. See also **means**.

Enemy Capabilities: Those courses of action of which the enemy is physically capable and, if adopted, would affect the accomplishment of the mission. The term "capabilities" includes not only the general courses of action open to the enemy, such as attack, defense, or withdrawal, but also all the particular courses of action possible under each general course of action. Enemy capabilities are considered in the light of all known factors affecting military operations including time, space, weather, terrain, and the strength and disposition of enemy forces. In strategic thinking, the capabilities of a nation represent the courses of action within the power of the nation for accomplishing its national objectives in peace or war.

Engagement: In air defense, an attack with guns or air-to-air missiles by an interceptor aircraft, or the launch of an air defense missile

by air defense artillery and the missile's subsequent travel to
intercept.

Enlarged Sanctuarization: See **Méry Plan.**

Enriched Material: Material in which the given isotope naturally
present has been artificially increased to a higher percentage
than that normally found. Enriched uranium contains more of
the fissionable isotope uranium-235 than the naturally occur-
ring percentage (0.7 percent).

Enrichment Plant: A facility that increases the ratio of U-235 to
U-238 from 0.7 percent to 99 percent. Alteration of the isotopic
composition of an element is accomplished through isotopic
separation. The two most common types of enrichment plants
are gaseous diffusion and gas centrifuge. Uranium must be
enriched for nuclear explosive use.

Equivalent Megatonnage (EMT): A measure used to compare the
destructive potential of differing combinations of nuclear warhead yields against relatively soft countervalue targets. EMT is a
computed function of yield (given in megatons) that compen-
sates approximately for the fact that blast damage resulting from
a nuclear detonation does not increase linearly with an increase
in yield. EMT calculations are useful in estimating the effects of
small numbers of smaller-yield warheads against the same targets.

   EMT is computed from the expression: $EMT = NY^x$, where N
equals the number of actual warheads of yield Y; Y equals the
yield of the actual warheads in metagons; and x equals the
scaling factor. Scaling factors vary with the size and characteristics of the target base and the number of targets attacked.

Escalation: An increase in scope or violence of a conflict, deliberate
or unpremeditated: 1. One side moving from a conventional
conflict to strategic nuclear strikes. 2. A move from local to
general war.

Escalation Ladder: Successive levels of intensity in the conflict
spectrum. See also **conflict spectrum.**

Escort: Cruisers, destroyers, frigates, and other surface warships
expressly configured to defend other ships against enemy attack.
May be multipurpose (antiair, antisubmarine) or unipurpose.
May also be assigned independent offensive missions. See also
cruiser; destroyer; frigate.

Essential Equivalence: A policy that stipulates a need for approximately equal capabilities and effectiveness but not numerical
equality between the central strategic systems of the United

States and the Soviet Union. Essential equivalence is a synonym for parity. See also **parity**; **Strategic Sufficiency**; **overkill**.

Essential Industry: Any industry necessary to a civilian or war economy. Includes the basic industries as well as the necessary portions of those other industries that transform crude, basic raw materials into useful intermediate or end products; e.g., the iron and steel industry, the food industry, and the chemical industry.

Exemplary Attack: An isolated attack against a military or civilian target demonstrating a particular capability; designed primarily for psychological effect. Hiroshima and Nagasaki were exemplary attacks. See also **symbolic attack**.

Exercise: A military maneuver or simulated wartime operation involving planning, preparation and execution that is carried out for the purpose of training and evaluation. May be a combined, unified joint, or single service exercise, depending on participating organizations.

Existence Load: Consists of items other than those in the fighting load that are required to sustain or protect the combat soldier, that may be necessary for increased personal and environmental protection, and that are not normally carried by the individual. See also **fighting load**.

Exoatmosphere: Higher than about forty nautical miles above sea level.

Explosive Energy Yield of a Nuclear Warhead: Energy released through detonation measured as equal to a given number of tons of TNT. (One kiloton equals 4.2 terajoules.) The drawback of this indicator is that it does not reflect the actual amount of potential damage from a blast because the area exposed to damage increases in proportion to two-thirds the power of the weapons yield.

Exposure Dose: The exposure dose at a given point is a measurement of the ability of the radiation to produce ionization. The unit of measurement of the exposure dose is the roentgen.

Extended Deterrence: Deterrent power of a state extended to include its allies or its own troops stationed abroad.

F

F-4: Air Force, Navy, and Marine Corps fighter or attack aircraft.

F-4G ("Wild Weasel"): Air Force fighter or attack aircraft equipped with warning and attack systems to seek out and destroy enemy SAMs (surface-to-air missiles).

F-14: Navy air superiority fighter.

F-15: Air Force air superiority fighter.

F-16: Air Force fighter or attack aircraft.

F-18: Navy fighter or attack aircraft.

F-111: Air Force night or bad weather attack aircraft.

FB-111: Medium bomber procured in small numbers in the late 1960s to supplement the B-52 force. Although capable of supersonic low-level flight, the aircraft's small range and payload limit its effectiveness. Modified, stretched FB-111H bombers may be added to the bomber force in the 1980s.

Fail-Safe: A plan that prevents an intercontinental bomber carrying nuclear weapons from continuing on a mission against the enemy if, at a geographically fixed point, the bomber commander has not received orders confirming the mission.

Fallout: The precipitation to earth of radioactive particulate matter from a nuclear cloud; also applied to the particulate matter itself.

Fallout-Safe Height of Burst: The height of burst at or above which no militarily significant fallout will be reproduced as a result of a nuclear weapon detonation. See also **types of burst**.

Fallout Shelter: Natural or man-made structures that afford protection against radioactive debris caused by a nuclear blast.

Fast Breeder Reactor: A reactor that uses plutonium and natural uranium. It produces more fissionable plutonium than it consumes as it generates electric power by converting the uranium 238 into plutonium 239.

Fast Reactor: A reactor in which the fission chain reaction is sustained by fast neutrons rather than by thermal or intermediate neutrons. Fast reactors contain little or no moderator to slow down the neutrons from the speeds at which they are ejected from fissioning nuclei.

Fertile Material: A material, not itself fissionable by thermal neutrons, that can be converted into a fissile material by irradiation in a reactor. There are two basic fertile materials, uranium 238 and thorium 232. When these fertile materials capture neutrons, they are partially converted into fissile plutonium 239 and uranium 232, respectively.

Field Army: Administrative and tactical organization composed of a headquarters, certain organic Army troops, service support troops, a variable number of corps, and a variable number of divisions. See also **division**.

Fighter Aircraft: Tactical aircraft used primarily to gain and maintain air superiority.

Fighting Load: Consists of items of individual clothing, equipment, weapons, and ammunition that are carried by, and are essential to, the effectiveness of the combat soldier on foot and the accomplishment of the immediate mission of his unit. See also **existence load**.

Finite Deterrence: Deterrence based on a minimum deterrent capability corresponding to specific calculable needs. Under a strategy of finite deterrence, only cities, of which there are a finite number, are targeted.

Fireball: The luminous sphere of hot gases that forms a few millionths of a second after detonation of a nuclear weapon and immediately starts expanding and cooling.

Firebreak: A psychological barrier that inhibits escalation from one type of warfare to another, such as from conventional to nuclear combat. See also **threshold**.

Firepower: 1. The amount of fire that may be delivered by a position, unit, or weapon system. 2. Ability to deliver fire.

Fire Power Umbrella: An area of airspace with specified dimensions and defined boundaries over a naval force at sea within which special procedures have been established for the identification and operation of friendly aircraft.

First Strike: The launching of an initial strategic nuclear attack before the opponent has used any strategic weapons himself. See also **preemptive strike**.

First-Strike Capability: A nuclear capability that makes a first strike possible yet may be insufficient for a credible second strike.

First-Strike Strategy: Strategy based on the notion that only by striking first can a nuclear power gain the advantage and prevent defeat.

First Use: The initial employment of specific military measures, during the conduct of war, such as nuclear weapons. A belligerent could execute a second strike in response to aggression, yet be the first to employ nuclear weapons. See also **first strike; second strike**.

Fission: The splitting of an atomic nucleus of certain heavy elements like uranium and plutonium by bombardment with neutrons, which results in the release of substantial quantities of energy. See also **fusion**.

Fissionable Material: Commonly used as a synonym for fissile material. The meaning of this term also has been extended to include material that can be fissioned by fast neutrons only, such as uranium 238. Used in reactor operations to mean fuel.

Fission-to-Yield Ratio: The ratio of the yield derived from nuclear fission to the total yield; frequently expressed in percentage.

Fission Yield: 1. The amount of energy released by fission in a thermonuclear (fusion) explosion as distinct from that released by fusion. **2.** The amount (percentage) of a given nuclide produced by fusion.

Flare Dud: A nuclear weapon that, when launched at a target, detonates with anticipated yield but at an altitude appreciably greater than intended.

Flash Burn: A burn caused by excessive exposure of bare skin to thermal radiation.

Fleet: An organization of ships, aircraft, marine forces, and shore-based fleet activities, all under the command of a commander or commander-in-chief who may exercise operational as well as administrative control.

Fleet Ballistic Missile Submarine: A nuclear-powered submarine designed to deliver ballistic missile attacks against assigned targets from either a submerged or surfaced condition. See also **ballistic missile; SBLM (Submarine-launched ballistic missile)**.

Fleet-in-Being: A fleet or force that avoids decisive action but that, because of its strength and location, causes or necessitates counterconcentrations and thus reduces the number of opposing units available for operations elsewhere.

Fleet Marine Force: A balanced force of combined arms comprising land, air, and service elements of the U.S. Marine Corps. A Fleet Marine Force is an integral part of a U.S. fleet and has the status of a type command.

Flexibility: Capabilities that afford countries and weapons systems a range of options, and facilitate smooth adjustment when situations change. See also **flexible response**.

Flexible Response: A strategy predicated on capabilities to act effectively across the entire spectrum of war at times, places, and in manners of the power's choosing. See also **graduated response**.

FLIR (Forward-looking infrared): A TV-Like system capable of detecting objects by their infrared radiation.

Force de Frappe: Strategic nuclear weapons systems designed to give France an independent minimum deterrent force. See also **minimum deterrence**.

Foreign Internal Defense: Participation by civilian and military agencies of another government in any of the action programs taken by their government to free and protect its society from subversion, lawlessness, and insurgency.

Foreign Military Sales: That portion of U.S. military assistance authorized by the Foreign Assistance Act of 1961, as amended. This assistance is for both defense articles and services (including training). This assistance differs from Military Assistance Program Grant Aid in that it is purchased by the recipient country.

Foreign Policy: Foreign policy comprises the totality of purposes and international commitments by which a nation through its constitutional or otherwise designated authority seeks by means of influence, power, and sometimes violence to deal with foreign states and problems in the international environment.

Forward Base: A military installation maintained on foreign soil or on a distant possession that is conveniently located with regard to actual or potential areas of operations.

Forward-Based Systems (FBS): Introduced by the Soviet Union to refer to those U.S. nuclear systems based in other countries or on aircraft carriers and capable of delivering a nuclear strike against the territory of the Soviet Union. The Soviet Union took the position in both SALT I and early in SALT II that U.S. tactical forces capable of delivering nuclear strikes against the territory of the Soviet Union had to be included in any permanent agreement on strategic arms; however, it was agreed at Vladivostok in 1974 that FBS would not be a SALT issue.

Forward Defense: Protective measures taken to contain or repulse military aggression as close to the original line of contact as possible.

Forward Edge of the Battle Area: The foremost limits of a series of areas in which ground combat units are deployed, excluding the areas in which the covering or screening forces are operating, designated to coordinate fire support, the positioning of forces, or the maneuver of units.

Fourquet Plan: Publicized by French Chief of Staff General Michel Fourquet in the spring of 1969 (but conceived in 1968, following the invasion of Czechoslovakia by East-bloc troops). The Fourquet Plan revised the **Ailleret Doctrine** by identifying a potential enemy and by rejecting the notion that an independent French nuclear arsenal would ensure French neutrality and security in an East-West war. The Fourquet plan stressed a carefully graduated flexible response strategy—*la réplique graduée*—and relied heavily on tactical nuclear weapons (partially in order to establish a triggering link with the American strategic deterrent), with strategic weapons serving as the ultimate deterrent against an all-out attack on French territory. The Fourquet

Plan was modified by the **Méry Plan.**

Fractional Orbital Bombardment System (FOBS): A missile that achieves an orbital trajectory, but fires a set of retrorockets before the completion of one revolution in order to slow down, reenter the atmosphere, and release the warhead it carries into a normal ballistic trajectory toward its target. While a normal ICBM follows a parabolic path to target, highly visible to defending radars, a weapon in low orbit, can make a sharp descent to earth, cutting radar warning time substantially. A FOBS path accordingly consists of a launch into low orbit, a partial circle to the earth target, and a rapid descent.

Free Rocket: A missile with a completely self-contained propellant package that is neither guided nor controlled in flight.

Frigate: A warship designed to operate independently, or with strike, antisubmarine warfare, or amphibious forces against submarine, air, and surface threats. (Normal armaments consist of three- and five-inch dual-purpose guns and advanced antisubmarine warfare weapons.) Designated as DL. See also **guided missile frigate.**

FROD (Functionally Related Observable Differences): A concept developed by American SALT negotiators to deal with certain verification problems, most specifically how to distinguish between two aircraft of the same type where one is being utilized as a heavy bomber and the other is not. Indications are that the SALT II agreement will permit the use of bomber aircraft in multiple roles, but require that all such aircraft be counted as heavy bombers unless there are observable differences related to the function of the aircraft.

Front: 1. The lateral space occupied by an element, measured from the extremity of one flank to the extremity of the other flank. 2. The direction of the enemy. 3. The line of contact of two opposing forces. 4. When a combat situation does not exist or is not assumed, the direction toward which the command is facing.

Frontal Attack: A form of attack in which the main action is directed against the front of the enemy forces.

Fratricide: The phenomenon whereby nuclear warhead explosions create such turbulent local conditions that other incoming warheads are damaged, destroyed, or made to deviate from their intended trajectories.

Fuel: Fissionable material for use in a reactor to produce energy. Also applied to a mixture, such as natural uranium, in which only part of the atoms are readily fissionable, if the mixture can be made to sustain a chain reaction.

Fuel Cycle: The series of steps involved in supplying fuel for nuclear power reactors. It includes mining, refining, the original fabrication of fuel elements, their use in a reactor, chemical processing to recover the fissionable material remaining in the spent fuel, reenrichment of the fuel material, and refabrication into new fuel elements.

Full Mobilization: Expansion of the active armed forces resulting from action by Congress and the president to mobilize all Reserve Component units in the existing approved force structure, all individual reservists, and the materiel resources needed for their support. See also **mobilization**.

Fusion: The process whereby the nuclei of light elements, especially those of the isotopes of hydrogen (deuterium and tritium), combine to form the nucleus of a heavier element, with the release of substantial amounts of energy. The fusion process constitutes the basis of the thermonuclear weapon that is vastly more powerful than the fission-type nuclear weapon. See **fission**.

Fusion Weapon: An atomic weapon using the energy of nuclear fusion, such as a hydrogen bomb.

G

Gamma Rays: High energy electromagnetic radiation emitted from atomic nuclei during a nuclear reaction. Gamma rays and very high energy X-rays differ only in origin, the latter being produced in other ways.

Gap Filler Radar: Unattended air defense surveillance radar once used to supplement the coverage of long-range radar in areas where coverage is inadequate.

Gaseous Diffusion: A method of isotopic separation based on the fact that gas atoms or molecules with different masses will diffuse through a porous barrier at different rates. The method is used to separate uranium 235 from uranium 238; it requires large gaseous diffusion plants and enormous amounts of electric power.

GCI (Ground Control Intercept): A system of controlling the operations of interceptors from ground radar stations.

General Disarmament: Reduction of armed forces by nations to a level required for internal security only.

General Purpose Forces: All combat forces not designed primarily to accomplish strategic offensive, defensive, or mobility missions. See also **strategic defense; strategic mobility; strategic offense**.

General Staff: A group of officers in the headquarters of Army or

Marine divisions, Marine brigades, aircraft wings, or similar or larger units that assist their commanders in planning, coordinating, and supervising operations. A general staff may consist of four or more principal functional sections: personnel (G-1), military intelligence (G-2), operations and training (G-3), logistics (G-4), and (in Army organizations) civil affairs or military government (G-5). (A particular section may be added or eliminated by the commander, depending upon need.) The comparable Air Force staff is found in the wing and larger units, with sections designated as above. G-2 Air and G-3 Air are Army officers assigned to G-2 or G-3 at division, corps, or Army headquarters level, who assist in planning and coordinating joint operations of ground and air units. Naval staffs ordinarily are not organized along these lines, but when they are, they are designated N-1, N-2, etc. Similarly, a joint staff may be designated J-1, J-2, etc. In Army brigades and smaller units and in Marine Corps units smaller than a brigade or aircraft wing, staff sections are designated S-1, S-2, etc., with corresponding duties; referred to as a unit staff in the Army and as an executive staff in the Marine Corps.

General War: Armed conflict between major powers in which the total resources of the belligerents are employed and the national survival of the belligerents is in jeopardy. Commonly reserved for a showdown between the United States and the Soviet Union, featuring nuclear weapons.

Generated Alert: A condition where forces are placed in a high state of readiness, with the vast majority of the bomber force on ground alert ready for rapid take-off and the vast majority of the submarine force at sea.

Glide Bomb: A bomb, fitted with airfoils to provide lift, that is carried and released in the direction of a target by an airplane.

Global Positioning Satellites: A system of orbiting satellites that by the early 1980s will be able to give ships, aircraft, missiles, and other vehicles precise information on their position and velocity.

Graduated Deterrence: A range of deterrent power that affords credible capabilities to inhibit aggression across all, or a considerable portion of, the conflict spectrum.

Graduated Response: The incremental application of national power in ways that allows the opposition to accommodate one step at a time. See also **flexible response**.

Grey Propaganda: Propaganda that does not specifically identify any source.

Gross Error: A nuclear weapon detonation at such a distance from the desired ground zero as to cause no nuclear damage to the target.

Ground Fire: Small arms ground-to-air fire directed against aircraft.

Ground Zero: The point on the surface of the earth at, vertically below, or above the center of a planned or actual nuclear detonation.

Guerrilla Warfare: Military and paramilitary operations conducted in enemy-held or hostile territory by irregular, predominantly indigenous forces.

Guidance System: A system that evaluates missile flight information, correlates it with target data, determines the desired flight path, and communicates the necessary commands to the missile flight control system.

Guided Missile: An unmanned vehicle moving above the surface of the earth whose trajectory or flight path is capable of being altered by an external or internal mechanism. See also **aerodynamic missile; ballistic missile**.

Guided Missile Cruiser: With exception of CGNs, these ships are full conversion of heavy cruisers. All guns are removed and replaced with Talos or Tartar missile launchers. The CGN is a nuclear-powered, long-range ship equipped with Talos or Terrier missile and ASROC (antisubmarine rocket) launchers. Designated as CG and CGN. For designed mission, see **heavy cruiser**.

Guided Missile Destroyer: This destroyer type is equipped with Terrier or Tartar guided missile launchers, improved naval gun battery, long-range sonar, and antisubmarine warfare weapons, including ASROC (antisubmarine rocket). Designated as DDG. For designed mission, see **destroyer**.

Guided Missile Frigate: Equipped with Terrier or Tartar missile launchers and 5"/54-gun battery. Designated as DLG and DLGN. The DLGN is nuclear powered. For designed mission, see **frigate**.

Guided Missile Heavy Cruiser: These ships are converted heavy cruisers with one triple 8"/55 turret removed and replaced with a twin Terrier missile launcher. Designated as CAG. For designed mission, see **heavy cruiser**.

Guided Missile Light Cruiser: Converted light cruisers. In addition to 6"/47 guns, either Terrier or Talos missile launchers have been added to main armament. Designated as CLG. For designed mission, see **light cruiser**.

Guided Missile Submarine: A submarine designed to have an additional capability to launch guided missile attacks from surfaced condition. Designated as SSG and SSGN. The SSGN is nuclear powered.

Gun: 1. A cannon with a relatively long barrel, operating with a relatively low angle of fire, and having a high muzzle velocity. 2. A cannon with a tube length thirty to fifty calibers or more. See also **howitzer; mortar.**

Gun, Heavy, 175 mm: A full-tracked, self-propelled gun with a maximum range of 32,000 meters.

Gun-type Weapon: A device in which two or more pieces of fissionable material, each less than a critical mass, are brought together very rapidly so as to form a supercritical mass.

Gun, Very Heavy Artillery, 280 mm: A mobile cannon designed specifically to fire a nuclear projectile. Mobility for this weapon is provided by a "double-ender" transporter.

H

Half-Life: The time required for the activity of a given radioactive substance to decrease to half of its initial value due to radioactive decay. The half-life is a characteristic property of each radioactive substance and is independent of its amount or condition. The effective half-life of a given isotope is the time in which the quantity in any body will decrease to half its initial value as a result of both radioactive decay and biological elimination.

Harbor Defense: The defense of a harbor or anchorage and its water approaches against external threats such as: (1) submarine, submarine-borne, or small surface craft attack; (2) enemy mine-laying operations; and (3) sabotage. The defense of a harbor from guided or dropped missiles while such missiles are airborne is considered to be a part of air defense.

Hard Base: A launching base that is protected against a nuclear explosion.

Hardened Site: A site constructed to withstand the blasts and associated effects of a nuclear attack and likely to be protected against a chemical, biological, or radiological attack. See also **hard target.**

Hardening of Silos: Protection of a missile site with concrete and earth and other measures so as to withstand blast, heat, or radiation from a nuclear attack. The term is most commonly applied to missiles housed in underground concrete silos mounted on steel springs and fitted with armored blast doors, whose associated command and control facilities are similarly protected. Although "hardness" is attributed to any protective structures that can withstand even a few pounds per square inch of over-pressure, strategic missile silos are protected against greater blast effects.

Hard Missile Base: A launching base that is protected against a nuclear explosion.

Hardness: The amount of protection afforded by structural shielding against blast, heat, and radiation effects of nuclear explosions, usually measured in pounds per square inch.

Hard-Site Defense: Terminal ABM defense designed to protect ICBM sites or other hardened facilities from nuclear attack. This concept is also known as hard-point defense.

Hard-Site ICBM: Any ICBM in a silo that provides substantial protection against nuclear attack. See also **hard target; ICBM (intercontinental ballistic missile)**.

Hard Target: A point or area protected to some significant degree against the blast, heat, and radiation effects of nuclear explosions of particular yields. See also **overpressure; soft targets**.

Harmonization: The process or results of adjusting differences or inconsistencies to bring significant features into agreement.

Harpoon (SLCM): The Harpoon anti-ship missile is a tactical cruise missile measuring 34 centimeters in diameter, 3.84 meters in length, has a total volume of .3 cubic meters, and is powered by a turbojet engine that has a thrust of 660 pounds. With a fuel consumption rate of 1.5 pounds of fuel per pound of thrust per hour of flight, the Harpoon has a maximum range of 100 kilometers at a speed of Mach .85.

Hawk Program: Early in 1958 Belgium, France, the Federal Republic of Germany, Italy, and the Netherlands accepted the offer to use U.S. government-owned property rights to facilitate industrial contracts for the manufacture in Europe of the ground-to-air missile system, the Hawk. Five European firms combined to form an international company known as SETEL (Société Européenne de Téléguidage—European Society of Teleguidance) to act as the European prime contractor. Production was allocated in proportion to the number of complete weapons systems that each nation agreed to buy. The initial production program, which included over 4,000 missiles and associated equipment, was completed in 1967.

In November 1967 the participating countries started a new program, the Hawk European Limited Improvement Program (HELIP), which took as its basis the American Hawk Improvement Program. This program adapted the Hawk weapon system to the air environment of the next decade in order to prolong its use. Early in 1974, the decision to launch the HELIP Production Phase was taken by Denmark, France, Greece, Italy, the Netherlands, and the Federal Republic of Germany. The launching of the Production Phase can be considered as a great achievement in terms of improvement of the basic Hawk System from an operational point of view, in terms of standardization and the introduction of a new technology into European industry.

Heavy Assault Weapon: A weapon, capable of being operated from ground or vehicle, used to defeat armor and other materiel targets.

Heavy Bomber: A multiengine aircraft with intercontinental range, designed specifically to engage targets whose destruction would reduce an enemy's capacity or will to wage war. See also **medium bomber.**

Heavy Cruiser: A warship designed to operate with strike, anti-submarine, or amphibious forces against air and surface threats. Full load displacement is approximately 21,000 tons. Designated as CA.

Heavy Division: An armored or mechanized division, so called because of the equipment.

Heavy ICBM: The 1972 SALT I Interim Agreement on the limitation of selected strategic offensive systems identified heavy ICBMs as those having a volume significantly greater than that of the largest light ICBM. The U.S. Titan II and the Soviet SS-7, SS-8, SS-9, SS-18, and SS-19 are heavy ICBMs.

Heavy-Lift Ship: A ship especially designed for the loading and unloading of heavy and bulky items. It has booms of sufficient capacity to accommodate a single lift of 100 tons.

Heavy Tank: Tanks weighing more than sixty tons are generally designated as "heavies," although the United States no longer uses "heavy," "medium," and "light" as classifications.

Heavy Water: Water containing significantly more than the natural proportion (one in 6500) of heavy hydrogen (deutrium) atoms to ordinary hydrogen atoms. Heavy water is used as a moderator in some reactors because it slows down neutrons effectively. See also **moderator.**

Height of Burst: The vertical distance from the earth's surface or target to the point of burst. See also **optimum height of burst.**

H-Hour: The specific hour on D-day at which a particular operation commences. The operation may be the commencement of hostilities; the hour at which an operation plan is executed or is to be executed (as distinguished from the hour the order to execute is issued); or the hour the operations phase is implemented, either by land assault, parachute assault, amphibious assault, air, or naval bombardment. The highest command or headquarters coordinating the planning will specify the exact meaning of H-hour.

High Airburst: The fallout-safe height of burst of a nuclear weapon that increases damage to or casualties on soft targets, or reduces induced radiation contamination at actual ground zero. See also **types of burst.**

High-Altitude Bombing: Horizontal bombing with the height of release over 15,000 feet.

High-Risk Areas: The most likely target areas in a nuclear first strike. They include major military and industrial installations, great metropolitan centers, and those cities located close to military, industrial, and transportation centers.

High-Speed Submarine: A submarine capable of submerged speeds of twenty knots or more.

High-Temperature Gas-cooled Reactor (HTGR): A type of reactor not widely used for power generation. It is more efficient than the light-water or heavy-water reactors. Fueled by highly-enriched uranium, the HTGR produces spent fuel of U-233 that after processing is usable in the production of nuclear explosives.

High Threshold: An intangible line between levels and types of conflict across which one or more antagonists plan to escalate with great reluctance after other courses of action fail, or across which they are compelled to move only if subjected to immense pressures. See also **low threshold; threshold.**

Hi-Lo Mix: 1. Mingling high-cost, high-performance items with relatively low-cost, low-performance items in any given weapon system to achieve the best balance between quantity and quality in ways that maximize capabilities and minimize expenses. 2. In the context of naval deployments, the acquisition of strike force ships with highly capable and effective weapons systems to operate in forward deployment areas and the procurement of a greater number of non-strike force ships that are smaller, less sophisticated, but at the same time highly effective for missions in areas of low-intensity conflict and coastal defense.

Holding Attack: An attack designed to hold the enemy in position, to deceive him as to where the main attack is being made, to prevent him from reinforcing the elements opposing the main attack, and to cause him to commit his reserves prematurely at an indecisive location.

Honest John: A short-range, unguided, truck-mounted rocket intended to deliver a nuclear weapon against enemy combat forces. Being phased out of the U.S. inventory.

"Hot Line" Agreement: An agreement between the United States and the Soviet Union (June 1963) that established an official teletype communications link between Washington and Moscow for use by heads of government in a crisis situation. Similar links were established between Paris and Moscow in 1966 and between London and Moscow in 1967.

Howitzer: 1. A cannon that combines certain characteristics of guns and mortars. It delivers projectiles with medium velocities either with low or high trajectories. 2. A cannon with tube length of twenty to thirty calibers. See also **gun; mortar.**

Hunter-Killer Force: A naval force consisting of an antisubmarine warfare carrier, associated aircraft and escorts combining specialized searching, tracking, and attacking capabilities of air and surface antisubmarine warfare units operated as a coordinated group for the conduct of offensive antisubmarine operations in an area of submarine probability.

Hunter-Killer Operations: Offensive antisubmarine operations in a submarine probability area combining the best searching, tracking, and attacking capabilities of air, surface, and subsurface units and forces in coordinated action to locate and destroy submarines at sea.

Hydrogen Bomb: A nuclear weapon that derives its energy largely from fusion.

Hypergolic Fuel: Fuel that will spontaneously ignite with an oxidizer, such as aniline with fuming nitric acid; used as the propulsion agent in certain missile systems.

I

ICBM (Intercontinental Ballistic Missile): A land-based, rocket-propelled vehicle capable of delivering a warhead within intercontinental ranges (in excess of about 3,000 nautical miles). The SALT I agreement defined ICBMs as strategic ballistic missiles capable of ranges in excess of the shortest distance between the northeastern border of the continental United States and the northwestern border of the continental USSR (about 3,000 nautical miles). The U.S. Minuteman III and the Soviet SS-11 are examples of ICBMs.

ICBMs fly to a target on an elliptical trajectory outside the atmosphere. The missile is guided only during the initial powered phase of the trajectory with the altitude, bearing, and velocity setting the missile on a programmed course to an apogee and then descending to target. Terminal guidance can be provided for the reentry system. ICBMs consist of a booster stage, one or more sustainer propulsion stages, a reentry vehicle, possible penetration aids, and in the case of a MIRVed missile, a post-boost vehicle. See also **bus**; **MIRV**; and **MARV**.

Imagery: Representations of objects reproduced electronically or by optical means on film, electronic display devices, or other media.

Immediate Air Support: Air support to meet specific requests that arise during the course of a battle—requests that by their nature cannot be planned in advance.

Immediate Nuclear Support: Nuclear support to meet specific requests that arise during the course of a battle—requests that by their nature cannot be planned in advance. See also **nuclear support**.

Impact Action Fuze: A fuse that is set in action by the striking of a projectile or bomb against an object; e.g., percussion fuse, contact fuse.

Implosion Weapon: A device in which a quantity of fissionable material, but less than a critical mass, has its volume suddenly decreased by compression so that it becomes supercritical and an explosion can take place. The compression is achieved by means of a spherical arrangement around fissionable material of specially fabricated shapes of ordinary high explosives that produce an inwardly directed implosion wave.

Incidents: Brief clashes or other military disturbances generally of a transitory nature and not involving protracted hostilities.

Independent European Programme Group (IEPG): Stemmed from a 1975 decision by Eurogroup ministers in the Hague to establish a new independent forum for European cooperation in defense equipment procurement in which France could participate. The IEPG has no formal charter or terms of reference. However, at its first meeting in Rome in February 1976 the group agreed that the purpose of equipment collaboration was to permit more effective use of funds for research, development, and procurement; to increase standardization and interoperability of equipment, which would also facilitate cooperation in the fields of logistics and training; to ensure maintenance of a healthy European defense through a shared industrial and technological base; and to strengthen Europe's position in its relationship with the United States and Canada. Members of the IEPG are Belgium, Denmark, the Federal Republic of Germany, France, Greece, Italy, Luxembourg, the Netherlands, Norway, Portugal, Turkey, and the United Kingdom.

Indirect Strategy: Employment of all means (political, diplomatic, economic, psychological, and threat of force) other than the application of military force in conflict situations.

Induced Radiation: Radiation produced as a result of exposure to radioactive materials, particularly the capture of neutrons. See also **contamination; residual radioactivity**.

Industrial Mobilization: The transformation of industry from its peacetime activity to the industrial program necessary to support national military objectives. It includes the mobilization of materiels, labor, capital, production facilities, and contributory items and services essential to the industrial program.

Industrial Preparedness: The state of preparedness of industry to produce essential materiel to support the national military objectives.

Industrial Preparedness Program: Plans, actions, or measures for the transformation of both government- and civilian-owned industry from its peacetime activity to the emergency program necessary to support the national military objectives. Includes such measures as contributory items and services for planning with industry, and modernization, expansion, and preservation of production facilities.

Inertial Guidance: A guidance system designed to project a missile over a predetermined path adjusted after launch by devices wholly within the missile and independent of outside information. The system measures and converts accelerations experienced to distance traveled in a certain direction. See also **guidance system**.

Inertial Guidance System: A guidance system designed to project a missile to a predetermined point on the earth's surface by measuring acceleration. The path of the missile is controlled during powered flight on the basis of acceleration measurements made with instruments wholly within the missile and independent of outside information. The system is thus insensitive to jamming, atmospheric conditions in the launching area, and other forms of interference.

Infyonics: On the battlefield, the application of sensor and communications technologies to small land units. These technologies include electronic detection barriers (ground sensors), radar-assisted rifles, hand-held radar, night vision scopes, and thermal imagers.

Initial Radiation: The nuclear radiation accompanying a nuclear explosion and emitted from the resultant fireball; immediate radiation.

Initiation: Action that sets off a chain reaction in a fissile mass that has reached the critical state generally by the emission of a "spurt" of neutrons.

INS (Inertial Navigation System): A system of navigation that keeps track of a vehicle's location by continuously measuring its acceleration in all directions; it can operate without any external reference.

Insurgency: A condition of revolt or insurrection against a constituted government that falls short of civil war.

Intelligence: The product resulting from the collection, collation, evaluation, analysis, integration, and interpretation of all collected information.

Intelligence Cycle: The steps by which information is assembled, converted into intelligence, and made available to consumers. The cycle is composed of four basic phases: (1) *direction*: the determination of intelligence requirements, the preparation of a collection plan, the assignment to collection agencies, and the continuous checking on the productivity of these agencies; (2) *collection*: the exploitation of information sources and the delivery of the collected information to the proper intelligence processing unit for use in the production of intelligence; (3) *processing*: the steps whereby information becomes intelligence through evaluation, analysis, integration, and interpretation; and (4) *dissemination*: the distribution of information or intelligence products (in oral, written, or graphic form) to departmental and agency intelligence consumers.

Intelligence Evaluation: Appraisal of an item of information in terms of credibility, reliability, pertinency, and accuracy. Appraisal is accomplished at several stages within the intelligence process in progressively different contexts. Initial evaluations, made by case officers and report officers are focused upon the reliability of the source and the accuracy of the information as judged by data available at or close to their operational levels. Later evaluations, by intelligence analysts, are primarily concerned with verifying accuracy of information and may, in effect, convert information into intelligence. Appraisal or evaluation of items of information or intelligence is indicated by a standard letter-number system. The evaluation of the reliability of sources is designated by a letter from A through F, and the accuracy of the information is designated by numeral 1 through 6. These are two entirely independent appraisals, and these separate appraisals are indicated in accordance with the system indicated below. Thus, information adjudged to be "probably true" received from a "usually reliable source" is designated "B-2" or "B2," and information about which the "truth cannot be judged" received from a "usually reliable source" is designated "B-6" or "B6."

Reliability of Source
A—Completely reliable
B—Usually reliable
C—Fairly reliable
D—Not usually reliable
E—Unreliable
F—Reliability cannot be
    judged

Accuracy of Information
1—Confirmed by other
    sources
2—Probably true
3—Possibly true
4—Doubtful
5—Improbable
6—Truth cannot be judged

Intention: The determination of a country or coalition to use capabilities in specific ways at specific times and places. Intentions are conditioned by many variables, including interests, objectives, policies, principles, commitments, and national will.

Interceptor Aircraft: A manned aircraft utilized for identification and engagement of aerodynamic threats (aircraft and cruise missiles).

Interceptor Missile: A missile designed to counter enemy offensive missiles, reentry vehicles, or aircraft.

Interchangeability: A condition that exists when two or more items possess such functional and physical characteristics as to be equivalent in performance and durability, and are capable of being exchanged one for the other without alteration of the items themselves, or of adjoining items, except for adjustment, without selection for fit and performance.

Interconnection: The linking together of interoperable systems.

Intercontinental Ballistic Missile (ICBM): See **ICBM (intercontinental ballistic missile).**

Interdict: To prevent or hinder by any means the enemy use of an area or route.

Interdiction-type Targets: Targets that are essential to the movement or employment of enemy forces, the destruction or damage of which will interrupt or impede further enemy military operations.

Intermediate-Range Ballistic Missile (IRBM): This term usually refers to a ballistic missile with a range capability of from about 1,500 to 3,000 nautical miles. The United States has no IRBMs. The Soviet SS-5 is an example of an IRBM.

Intermediate-Range Bomber Aircraft: A bomber designed for a tactical operating radius of between 1,000 to 2,500 nautical miles at design gross weight and design bomb load.

Internal Radiation: Nuclear radiation (alpha and beta particles and gamma radiation) resulting from radioactive substances in the body.

International Arms Control Organization: An appropriately constituted organization established to supervise and verify the implementation of arms control measures.

International Atomic Energy Agency (IAEA): Agency of the United Nations established in 1957 to induce nations to cooperate in the development of the peaceful use of atomic energy. The agency has established safeguards to prevent diversion of fissionable material for military use.

International Logistics: The negotiating, planning, and implementing of supporting logistics arrangements between nations and their forces and agencies. It includes furnishing logistic support (major end items, materiel, and services) to, or receiving logistic support from, one or more friendly foreign governments, international organizations, or military forces, with or without reimbursement. It also includes planning and actions related to the intermeshing of a significant element, activity, or component of the military logistics systems or procedures of the United States with those of one or more foreign governments, international organizations, or military forces on a temporary or permanent basis. It includes planning and actions related to the utilization of U.S. logistics, policies, systems, and procedures to meet requirements of one or more foreign governments, international organizations, or forces.

International Nuclear Information System (INIS): An IAEA (International Atomic Energy Agency) program for the exchange of scientific and technological information.

Interoperability: 1. The ability of systems, units, or forces to provide services to and accept services from other systems, units, or forces and to use the services so exchanged to enable them to operate effectively together. **2.** The condition achieved among communications-electronics systems, or items of communications-electronics equipment, when information or services can be exchanged directly and satisfactorily between them or their users.

Intrawar Deterrence: Deterrence exercised during a limited or local war designed to inhibit enemy escalation and to limit damages.

Ionization: The process of producing ions by the removal of electrons of atoms or molecules.

Ionosphere: The region of the atmosphere, extending from roughly 40 to 250 miles altitude, in which there is appreciable ionization. The presence of charged particles in this region profoundly affects the propagation of electromagnetic radiations of long wavelengths (radio and radar waves).

Irradiation: Exposure to radiation, as in a nuclear reactor.

Isotopic Separation: The process of separating isotopes from one another or changing their relative abundances, as by gaseous diffusion or electromagnetic separation. All systems are based on the mass differences of the isotopes. Isotope separation is a step in the isotopic enrichment process.

J

Joint: Connotes activities, operations, etc., in which elements of more than one service of the same nation participate.

Joint Amphibious Operation: Amphibious operation conducted by significant elements of two or more services.

Joint Force: A general term applied to a force that is composed of two or more significant elements of the Army, the Navy or the Marine Corps, or the Air Force operating under a single commander exercising unified command or operational control over such joint forces.

Joint Intelligence Estimate for Planning (JIEP): A worldwide series of strategic estimates prepared annually by the Defense Intelligence Agency (DIA) for the Joint Chiefs of Staff (JCS); it is intended to be used as a base for developing intelligence annexes for JCS plans.

Joint Strategic Capabilities Plan (JSCP): A short-range, current capabilities plan that translates U.S. national objectives and policies for the next fiscal year into terms of military objectives and strategic concepts, and defines military tasks that are in consonance with actual U.S. military capabilities. See also **national objectives.**

Joint Strategic Objectives Plan: A midrange objectives plan that translates future U.S. national objectives and policies (within the time frame of five to eight years) into military objectives and strategic concepts and defines basic undertakings that may be accomplished with the objective force levels. See also **Joint Strategic Capabilities Plan (JSCP)**.

Joule: The energy released by detonating a given number of tons of TNT. One kiloton equals 4.2 terajoules.

K

K-Day: The basic date for the introduction of a convoy system or any particular convoy lane. See also **D-day**.

Kill Probability: A measure of the probability of destroying a target.

Kiloton: A measure of the yield of a nuclear weapon equivalent to 1000 tons of TNT (trinitrotoluene). The bomb detonated at Hiroshima in World War II had an approximate yield of 14 kilotons.

Kiloton Weapon: A nuclear weapon, the yield of which is measured in terms of thousands of tons of trinitrotoluene (TNT) explosive equivalents, producing yields from 1 to 999 kilotons. See also **nominal weapon; subkiloton weapon**.

L

Lance: A short-range inertially-guided tactical missile, mounted on a tracked vehicle or trailer, capable of delivering a nuclear weapon against enemy combat forces.

Land Control Operations: The employment of ground forces to achieve military objectives in vital land areas, supported by naval and air forces, as appropriate. Such operations include destruction of opposing ground forces, securing key terrain, protection of vital land lines of communication, and establishment of local military superiority in areas of land operations.

Landing Attack: An attack against enemy defenses by troops landed from ships, aircraft, boats, or amphibious vehicles. See also **assault**.

Landing Craft: A craft specifically designed for carrying troops and equipment employed in amphibious operations, for beaching, unloading, and retracting. Also used for logistic cargo resupply operations.

Landing Force: A task organization of aviation and ground units assigned to an amphibious assault. It is the highest troop echelon in the amphibious operation. See also **amphibious force**.

Land, Sea, or Aerospace Projection Operations: The employment of land, sea, air forces, or an appropriate combination to project

U.S. military power into areas controlled or threatened by enemy forces. Operations may include penetration of such areas by amphibious, airborne, or land transported means, as well as air combat operations by land-based or carrier air groups.

Laser (Light Amplification by Stimulated Emission of Radiation): The use of focused light beams to provide force for application in a military mode.

Launcher: A structural device designed to support and hold a missile in position for firing. See also **cold launch; transporter-erector-launcher (TEL)**.

Launch-on-Warning: A doctrine calling for the launch of ballistic missiles when a missile attack against them is detected and before the attacking warheads reach their targets.

Launch-through-Attack: Involves delaying the firing of missiles until some have arrived precluding a launch on false warning.

Laydown Bombing: A very low level bombing technique wherein delay devices are used to allow the attacker to escape the effects of the bomb.

Lifeguard Submarine: A submarine employed for rescue in an area that cannot be adequately covered by air or surface rescue forces because of enemy opposition, distance from friendly bases, or other reasons. It is stationed near the objective and sometimes along the route to be flown by the strike aircraft.

Light Cruiser: A warship with six inch naval guns as main battery. It is designed to operate with strike, antisubmarine, or amphibious forces against air and surface threats. Full load displacement is approximately 18,000 tons. Designated as CL. See also **guided missile light cruiser**.

Light Division: An infantry division, lacking the heavy equipment of armored or mechanized divisions.

Light Tank: Tanks weighing less than forty tons are generally designated as "light," although the United States no longer uses "heavy," "medium," and "light" as classifications. See also **heavy tank, medium tank**.

Light-Water Reactor (LWR): The most common nuclear reactor fueled by enriched uranium (U-235); produces spent fuel of plutonium that, after processing, is usable in the production of nuclear explosives.

Limited Nuclear Retaliation: Limited nuclear strategic retaliatory attacks designed to reduce the adversary's resolve rather than his strategic forces.

Limited Strategic War: A form of general war in which one or more belligerents exercise voluntary restraints to restrict casualties and damage. See also **general war; limited war.**

Limited War: Armed encounters, exclusive of incidents, in which one or more major powers or their proxies voluntarily exercise various types and degrees of restraint to prevent unmanageable escalation. See also **escalation; limited strategic war.**

Line of Communication: Land, sea, and aerospace routes essential to the conduct of international security affairs, particularly the deployment of armed forces and associated logistic support.

Liquid Propellant: Any liquid combustible fed to the combustion chamber of a rocket engine.

Local War: War confined to a geographically limited theater where conventional as well as nuclear weapons may be used.

Logistics: The science of planning and carrying out the movement and maintenance of forces. In its most comprehensive sense, logistics deals with those aspects of military operations related to: (1) design and development, acquisitions, storage, movement, distribution, maintenance, evacuation, and disposition of materiel; (2) movement, evacuation, and hospitalization of personnel; (3) acquisition or construction, maintenance, operation, and disposition of facilities; and (4) acquisition or furnishing of services.

Long-Range Bomber Aircraft: A bomber designed for a tactical operating radius of over 2,500 nautical miles at design gross weight and design bomb load. See also **bomber; medium bomber.**

Long-Term Defense Program (LTDP): A NATO program proposed by the United States at the May 1977 meeting of the NATO defense ministers. The focus of the LTDP was agreed to be a limited number of high-priority measures in ten critical fields. The purpose was to develop long-term plans for national and cooperative programming in these areas to insure that actions taken will be complementary and responsive to agreed priorities and phasing. Initial planning has been placed in the hands of separate NATO task forces, which report to the NATO defense ministers and to the NATO heads of government. The ten selected high-priority program areas are: readiness; reinforcement; reserve mobilization; maritime; air defense; command, control, and communications; electronic warfare; rationalization; logistics; and nuclear planning.

Low Airburst: The fallout-safe height of burst of a nuclear weapon that maximizes damages to or casualties on surface targets. See also **types of burst.**

Low-altitude Bombing: Horizontal bombing with the height of release between 900 and 8,000 feet.

Low Threshold: An intangible line between levels and types of conflict across which one or more antagonists plan to escalate with scant regret or across which they would be compelled to move quickly if subjected to pressures. See also **high threshold; threshold.**

M

MAGCOM (Magnetic Contour Matching System): Because of the ineffectiveness of the TERCOM system to operate over water, the MAGCOM system was developed as an alternative. MAGCOM incorporates techniques similar to those of TERCOM, but uses the contours of the earth's magnetic field for comparison instead of the physical contours of the terrain. See also **TERCOM (terrain contour matching system).**

Magnetic Anomaly Detection: Antisubmarine warfare systems that locate hostile submarines through detection of disturbances in the magnetic force fields.

Main Attack: 1. The principal attack or effort into which a commander throws the full weight of the offensive power at his disposal. 2. An attack directed against the chief objective of the campaign or battle.

Main Battle Tank: A tracked vehicle providing heavy armor protection and serving as the principal assault weapon of armored and infantry troops. See also **heavy tank; light tank; medium tank.**

Major Fleet: A principal, permanent subdivision of the operating forces of the Navy with certain supporting shore activities. Presently there are two such fleets: the Pacific Fleet and the Atlantic Fleet. See also **fleet.**

Major NATO Commanders: The major NATO commanders are Supreme Allied Commander Atlantic, Supreme Allied Commander Europe, Allied Commander-in-Chief Channel.

Major Nuclear Power: Any nation that possesses a nuclear striking force capable of posing a serious threat to every other nation.

Maneuver: 1. A movement to place ships, troops, materiel, or fire in a better location with respect to the enemy. 2. A tactical exercise carried out at sea, in the air, on the ground, or on a map in imitation of war. 3. The operation of a ship, aircraft, or vehicle to cause it to perform desired movements.

Maneuvering Reentry Vehicle (MARV): A ballistic missile reentry vehicle equipped with its own navigation and control systems capable of adjusting its trajectory during reentry into the atmosphere. The advantages of MARV are twofold. First, the onboard guidance and control systems give some MARVs a greater ultimate potential for accuracy due to corrections in the terminal reentry phase. Such accuracy may be essential if the intent is to strike key targets while avoiding or minimizing collateral damage. Second, other MARVs have high maneuverability and thus the inherent ability to evade terminal ABM defense interceptor missiles.

Manhattan Project: The War Department's program during World War II that produced the first atomic bombs. The term originated in the code name, "Manhattan Engineer District," which was used to conceal the nature of the secret work underway. The Atomic Energy Commission, a civilian agency, succeeded the military unit January 1, 1947.

MAP (Multiple Aim Point System): A deceptive mobile basing mode (for the M-X—Missile X ICBM) designed to increase the number of aim points or targets that the Soviet Union would have to attack if it desired to destroy the American land-based missile force. This is accomplished by having more hardened silos than there are missiles, the missiles being continuously shifted among the silos.

Marine Amphibious Corps: A Marine air-ground task force built around two Marine divisions and two Marine aircraft wings. The Marine amphibious corps normally employs the full combat resources of two Marine division or wing teams.

Maritime Area: A maritime theater of operations can be divided for the purposes of decentralization of command into maritime areas and subareas; e.g., Atlantic theater, which is divided into maritime area and subarea commands.

Maritime Control Area: An area generally similar to a defensive sea area in purpose except that it may be established any place on the high seas. Maritime control areas are normally established only in time of war. See also **defensive sea area**.

MARV (Maneuvering Reentry Vehicle): See **maneuvering reentry vehicle (MARV)**.

Mass Destruction: Conflict and instruments of conflict capable of creating casualities and devastation indiscriminately on a colossal scale; particularly, chemical, biological and nuclear weapons and warfare. See also **nuclear weapon**.

Massive Retaliation: The act of countering aggression of any type with tremendous destructive power, particularly a crushing nuclear response to any provocation deemed serious enough to warrant military action. The doctrine was first set forth by Secretary of State John Foster Dulles in an address delivered by him on January 12, 1954. This doctrine, essentially seen by many as a cost-cutting measure, was part of the Eisenhower administration's "new look" approach to defense.

Material Unaccounted For (MUF): The shrinkage of nuclear material as it goes through the fuel cycle, leading to discrepancies between physical inventory and book inventory of fissionable materials. MUF is important with respect to possible diversion of significant quantities of fissionable material since IAEA (International Atomic Energy Agency) safeguards require that each state establish its own system of accounting for and controlling all nuclear material on the basis of the nonproliferation treaty.

Materiel Readiness: The availability of materiel required by a military organization to support its wartime activities or contingencies, disaster relief (flood, earthquake, etc.), or other emergencies.

Maximum Effective Range: The maximum distance at which a weapon may be expected to fire accurately to achieve the desired result.

Maximum Range: The greatest distance a weapon can fire without consideration of dispersion.

M-Day: The term used to designate the day on which mobilization is to begin. See also **D-day**.

Means: Money, manpower, materiel, and other resources converted into capabilities that contribute to the accomplishment of national securities aims. See also **capability; ends**.

Median Incapacitating Dose: The amount or quantity of chemical agent which when introduced into the body will incapacitate fifty percent of exposed unprotected personnel.

Median Lethal Dose: 1. Nuclear: the amount of radiation over the whole body that would be fatal to fifty percent of the animals or organisms in question in a given period of time. **2.** Chemical: the dose of a toxic chemical agent that will kill fifty percent of exposed unprotected personnel; expressed in milligram minutes per cubic centimeter.

Medium Altitude Bombing: Horizontal bombing with the height of release between 8,000 and 15,000 feet.

Medium Atomic Demolition Munition: A low-yield, team-portable atomic demolition munition that can be detonated either by remote control or a timer device.

Medium Bomber: 1. A multiengined aircraft that lacks intercontinental range without in-flight refueling but is suitable for strategic bombing on one-way intercontinental missions, even without tanker support. 2. A bomber designed for a tactical operating radius of under 1,000 nautical miles at design gross weight and design bomb load. See also **bomber**; **long-range bomber aircraft**.

Medium-Range Ballistic Missile (MRBM): This term usually refers to a ballistic missile with a range capability of about 600 to 1,500 nautical miles. The United States has no MRBMs. The Soviet SS-4 is an example of an MRBM.

Medium Tank: Tanks weighing between forty and sixty tons generally are designated as "mediums," although the United States no longer uses "heavy," "medium," and "light" classifications. See also **heavy tank**; **light tank**.

Megaton Weapon: A nuclear weapon, the yield of which is measured in terms of millions of tons of TNT (trinitrotoluene) equivalents (one million tons of TNT equals 1,000 kilotons).

Merchant Marine: All non-military vessels of a nation, publicly and privately owned together with their crews, that engage in domestic or international trade and commerce.

Méry Plan: In March 1976, General Guy Méry, French chief of staff of the armed forces, announced a revision of French nuclear strategy. He presented the concept of an "enlarged sanctuarization" as a middle course between a global strategic posture and a narrow national one. Méry reaffirmed the principle of a "graduated response" and the importance of tactical nuclear weapons and suggested that, although France would not participate in NATO's forward defense preparation in times of peace, France would take part in the forward "first" battle.

MICV (Mechanized Infantry Combat Vehicle): An Army armored fighting vehicle.

Midcourse Correction: Adjustment of the flight path of a ballistic missile between boost phase and reentry phase.

Militarily Significant Fallout: Radioactive contamination capable of inflicting radiation doses to personnel that may result in a reduction of their combat effectiveness.

Military Assistance Advisory Group: A joint service group, normally under the military direction of a commander of a unified command and representing the secretariat of defense, that primarily administers U.S. military assistance, planning, and programming in a host country.

Military Assistance Program (MAP): The U.S. program for providing military assistance under the Foreign Assistance Act of 1961, as amended, as distinct from Economic Aid and other programs authorized by the act; includes the furnishing of defense articles and defense services through MAP Grant Aid or military sales to eligible allies, as specified by Congress.

Military Balance: The comparable combat power of two competing countries or coalitions. See also **combat power**.

Military Cybernetics: In Soviet usage, a military-technical science that is a branch of cybernetics. Military cybernetics deals with the structure and laws of operation of systems for the control of troops and weapons, and also defines the tactico-technical requirements that the technological equipment of such systems must meet.

Military Intervention: The deliberate act of a nation or group of nations to introduce its military forces into the course of an existing controversy.

Military Necessity: The principle whereby a belligerent has the right to apply any measures required to bring about the successful conclusion of a military operation that are not forbidden by the laws of war.

Military Occupation: A condition in which a territory is under the effective control of a foreign armed force. See also **occupied territory**.

Military Posture: The military disposition, strength, and condition of readiness as they affect its capabilities.

Military Science: In Soviet usage, the methodology is dialectical and historical materialism. A profound knowledge of Marxist-Leninist philosophy and its skillful application to military research emerge as important conditions for the rigorous, scientific nature of Soviet military theory. The Soviet Union states that the methodology of bourgeois military science is based on idealism and metaphysics, accounting for its limitations and inconsistency.

Military Strategy: The art and science of employing military power under all circumstances to attain national security objectives by applying force or the threat of force. See also **national objectives; national security; strategy; tactics.**

Mine: An explosive or other material, normally encased, designed to destroy or damage ground vehicles, boats, or aircraft, or designed to wound, kill, or otherwise incapacitate personnel. It may be detonated by the action of its victim, by the passage of time, or by controlled means.

Mine Countermeasures: Includes all methods for preventing or reducing damage or danger to ships, personnel, aircraft, and vehicles from mines.

Mine Warfare: The strategic and tactical use of mines and their countermeasures.

Mine Warfare Forces: Navy forces charged with the strategic and tactical use of naval mines and their countermeasures. Such forces are capable of offensive and defensive measures in connection with laying and clearing mines.

Minimum Altitude Bombing: Horizontal or glide bombing with the height of release under 900 feet. See also **skip bombing**.

Minimum Attack Altitude: The lowest altitude determined by the tactical use of weapons, terrain consideration, and weapons effects that permits the safe conduct of an air attack and minimizes effective enemy counteraction.

Minimum Deterrence: Deterrent strategy based on the possession of a small and limited strategic nuclear capability sufficient to deter any nuclear power from rational attack as the penalty for aggression would be unacceptable. See also **force de frappe**.

Minimum Energy Trajectory: The missile flight path that reaches a given range with the least expenditure of propellant energy.

Minimum Normal Burst Altitude: The altitude below which air defense nuclear warheads are not normally detonated.

Minimum Residual Radioactivity Weapon (MRR Weapon): A nuclear weapon designed to have optimum reduction of unwanted effects from fallout, rainout, and burst site radioactivity. This term is replacing the term "clean weapon." See also **salted weapon**.

Mini-Nukes: Small tactical nuclear weapons of yields as low as .01 kilotons. This weapon system is fitted with a precision guidance system and is target deliverable with a circular error probability (CEP) of almost zero.

Minuteman: A three-stage, solid-propellant, second-generation intercontinental ballistic missile equipped with a nuclear warhead, designed for deployment in a hardened and dispersed configuration and in a mobile mode on railroad trains. It is a simpler, smaller, lighter missile than earlier intercontinental ballistic missiles and is designed for highly automated remote operation. Designated as LGM-30. See also **ballistic missile; hardened site; hard target; ICBM (intercontinental ballistic missile); mobile missile**.

MIRV (Multiple Independently Targetable Reentry Vehicle): See **multiple independently targetable reentry vehicle (MIRV)**.

Missile: A non-manned delivery vehicle that can be guided after having left its launching base during part or the whole of its trajectory. Strategic missiles are classified as follows: intercontinental ballistic missile (ICBM); intermediate range ballistic missile (IRBM); medium range ballistic missile (MRBM); submarine-launched ballistic missile (SLBM); and modern large ballistic missile (MLBM).

Missile Control System: A system that serves to maintain altitude stability and to correct deflections. See also **guidance system**.

Missile Destruct System: A system that, when operated by external command or preset internal means, destroys the missile or similar vehicle.

Missile Intercept Zone: That geographical division of the destruction area where surface-to-air missiles have primary responsibility for destruction of airborne objects.

Missile Release Line: The line at which an attacking aircraft could launch an air-to-surface missile against a specific target.

Mission: A function or task assigned to specific armed forces.

MK-12A: A higher yield, more accurate warhead designed to replace the MK-12 warhead presently deployed on Minuteman III missiles. MK-12A warheads may also be deployed on M-X ICBMs and Trident II SLBMs. See also **M-X**; **Trident**.

MLNF (Multilateral Nuclear Force): A proposal for a fleet of twenty-five surface ships armed with Polaris nuclear missiles that would be deployed in the Mediterranean and North Seas. These ships were to be committed to the nuclear defense of NATO, their missiles only launched upon unanimous approval of the participant states.

Mobile Defense: Defense of an area or position in which maneuver is used with organization of fire and utilization of terrain to seize the initiative from the enemy.

Mobile Missile: Any ballistic or cruise missile mounted on or fired from a movable platform, such as a truck, train, ground effects machine, ship, or aircraft.

Mobility: The capability of military forces to move from place to place while retaining their ability to fulfill their primary mission.

Mobility Forces: The transport, cargo and tanker ships, and aircraft used to move U.S. forces abroad and support them where deployed. Also called airlift/sealift forces.

Mobilization: The act of preparing for war or other emergencies by assembling and organizing raw materials; focusing industrial efforts on national security objectives; marshalling and readying

Reserves, National Guard units, and individuals for active military organizations filled with personnel inducted from civilian life.

Mobilization Base: The total of all resources available, or that can be made available, to meet foreseeable wartime needs. Such resources include the manpower, materiel resources, and services required for the support of essential military, civilian, and survival activities, as well as the elements affecting their state of readiness, such as (but not limited to) the following: manning levels, state of training, modernization of equipment, mobilization of materiel reserves and facilities, continuity of government civil defense plans and preparedness measures, psychological preparedness of the people, international agreements, planning with industry, dispersion, and stand-by legislation and controls. See also **combat power**.

Moderator: A material, such as ordinary water, heavy water, or graphite, used in a reactor to slow down high-velocity neutrons, thus increasing the likelihood of further fission.

Modern Large Ballistic Missile (MLBM): An intercontinental ballistic missile (ICBM) of a type deployed since 1964 and having a volume significantly greater than the largest light ICBM operational in 1972 (the Soviet SS-11). The United States has no MLBMs. The Soviet SS-9 (deployed) and the SS-18 (under development) are MLBMs.

Monad: A single leg of a triad.

Mopping Up: The liquidation of remnants of enemy resistance in an area that has been surrounded or isolated, or through which other units have passed without eliminating all active resistance.

Mortar: Normally a muzzle-loading weapon with either a rifled or smooth bore. It usually has a shorter range than a howitzer, employs a higher angle of fire, and has a tube length of ten to twenty calibers. See also **gun; howitzer**.

Motorized Unit: A unit equipped with complete motor transportation that enables all of its personnel, weapons, and equipment to be moved at the same time without assistance from other sources.

Moving Havens: Restricted areas established to provide a measure of security to submarines and surface ships in transit through areas in which the existing attack restrictions would be inadequate to prevent attack by friendly forces.

Multilateral Force (MLF): Military arrangement combining troops and weapons systems of different nations, in an institutional structure under combined command and control.

Multinational Force: Military arrangement in which several nations participate, where the national contributions remain separate but coordinated.

Multiple Independently Targetable Reentry Vehicle (MIRV): Two or more reentry vehicles carried by a single missile and capable of being independently targeted. A MIRVed missile employs a **bus** or other warhead dispensing mechanism. The dispensing mechanism maneuvers to achieve successive desired positions and velocities to dispense each reentry vehicle (RV) on a trajectory to attack the desired targets. Thus, the RVs are aimed at separate targets over a large geographical area called the "MIRVed missile's footprint." The exact size of the footprint depends on a number of factors, including the amount of propellant in the dispenser (bus) and the time period over which individual RVs are dispensed. U.S. MIRV missiles currently deployed are the Minuteman III ICBM and the Poseidon (C-3) SLBM. The Soviet Union is known to be testing several types of MIRV ICBMs and has initiated deployment.

Multiple Reentry Vehicle (MRV): A ballistic missile reentry vehicle having two or more reentry vehicles not capable of being independently targeted. A MRV system has two primary objectives: (1) the ability to distribute the warhead's nuclear effects over a large area target more efficiently; and (2) the ability to present multiple targets to an ABM defense. The United States deployed the Polaris A-3 SLBM in the late 1960s, the first operational ballistic missile to employ the concept of multiple reentry vehicles (MRV). The Soviet Union has also deployed MRV payloads.

Multipurpose Close Support Weapon: A ground close-support weapon capable of defilade delivery of a variety of warheads including nuclear.

Multipurpose Weapons: Weapons with the capability for effective application in different modes and levels of conflict.

Mutual and Balanced Force Reductions (MBFR): The MBFR negotiations have been in progress in Vienna since November 1973. These negotiations are considering proposals for exchanges of information and real reductions and limitations of forces. NATO nations directly participating in these talks are Belgium, Canada, the Federal Republic of Germany, Luxembourg, the Netherlands, the United Kingdom, and the United States. Warsaw Pact direct participants are Czechoslovakia, the German Democratic Republic, Poland, and the Soviet Union. Direct participants are those states with forces in the geographic area to be covered—the so-called "reductions area." It includes the territory of the Federal Republic of Germany, the German Democratic Republic, the Benelux countries, Poland, and Czechoslovakia. Eight other nations are also participating: Denmark, Greece, Italy, Norway, and Turkey on the Western side; Bulgaria, Romania, and Hungary on the East. However, forces in the territory of these nations will not be reduced, although the West has reserved the right to address the status of forces in Hungary further.

At the outset of the negotiations, the Western nations provided an estimate of major disparities favoring the Warsaw Pact in geography, manpower, and the structure and equipment of opposing forces. Accordingly, the NATO allies have proposed to the East that the final outcome of the reduction process be approximate parity in the form of a common collective ceiling on the overall ground and air manpower of each side, and that the major imbalance in tanks be diminished at the outset. The common ceiling, according to the West's proposal, would be reached through two phases of reductions. The first phase would result in reduction of a Soviet tank army of 68,000 men and 1,700 tanks and reduction of 29,000 U.S. ground force personnel. The 1,000 U.S. nuclear warheads, 54 F-4 Phantom nuclear-capable aircraft, and 36 Pershing surface-to-surface missile launchers would be reduced as part of the first phase of reductions. All the direct participants would join in a second phase of reductions to achieve the common collective ceiling on forces in the reductions area. The West has indicated that this ceiling might, illustratively, be set at about 700,000 men in ground forces and 900,000 in air and ground forces combined.

To maintain undiminished security while increasing stability, other measures associated with the reductions would be needed to verify compliance, and to assure that forces withdrawn from the central region are not used to increase the threat to nations on the northern and southern flanks. In addition, the West has suggested measures like prior notification of troop movements. These proposed measures are intended to diminish the risk of miscalculation and to reduce ambiguities about the activities of forces remaining after reductions have been completed.

The initial Eastern approach in the MBFR talks was essentially to propose equal percentage reductions of about seventeen percent in ground and air forces and their armaments, including nuclear weapons, of all direct participants. The reductions would be carried out in three stages of about two percent, five percent, and finally 10 percent. The Western nations opposed this approach, as it would have implicitly codified in an international agreement the major source of NATO concern in central Europe—the disparity in ground forces, particularly in tanks—and it would have even tended to aggravate that imbalance if accepted.

In February 1976, the Eastern negotiators presented a new proposal. This proposal provided for reduction of U.S. and Soviet troops in a first stage, with the other participants freezing their forces until reduction in a second stage. This new proposal appears to retain many of the basic deficiencies of the original Eastern approach. In particular, the proposed manpower and equipment reductions do not eliminate or even reduce the disparities in ground force personnel and tanks. Major differences remain between the Eastern and Western positions. The discussions did not produce any agreements on major issues during 1977, but the participants are continuing to actively pursue an accord.

Mutual Assured Destruction: A condition in which an assured destruction capability is possessed by opposing sides. See also **assured destruction; unacceptable damage**.

Mutual Deterrence: A stable situation in which two or more countries or coalitions of countries are inhibited from attacking each other because the casualties or damage resulting from retaliation would be unacceptable. See also **deterrence; nuclear deterrence**.

M-X (Missile X ICBM): Being developed as the next generation of U.S. ICBMs. It would provide enhanced survivability and increased capability. The M-X is currently planned to have approximately four times greater throw-weight, significantly greater accuracy, and more numerous higher-yield warheads than Minuteman III. These characteristics are expected to give each M-X warhead a very high probability of destroying very hard targets. The M-X is also being designed to permit deceptive mobile basing, sometimes called the "shell game." This involves the random movement of missiles and launch control facilities among hardened above-ground shelters or in hardened, covered trenches. The ultimate deployment scheme has not yet been selected, but the trench concept appears to be the preferred candidate. Mobile basing for the M-X is expected to improve the survivability of the system significantly over fixed-based ICBMs.

It would require the Soviets to attack all shelters or trench areas in which the M-X could possibly be housed. To conduct such an attack, the Soviets would have to expend more ICBMs than the number of M-X they would destroy. This reduces the Soviet incentive to attack the system.

N

Napalm: 1. Powdered aluminum soap or similar compound used to gelatinize oil or gasoline for use in bombs or flame throwers. 2. The resultant gelatinized substance.

Nassau Agreement: An agreement reached in Nassau in December 1962 between the United States and Great Britain, which provided that the United States would sell Britain Polaris missiles, on the condition that Britain would assign Polaris-equipped submarines to a NATO command, *whenever established,* as the nucleus of a NATO nuclear force. This agreement circumvented the unattractive choices posed to the British as a result of the Skybolt cancellation and prolonged the life of Britain's independent nuclear deterrent. See **minimum deterrence; Skybolt.**

National Command Authorities: The top national security decision-makers of a country. In the United States they are limited to the president, the secretary of defense, and their duly deputized alternates or successors.

National Component: Any national forces of one or more services under the command of a single national commander that are assigned to any NATO commander.

National Emergency: A condition declared by the president or Congress by virtue of their powers to authorize certain emergency actions to be undertaken in the national interest. Actions to be taken may include partial or total mobilization of national resources.

National Forces for the Defense of the NATO Area: Nonallocated forces whose mission involves the defense of a zone within the NATO area of responsibility.

National Infrastructure: Infrastructure provided and financed by a NATO, SEATO or CENTO (Central Treaty Organization) member in its own territory solely for its own forces (including those forces assigned to or designated for NATO, SEATO, or CENTO).

National Intelligence Estimate: A strategic estimate of capabilities, vulnerabilities, and probable courses of action of foreign nations that is produced at the national level as a composite of the views of the intelligence community. See also **strategic intelligence**.

National Interests: A highly generalized concept of elements that constitute a state's compelling needs, including self-preservation, independence, national integrity, military security, and economic well-being.

National Objectives: The fundamental aims, goals, or purposes of a nation toward which policies are directed and energies are applied. These may be short-, mid-, or long-range in nature.

National Policies: Broad courses of action or statements of guidance adopted by a government in pursuit of national objectives.

National Power: The sum total of any nation's capabilities or potential derived from available political, economic, military, geographic, social, scientific, and technological resources. See also **combat power**.

National Security: The protection of a nation from all types of external aggression, espionage, hostile reconnaissance, sabotage, subversion, annoyance, and other inimical influences.

National Security Agency (NSA): Established by President Harry S Truman, October 24, 1952, to replace the Armed Forces Security Agency (AFSA).

National Security Goals (United States): To deter the use, or threat of use, of nuclear or conventional forces against the United States, its allies, and friends. If deterrence fails, to terminate the conflict on terms favorable to the United States and its allies.

National Security Interests: Those national interests primarily concerned with preserving a state from harm. See also **national interests; national security**.

National Security Objectives: Those national objectives primarily concerned with shielding national interests from threats, both foreign and domestic. See also **national objectives; national security**.

National Security Policies: Those national policies which provide guidance primarily for attaining national security objectives. See also **national policies; national security**.

National Strategy: The art and science of developing and using the political, economic, and psychological powers of a nation, together with its armed forces, during peace and war, to secure national objectives. See also **strategy**.

National Technical Means of Verification: Techniques that are under national control for monitoring compliance with the provisions of an agreement.

National Will: The temper and morale of the people as they influence a nation's ability to satisfy national security interests or attain national security objectives.

NATO (North Atlantic Treaty Organization): The North Atlantic Treaty (1949) established a regional military organization to provide for the security of its signatories in the North Atlantic area. The fifteen members of the alliance include: Belgium, Great Britain, Denmark, France, West Germany, Greece, Iceland, Italy, Luxembourg, the Netherlands, Norway, Portugal, Turkey, and the United States. The mission of the alliance is chiefly military—to deter and if necessary defend against Warsaw Pact military aggression in central Europe through the combined conventional forces of the members assigned to NATO and the protection afforded by the American nuclear deterrent.

NATO Exercises: In order to increase the effectiveness and combat value of the NATO armed forces and to further cooperation among the different nations, test plans, or study strategic problems international exercises are organized periodically by the Supreme Allied Commanders Europe and Atlantic, or by the Commander-in-Chief Channel, in conjunction with member governments. The exercises are planned in advance in order to prevent overlapping, to ensure that the necessary forces will be available, and to give member governments an opportunity to coordinate national exercises with NATO exercises. There are different types of exercises, each of which is given a specific name, and the number of forces participating varies considerably. They fall into two main categories: those in which no forces take part, which are called command post exercises (CPX), and those in which actual forces participate.

The aims of CPX are to familiarize commanders and staff officers with wartime problems, to test and evaluate plans and executive bodies, to study tactical and other questions, and to test communications facilities. The objectives of a CPX are to define, examine, and solve military defense problems. It may consist of a series of group discussions in which the "exercise director" describes the problems chosen for study and during which the different commanders and their staffs present their views. Or, it may consist of a staff exercise, undertaken at any or all levels, in which tactics and procedures are acted out without the use of actual troops. Live exercises (those in which forces do take part) are carried out either in a limited area, in which case they are organized by supreme or subordinate commanders, or on a NATO-wide scale where they are jointly conducted by the Supreme Allied Commander, and the Commander-in-Chief Channel. These maneuvers have increased in scale with additions to the strength of forces assigned to NATO commands.

NATO Industrial Advisory Group (NIAG): Established in 1968, the objectives of NIAG are to provide a forum for free exchange of views on the various industrial aspects of NATO armaments questions; to foster a deeper feeling of international involvement in research, development, and production; to seek closer cooperation among the industries of member countries; and to encourage the timely and efficient exchange of information between member governments and their defense industries.

NATO Preparation Time: In the event of an impending attack, the time between the receipt of authorization from NATO political authorities by major NATO commanders to implement military measures and the start of the attack.

NATO Unified Product: A standardized product that is used or fully suitable for use by all NATO nations for a given end use.

NATO Warning Time: The time between recognition by a major NATO commander or higher NATO authority that an attack is impending and the start of the attack.

NATO-Wide Communications: In the late 1960s steps were taken to improve NATO's communications capability. In December 1967 a decision was made to establish the first NATO special communications network for political consultation, for the exchange of intelligence and other data, and for expediting critical NATO decisions on the use of nuclear weapons. This was called colloquially the "NATO-Wide Communications System" and provided direct telegraph links between NATO headquarters at Evere, the NATO capitals (except Paris), and the major NATO command headquarters. Also, in the late 1960s, NATO adopted a U.S. proposal to enhance the survivability, reliability, and speed of NATO's vital communications with the use of the most modern telecommunications system, that of satellites.

In March 1970 the first of two communications satellites of Phase II of the NATO Satellite Communications Program was launched, and later the same year the first of the twelve satellite ground terminals was brought into service. The ground stations of this system were established on the territory of each of the member nations (except France, Iceland, and Luxembourg). The coverage of the system extends over the whole of the NATO area, providing increased communication capabilities between NATO headquarters in Brussels, each of the member nations, and the NATO military commands. These capabilities will be greatly enhanced by the planned Phase III, which provides for additional satellite ground terminals and a satellite space segment of greatly increased power. The Phase III system, which will eventually form part of the new NATO Integrated Communications System (NICS), is due to become operational in the late 1970s.

NATO-Wide Exercise: An exercise involving all three major NATO commanders with a majority of subordinate commanders and national defense staffs concerned.

Naval Campaign: An operation or a connected series of operations conducted essentially by naval forces including all surface, subsurface, air, and amphibious troops, for the purpose of gaining, extending, or maintaining control of the sea.

Naval Operation: 1. A naval action, or the performance of a naval mission, that may be strategic, tactical, logistic, or training. 2. The process of carrying on or training for naval combat to gain the objectives of any battle or campaign.

Naval Superiority: Dominance on the high seas to a degree that permits friendly land, aerospace, and naval forces to operate at specific times and places on, over, or adjacent to the high seas without prohibitive interference by enemy naval elements. See also **sea control**.

Navstar: A proposed global positioning system comprised of twenty-four satellites to be placed in synchronous orbits, designed to provide nearly continuous signals that may be monitored by passive receivers on board ICBMs. Four such signals, plus orbital details from satellites, will enable a missile to determine its position to within twenty to thirty feet and to correct its altitude or velocity.

Neutral State: In international law, a state that pursues a policy of neutrality during war. See also **neutrality**.

Neutrality: In international law, the attitude of impartiality during periods of war adopted by third states toward belligerents and recognized by them, creating rights and duties between the impartial states and the warring nations. In a United Nations enforcement action, the rules of neutrality apply to impartial members of the United Nations in so far as they are excluded by their obligations under the United Nations charter. See also **nonalignment**.

Neutron-Induced Activity: Radioactivity induced in the ground or in an object as a result of direct irradiation by neutrons.

Neutron Warhead: An enhanced-radiation warhead for delivery by the Lance surface-to-surface missile for destruction of battlefield personnel by high-neutron content radiation. Blast and heat are minimized. The warhead provides for target destruction while reducing collateral damage to surrounding areas and population. See also **Lance**.

Nike Hercules: A mobile or fixed site, surface-to-air guided missile system with nuclear warhead capability, designed to intercept and destroy manned bombers and air-breathing missiles at greater ranges and altitudes than the Nike Ajax. It also has a surface-to-surface capability.

No-Cities Strategy: Essentially a counterforce strategy. In the event of a nuclear strike, the strategic forces of the enemy rather than enemy population centers are to be targeted.

Nominal Weapon: A nuclear weapon producing a yield of approximately twenty kilotons. See also **kiloton weapon; subkiloton weapon**.

Nonalignment: The political attitude of a state that does not associate or identify itself with the political ideology or objective espoused by other states, groups of states, or international causes, or with the foreign policies stemming from them. It does not preclude involvement, but expresses the attitude of no pre-commitment to a particular state, bloc, or policy before a situation arises. See also **neutrality**.

Noncentral Systems: A U.S. term for nuclear weapons sytems other than central systems; generally tactical systems that are alliance or regionally oriented. The major categories of noncentral systems are: (1) **Missiles**. In this category are the intermediate-range, medium-range, and short-range ballistic missiles. The USSR has an advantage in numbers over the United States in this area, with over 600 intermediate range and medium-range ballistic missiles (such as the SS-4, SS-5, and SS-20); the United States has none. (2) **Aircraft**. Comprised of medium bombers and light bombers or fighters generally assigned to tactical or air defense units. (3) **Sea-based forces**. Includes various types that are inherently mobile and capable of delivering a variety of nuclear weapons. The United States has carrier-based aircraft; the Soviets currently have none. While both the United States and the Soviet Union deploy cruise missiles, technological asymmetries separate the cruise missile systems of the two powers. In contrast to the American system, the Soviet SS-N-3 Shaddock (deployed on cruise missile carriers and Echo-class submarines) is a relatively inaccurate missile, propelled by an inefficient turbojet engine over a range not exceeding 550 nautical miles. It measures forty feet in length and six feet in diameter. The SS-N-12, the follow-on system to the Shaddock, is the same size, but is reportedly capable of ranges approaching 2000 nautical miles. (4) **Special-use forces.** Both sides have some battlefield nuclear weapons deployed in support of conventional land forces. These weapons systems include nuclear artillery rounds, battlefield support missile and howitzer systems, atomic demolition munitions, and unguided rockets of a relatively short range.

Normal Operations: Generally and collectively the broad functions that the commander of a unified combatant command undertakes when he is assigned responsibility for a given geographic or functional area. Except as otherwise qualified in certain unified command plan paragraphs relating to particular commands, "normal operations" of a unified command commander include: planning for and execution of operations in contingencies; limited war and general war; planning and conduct of cold war activities; planning for and administration of military assistance; and maintaining the relationships, exercising the directive, or coordinating authority.

Nth Country: A reference to additions to the group of powers possessing nuclear weapons; the next country of a series to acquire nuclear capabilities.

Nuclear Airburst: The explosion of a nuclear weapon in the air at a height greater than the maximum radius of the fireball. See also **types of burst.**

Nuclear Allocation: The apportionment of specific numbers and types of nuclear weapons to a commander for a stated time period as a factor in the development of war plans. (Additional authority is required for the actual deployment of allocated weapons to locations desired by the commander to support his war plans. Expenditures of these weapons are not authorized until released by proper authority.)

Nuclear-capable Artillery: Cannon artillery capable of firing artillery-fired atomic projectiles (AFAPs). See also **artillery-fired atomic projectile (AFAP).**

Nuclear Cloud: An all-inclusive term for the volume of hot gases, smoke, dust, and other particulate matter from the nuclear bomb itself, and from its environment, that is carried aloft in conjunction with the rise of the fireball produced by the detonation.

Nuclear Club: Collective term for the states having their own nuclear armaments.

Nuclear Column: A hollow cylinder of water and spray thrown up from an underwater burst of a nuclear weapon, through which the hot, high-pressure gases formed in the explosion are vented to the atmosphere.

Nuclear Coordination: A broad term encompassing all the actions involved with planning nuclear strikes, including liaison between commanders for the purposes of satisfying support requirements or because of the extension of weapons effects into the territory of another.

Nuclear Damage: *Light damage*: Damage that does not prevent the immediate use of equipment or installations for which they were intended, although some repair by the user may be required for full use. *Moderate damage*: Damage that prevents the use of equipment or installations until extensive repairs are made. *Severe damage*: Damage that prevents use of equipment or installations permanently.

Nuclear Damage Assessment: The determination of the damage effect to the population, forces, and resources resulting from an actual nuclear attack; performed during the transattack and post-attack periods. It does not include the function of evaluating the operational significance of nuclear damage assessments.

Nuclear Defense: The methods, plans, and procedures involved in establishing and exercising defensive measures against the effects of an attack by nuclear weapons or radiological warfare agents. It encompasses both the training for and the implementation of these methods, plans, and procedures. See also **radiological defense**.

Nuclear Delivery System: A nuclear weapon, together with its means of propulsion and associated installations. Includes carriers such as aircraft, ships, and motor vehicles.

Nuclear Deterrence: Measures to prevent rather than prosecute nuclear wars. Psychological (as opposed to physical) means prevail, but armed forces play a crucial role. See also **deterrence; mutual deterrence**.

Nuclear Device: A nuclear explosive used for peaceful purposes, tests, or experiments. The term is used to distinguish these explosives from nuclear weapons, which are packaged units ready for transportation or use by military forces.

Nuclear Dud: A nuclear weapon that, when launched at or emplaced on a target, fails to provide any explosion of that part of the weapon designed to produce the nuclear yield.

Nuclear Energy: The energy liberated by a nuclear reaction (fission or fusion) or by radioactive decay.

Nuclear Exoatmospheric Burst: The explosion of a nuclear weapon above the sensible atmosphere (about forty nautical miles) where atmospheric interaction is minimal and therefore the weapon's effects radius is large. See also **types of burst**.

Nuclear-Free Zones: Areas in which the production and stationing of nuclear weapons are prohibited. The Treaty for the Prohibition of Nuclear Weapons (Treaty of Tlateloco) in Latin America, which took effect on January 22, 1968, established a nuclear-free zone in Latin America. Parties to the treaty agreed "to use exclusively for peaceful purposes the nuclear material and facilities which are under their jurisdiction," and to prohibit the production and stationing of nuclear weapons appropriate for use for warlike purposes.

Nuclear Half-Life: The concept of half-life is basic to an understanding of radioactive decay of unstable nuclei. Unlike physical systems—bacteria, animals, men, and stars—unstable isotopes do not individually have a predictable life span. There is no way of forecasting when a single unstable nucleus will decay. Nevertheless, it is possible to get around the random behavior of an individual nucleus by dealing statistically with large numbers of nuclei of a particular radioactive isotope. In the case of thorium 232, for example, radioactive decay proceeds so slowly that 14 billion years elapse before one-half of an initial quantity decays to a more stable configuration. Thus the half-life of this isotope is 14 billion years. After the elapse of second half-life (another 14 billion years), only one-fourth of the original quantity of thorium 232 would remain, one-eighth after the third half-life, and so on. For the most common uranium isotope, U-238, the half-life is 4.5 billion years, about the age of the solar system. The much scarcer, fissionable isotope of uranium, U-235, has a half-life of 700 million years, indicating that its present abundance is only about one percent of the amount present when the solar system was born. Most man-made radioactive isotopes, however, have much shorter half-lives, ranging from seconds or days up to thousands of years. Plutonium 239 (a man-made isotope) has a half-life of 24,000 years.

Nuclear Incident: An unexpected event involving a nuclear weapon facility or component resulting in any of the following, but not constituting a nuclear weapon(s) accident: **1.** An increase in the possibility of explosion or radioactive contamination. **2.** Errors committed in the assembly, testing, loading, or transportation of equipment, or the malfunctioning of equipment and materiel that could lead to an unintentional operation of all or part of the weapon arming or firing sequence, a substantial change in yield, or increased dud probability. **3.** An event of chance, unfavorable environment, or condition resulting in damage to the weapon, facility, or component.

Nuclear Initiation: Action that sets off a chain reaction in a fissile mass that has reached the critical state (generally by the emission of a "spurt" of neutrons).

Nuclear Nonproliferation: Arms control measures designed to prevent the acquisition of nuclear weapons and delivery means by nations that do not have a nuclear capability. See also **nuclear proliferation**.

Nuclear Operations Plan (NOP): The plan developed by the Supreme Allied Commander Europe (SACEUR) for the execution of nuclear strikes with the nuclear weapons under his command.

Nuclear Parity: A force structure standard that demands the nuclear capabilities of opposing powers be qualitatively similar though not necessarily quantitatively identical.

Nuclear Planning Group: In December 1966, NATO established the Nuclear Planning Group to provide a forum where non-nuclear alliance members could share information and participate in nuclear planning and decision-making. The Nuclear Planning Group consists of four standing members (the United States, Great Britain, Italy, and West Germany) and three to four rotating members (drawn from the other NATO members) who serve anywhere from nine to eighteen months. The secretary-general of NATO chairs the meetings.

Nuclear Plenty: Nuclear plenty indicates the availability of nuclear weapons in such quantities and sizes that their use need not be restricted to strategic targets, but can include tactical targets and tactical missions, including battlefield employment, antiair or antimissile defense, and antisubmarine warfare.

Nuclear Proliferation: The process by which one nation after another comes into possession of nuclear weapons (or into the right to determine their use).

Nuclear Radiation: Particulate and electromagnetic radiation emitted from atomic nuclei in various nuclear processes. The important nuclear radiations, from the weapons standpoint, are alpha and beta particles, gamma rays, and neutrons. All nuclear radiations are ionizing radiations, but the reverse is not true; X-rays, for example, are included among ionizing radiations, but they are not nuclear radiations since they do not originate from atomic nuclei.

Nuclear Reaction: A reaction involving a change in an atomic nucleus, such as fission, fusion, neutron capture, or radioactive decay, as distinct from a chemical reaction that is limited to changes in the electron structure surrounding the nucleus.

Nuclear Reactor: A device in which a fission chain reaction can be initiated, maintained, and controlled. Its essential component is a core with fissionable fuel. It usually has a moderator, a reflector, shielding, coolant, and control mechanisms. Sometimes called an atomic "furnace," it is the basic machine of nuclear energy.

Nuclear Safety Line: A line selected, if possible, to follow well-defined topographical features and used to delineate levels of protective measures, degrees of damage or risk to friendly troops, or to prescribe limits to which the effects of friendly weapons may be permitted to extend.

Nuclear Stability: Stability is a state of equilibrium or stalemate that encourages restraint and prudence by opponents facing the possibility of general war. Neither side has a first strike capability.

Nuclear Stalemate: A concept that postulates a situation wherein the relative strength of opposing nuclear forces results in mutual deterrence against employment of nuclear forces.

Nuclear Support: The use of nuclear weapons against hostile forces in support of friendly air, land, and naval operations. See also **immediate nuclear support.**

Nuclear Surface Burst: An explosion of a nuclear weapon at the surface of land or water or above the surface, at a height less than the maximum radius of the fireball. See also **types of burst.**

Nuclear Transmutation: Artificially induced modification (nuclear reaction) of the constituents of certain nuclei, thus giving rise to different nuclides.

Nuclear Underground Burst: The explosion of a nuclear weapon in which the center of the detonation lies at a point beneath the surface of the ground. See also **types of burst.**

Nuclear Underwater Burst: The explosion of a nuclear weapon in which the center of the detonation lies at a point beneath the surface of the water. See also **types of burst.**

Nuclear Vulnerability Assessment: The estimation of the probable effect on population, forces, and resources from a hypothetical nuclear attack. It is performed predominantly in the preattack period; however, it may be extended to the transattack or post-attack periods.

Nuclear War-Winning Capability: A condition resulting from the superior nuclear capabilities of a power, whereby sufficient strategic forces would survive an initial nuclear exchange to permit destruction of the remaining war-making potential of the other power.

Nuclear Weapon: A bomb, missile warhead, or other deliverable ordnance item (as opposed to an experimental device) that explodes as a result of energy released by atomic nuclei as a result of fission, fusion or both. See also **nuclear delivery system**.

Nuclear Weapon Debris: The residue of a nuclear weapon after it has exploded; that is, the materials used for the casing and other components of the weapon, plus unexpended plutonium or uranium together with fission products.

Nuclear Weapon Degradation: The degeneration of a nuclear warhead to such an extent that the anticipated nuclear yield is lessened.

Nuclear Weapon Exercise: An operation not directly related to immediate operational readiness. It encompasses removal of a weapon from its normal storage location, preparation for use, delivery to an employment unit, and movement in a ground training exercise, including the loading aboard an aircraft or missile and return to storage. It may include any or all of the operations listed above, but not launching or flying operations. Typical exercises involve aircraft generation exercises, ground readiness exercises, ground tactical exercises, and various categories of inspections designed to evaluate the capability of the unit to perform its prescribed mission.

Nuclear Weapons: A collective term for atomic bombs and hydrogen bombs. Any weapons based on a nuclear explosive.

Nuclear Weapons Accident: Any unplanned occurrence involving loss or destruction of, or serious damage to, nuclear weapons or their components that results in an actual or potential hazard to life or property.

Nuclear Weapons Design: Nuclear weapons depend on two fundamentally different types of nuclear reactions, each of which releases energy: fission, which involves the splitting of heavy elements like uranium; and fusion, which involves the combining of light elements like hydrogen. Fission requires that a minimum amount of material or "critical mass" be brought into contact for the nuclear explosion to take place. The more efficient fission weapons tend to fall within the yield range of tens of kilotons. Higher explosive yields become increasingly complex and impractical. Nuclear fusion permits the design of weapons of virtually limitless power. In fusion, according to nuclear theory, when the nuclei of light atoms like hydrogen are joined, the mass of the fused nucleus is lighter than the two original nuclei; the loss is expressed as energy. By the 1930s, physicists had concluded that this was the process which powered the sun and stars; but the nuclear fusion process remained only of theoretical interest until it was discovered that an atomic fission bomb might be used as a "trigger" to produce, within one- or two-millionths of a second, the intense pressure and temperature necessary to set off the fusion reaction.

Nuclear Yields: The energy released in the detonation of a nuclear weapon, measured in terms of the kilotons or megatons of trinitrotoluene (TNT) required to produce the same energy release. Yields are categorized as: very low—less than 1 kiloton; low—1 kiloton to 10 kilotons; medium—over 10 kilotons to 50 kilotons; high—over 50 kilotons to 500 kilotons; and very high—over 500 kilotons. The separate effects of the yield are blast, thermal radiation, and nuclear radiation.

Nuclear Zones: *Zone I*: A circular area, determined by using minimum safe distance I as the radius and the desired ground zero as the center, from which all armed forces are evacuated. If evacuation is not possible or if a commander elects a higher degree of risk, maximum protective measures will be required. *Zone II*: A circular area (less Zone I), determined by using minimum safe distance II as the radius and the desired ground zero as the center, in which all personnel require maximum protection. Maximum protection denotes that armed forces personnel are in "buttoned up" tanks or crouched in foxholes with improvised overhead shielding. *Zone III*: A circular area (less Zones I and II), determined by using minimum safe distance III as the radius and the desired ground zero as the center, in which all personnel require minimum protection. Minimum protection denotes that armed forces personnel are prone on open ground with all skin areas covered and with an overall thermal protection at least equal to that provided by a two-layer uniform.

Nucleon: The common name for a constituent particle of the atomic nucleus. It is applied to protons and neutrons, but it is intended to include any other particle that is found to exist in the nucleus.

Nuclide: All nuclear species of the chemical elements, both stable (about 270) and unstable (about 500), as distinguished from the two or more nuclear species of a single chemical element that are called isotopes.

Numerical Balance of Forces: The categories that follow are used in a study by the Library of Congress (*U.S./Soviet Military Balance, A Framework for Congress,* 1976) for computing the Soviet-American numerical balance of forces:

Strategic Nuclear	*Tactical Nuclear*	*Ground Forces*
Air defense	Artillery	Air defense
ALCMs	Fighter-attack	Antitank weapons
Bombers	aircraft	Artillery
ICBMs	Medium bombers	Divisions
MIRVs	Missiles	Helicopters
SLBMs		Logistical tail
SLCMs		Marines
Warheads		Personnel
		Tanks

Naval Forces	*Tactical Air Forces*	*Strategic Mobility*
Aircraft afloat	Airlift	*Forces*
Aircraft ashore	Attack fighters	Airlift
Aircraft carriers		Sealift
Attack submarines		
Combat boats		
Cruise missile ships		
Helicopter carriers		
Mine counter-		
measure ships		

O

Occupied Territory: Territory under the authority and effective control of a belligerent armed force. The term is not applicable to territory being administered pursuant to peace terms, treaty, or other agreement, expressed or implied, with the civil authority of the territory.

Office of Strategic Services (OSS): The United States intelligence service active during World War II. It was established by President Roosevelt in June 1942 and disbanded October 1, 1945.

Offset Bombing: Any bombing procedure that employs a reference or aiming point other than the actual target.

Offset Distance: The distance the desired or actual ground zero is offset from the center of an area target or from a point target.

Older Heavy Ballistic Missile Launcher: A ballistic missile launcher for an ICBM of a type deployed before 1964 that has a volume significantly greater than the largest light ICBM operational in 1972. U.S. Titan II and Soviet SS-7 and SS-8 launchers are examples.

Operating Forces: Those forces whose primary missions are to participate in combat and its integral supporting elements.

Operation: 1. A military action or the carrying out of a strategic, tactical, service, training, or administrative military mission. 2. The process of carrying on combat, including movement, supply, attack, defense, and maneuvers needed to gain the objectives of any battle or campaign.

Operational Interchangeability: Ability to substitute one item for another of different composition or origin without loss in effectiveness, accuracy, and safety of performance.

Operations and Maintenance: All activities of the armed forces, in peace and war, to carry out strategic, tactical, training, logistic, and administrative missions.

Optimum Height of Burst: For nuclear weapons, the optimum height of burst for a particular target (or area) is that at which it is estimated a weapon of a specified energy yield will produce a certain desired effect over the maximum possible area. See also **types of burst**.

Order of Battle: The identification, strength, command structure, and disposition of the personnel, units, and equipment of any military force.

Ordnance: Explosives, chemicals, pyrotechnic, and similar stores; e.g., bombs, guns and ammunition, flares, smoke, napalm.

Overkill: Destructive capabilities in excess of those that logically should be adequate to destroy specified targets or attain specific security objectives.

Over-the-Horizon: A radar system that makes use of the atmospheric reflection and refraction phenomena to extend its range of detection beyond line-of-sight. Over-the-horizon radars may be either forward-scatter or back-scatter systems.

Overpressure: The measure, expressed in pounds per square inch (psi) commonly used to determine the capability of an object to withstand the pressure exerted by a nuclear blast.

P

Panoply: A complete system of nuclear armament, including warheads, their delivery systems, and the corresponding systems of command and control.

Paramilitary Forces: Forces or groups that are distinct from the regular armed forces of any country, but resembling them in organization, equipment, training, or mission.

Parity: A condition in which opposing forces possess capabilities of certain kinds that are approximately equal in over-all effectiveness. See also **strategic; superiority.**

Partial Mobilization: Expansion of the active Armed Forces (short of full mobilization) resulting from action by Congress or the president to mobilize Reserve Component units or individual reservists to meet all or part of the requirements of a particular contingency, operational war plans, or to meet requirements incident to hostilities. See also **mobilization.**

Passive Air Defense: All measures, other than active defense, taken to minimize the effects of hostile air action. These include the use of cover, concealment, camouflage, deception, dispersion, and protective construction like missile site hardening. See also **active air defense; hardened site; hard target.**

Passive Defense: All measures other than the utilization of military forces taken to minimize the effects of hostile action.

Passive Deterrence: Deterrence of a nuclear first strike on a nuclear power by the threat of retaliation in kind. See also **active deterrence.**

Passive Electronic Countermeasures: Sometimes called Electronic Support Measures (ESM). ECM without active transmissions by the originator, such as intercept search for enemy electronic emissions and tactical evasion (measures taken to impede detection and tracking by the enemy).

Pattern Bombing: The systematic covering of a target area with bombs uniformly distributed according to a plan.

Pave Tack: A highly sophisticated forward-looking system that allows the acquisition of targets in conditions of darkness and weather that is lightly cloudy or hazy.

Payload: 1. The load (expressed in tons of cargo or equipment, gallons of liquid, or number of passengers) that the vehicle is designed to transport under specified conditions of operation, in addition to its unladen weight. 2. The warhead, its container, and activating devices in a military missile. **3.** The satellite or research vehicle of a space probe or research missile. **4.** The reentry vehicle(s) placed on ballistic trajectories by the main propulsion stages and bus. There are several general types of payload configurations, such as: (a) single reentry vehicles, (b) multiple reentry vehicles (MRV), (c) multiple independently targetable reentry vehicles (MIRV), and (d) maneuvering reentry vehicles (MARV). See **reentry vehicle (RV)**.

PBV (Post-Boost Vehicle): Permits a missile to make late-course powered corrections in trajectory for improved accuracy.

P-Day: That point in time at which the rate or production of an item available for military consumption equals the rate at which the item is required by the armed forces.

Peaceful Coexistence: The Soviet doctrine of peaceful coexistence is a revision of the Leninist concept of the inevitability of war. First presented by Khrushchev, the doctrine calls for the two super-powers to avoid nuclear war but to continue political and economic competition.

Penetration: A form of offensive maneuver which seeks to break through the enemy's defensive position, widen the gap created, and destroy the continuity of his positions.

Penetration Aids: Devices carried aboard offensive delivery vehicles to neutralize the effect of defensive systems. Both missiles and bombers may employ devices (decoys, chaff, electronic counter-measures—ECMs) to mislead enemy radar; bombers may employ defense suppression weapons.

Penetration Capability: The ability of offensive nuclear weapons to penetrate defenses.

Perimeter Defense: A defense without an exposed flank, consisting of forces deployed along the perimeter of the defended area.

Permissive Action Link: A device included in or attached to a nuclear weapon system to preclude arming or launching until the insertion of a prescribed discrete code or combination. It may include equipment and cabling external to the weapon or weapon system to activate components within the weapon or weapon system.

Pershing: A truck-mounted, inertially-guided short-range missile capable of delivering a nuclear weapon against enemy rear targets.

PGM (Precision Guidance Munitions): These weapons systems are successors to older surface-to-air missiles, such as the Navy's radar-guided Terrier and the Soviet infrared homing SA-2. PGM refers to bombs, missiles, and artillery projectiles with single-shot kill probabilities from ten to one hundred times greater than unguided munitions. This increase in accuracy is made possible by new guidance technologies that reduce the circular error probability of delivery vehicles to twenty meters or less.

Photoflash Bomb: A bomb designed to produce a brief and intense illumination for medium altitude night photography.

Pyrrhic Victory: A victory attained at such high cost that national interests suffer.

Pin-Down: A technique to neutralize enemy offensive ICBMs by detonating nuclear warheads periodically over their silos. Missiles launched in that environment are disrupted during boost phase by blast, heat, or radiation.

Pinpoint Target: In artillery and naval gunfire support, a target less than fifty meters in diameter.

Planned Nuclear Target: A nuclear target planned in an area or point in which a need is anticipated. A planned nuclear target may be scheduled or on call. Firing data for a planned nuclear target may or may not be determined in advance. Coordination and warning of friendly troops and aircraft are mandatory.

Plowshare: The Atomic Energy Commission program of research and development on peaceful uses of nuclear explosives.

Plutonium: A heavy, radioactive, man-made, metallic element with atomic number 94. Its most important isotope is fissionable plutonium 239, produced by neutron irradiation of uranium 238. It is used both for reactor fuel and in weapons.

Pod: An external container mounted on aircraft containing specialized systems.

Point Defense: Defense of a limited geographical area. Usually refers to defense of ICBM silos against attacking missiles.

Point Target: A target that requires the accurate placement of bombs or fire.

Polaris: 1. U.S. submarines that carry the first generation of submarine-launched Polaris missiles. Each submarine can carry sixteen missiles. Expected to begin leaving the force in the early 1980s. 2. An underwater surface-launched, surface-to-surface, solid-propellant ballistic missile with inertial guidance and nuclear warhead. Designated as UGM-27, with the following distinctions: UGM-27A—1,200 nautical mile range; UGM-27B—1,500 nautical mile range; and UGM-27C—2,500 nautical mile range.

Political Intelligence: Originally meant the arranging, coordinating, and conducting of covert operations so as to "plausibly" permit official denial of U.S. involvement, sponsorship, or support. Later this concept evolved so that it was employed by high officials and their subordinates to communicate information without using precise language that would reveal authorization and involvement in certain activities that would be embarrassing and politically damaging if publicly revealed.

Political Warfare: Offensive or defensive use of political tools to achieve national objectives.

Politico-Military Gaming: Simulation of situations involving the interaction of political, military, sociological, psychological, economic, scientific, and other appropriate factors.

Poseidon: U.S. submarines that carry the first generation of multiple-warhead submarine-launched Poseidon missiles. Each submarine can carry sixteen missiles. The thousands of warheads carried by these thirty-one submarines comprise the most survivable element of the U.S. nuclear retaliatory capability. Expected to be replaced by Trident submarines during the late 1980s and early 1990s. See also **Trident**.

Position Defense: The type of defense in which the bulk of the defending force is disposed in selected tactical localities where the decisive battle is to be fought. Principal reliance is placed on the ability of the forces in the defended localities to maintain their positions and to control the terrain between them. The reserve is used to add depth, to block, or restore the battle position by counterattack.

Postattack Period: In nuclear warfare, the period that extends from the termination of the final attack until political authorities agree to terminate hostilities.

Postlaunch Survivability: The ability of any given delivery system to breach enemy defenses and attack designated targets. See also **prelaunch survivability**.

Posture: The combined strategic intentions, capabilities, and vulnerabilities of a country or coalition of countries, including the strength, disposition, and readiness of its armed forces.

Power Projection: In naval terms, the launching of sea-based air and ground force attacks against enemy targets ashore.

Power Reactor: A reactor designed to produce useful nuclear power, as distinguished from reactors used primarily for research or for producing radiation or fissionable materials.

Precautionary Launch: The launching of nuclear-loaded aircraft under imminent nuclear attack so as to preclude friendly aircraft destruction and loss of weapons on the ground or carrier.

Precision Bombing: Bombing directed at a specific point target.

Preemptive Attack: An attack initiated on the basis of incontrovertible evidence that an enemy attack is imminent or under way.

Preemptive Strike: A nuclear attack initiated in anticipation of an opponent's decision to resort to nuclear war.

Preemptive War: A war initiated on the basis of incontrovertible evidence that an enemy attack is imminent.

Preferential Defense: Selective defense (by ballistic missile defense systems or hardening) of a land-based ballistic missile force where some silos are protected and others are not. In an attack, the aggressor could not know which silos would be defended and to what extent.

Prelaunch Survivability: The ability of any given delivery system to weather a surprise first strike successfully and retaliate. See also **postlaunch survivability**.

Pre-Position: To place military units, equipment, or supplies at or near the point of planned use or at a designated location to reduce reaction time and to insure timely support of a specific force during initial phases of an operation.

Pre-Positioned War Reserve Equipment: That portion of the war reserve materiel requirement that approved plans dictate be positioned or issued to the user prior to hostilities at or near the point of planned use to insure timely support of a specific project or designated force during the initial phase of war, pending arrival of replenishment shipments.

Pre-Positioned War Reserve Stock: That portion of the total war reserve stocks that is positioned against a pre-positioned war reserve requirement.

Prescribed Nuclear Load: A specified quantity of nuclear weapons to be carried by a delivery unit. The establishment and replenishment of this load after each expenditure is a command decision and is dependent upon the tactical situation, the nuclear logistical situation, and the capability of the unit to transport and utilize the load. It may vary from day to day and among similar delivery units.

Prescribed Nuclear Stockage: A specified quantity of nuclear weapons, components of nuclear weapons, and warhead test equipment to be stocked in special ammunition supply points or other logistical installations. The establishment and replenishment of this stockage is a command decision and is dependent upon the tactical situation, the allocation, the capability of the logistical support unit to store and maintain the nuclear weapons, and the nuclear logistical situation. The prescribed stockage may vary from time to time and among similar logistical support units.

Preventive War: A war initiated in the belief that military conflict, while not imminent, is inevitable, and that to delay would involve greater risk. See also **preemptive war.**

Principles of War: A collection of considerations amassed over the centuries that assist strategists and tacticians in setting priorities and courses of action.

1. Purpose (objective)	5. Economy	9. Security
2. Initiative	6. Maneuver	10. Simplicity
3. Flexibility	7. Surprise	11. Unity
4. Concentration	8. Exploitation	12. Morale

Probable Error Height of Burst: Error in height of burst in which projectile or missile fuses may be expected to exceed as often as not.

Production Reactor: 1. A reactor designed primarily for large-scale production of plutonium 239 by neutron irradiation of uranium 238. 2. A reactor used primarily for the production of radioactive isotopes.

Programs of Cooperation: Formal bilateral agreements between the United States and other nations that involve the transfer of delivery vehicles capable of nuclear delivery or deployment of nuclear weapons for use by the host nation under the direction of NATO Supreme Allied Commander Europe (SACEUR) or Supreme Allied Commander Atlantic (SACLANT). Host nations provide support for U.S. weapons and weapons provided for their use. The nuclear warheads remain in U.S. custody until release by the U.S. president in time of war.

Projectile: An object projected by an applied exterior force and continuing in motion by virtue of its own inertia, such as a bullet, shell, or grenade. Also applied to rockets and to guided missiles.

Proliferation: The acquisition of national nuclear weapons capabilities by nations not previously possessing them, either by the dissemination by the nuclear powers of weapons or information necessary for their manufacture, or by the development of domestic nuclear weapons programs.

Prompt Radiation: The gamma rays produced in fission as a result of other neutron reactions and nuclear excitation of the weapon materials that appear within a second or less after a nuclear explosion. The radiations from these sources are known either as prompt or instantaneous gamma rays. See also **induced radiation; initial radiation; residual nuclear radiation**.

Propellant: 1. The source that provides the energy required for propelling a projectile. Specifically, an explosive charge for propelling a projectile; **2.** A fuel, either solid or liquid, for propelling a rocket or missile.

Proximity Fuse: A fuse wherein primary initiation occurs by remotely sensing the presence, distance, or direction of a target or its associated environment by means of a signal generated by the fuse or emitted by the target, or by detecting a disturbance of a natural field surrounding the target.

Proxy War: A form of limited war in which great powers avoid a direct confrontation by furthering their national security interests and objectives through conflict between representatives or associates. See also **limited war**.

PSI Overpressure: Transient pressure above normal atmospheric pressure. The measure is commonly used to determine an object's ability to withstand the pressure from a nuclear blast.

PSP (Priority Strike Program): A plan that provides for the delivery of nuclear strikes against the highest priority targets in the nuclear operations plan (NOP).

Psychological Operations: Planned psychological activities in peace and war directed towards enemy, friendly, and neutral audiences in order to create attitudes and behavior favorable to the achievement of political and military objectives. These operations include psychological action, psychological warfare, and psychological consolidation and encompass those political, military, economic, ideological and information activities designed for achieving a desired psychological effect.

Psychological Warfare: The use of communications media and other psychological means in a declared emergency or in a war, designed to bring psychological pressure to bear on the enemy and to influence favorably the attitudes and behavior of hostile groups and other target audiences in areas under enemy control. The primary objectives are to support all efforts against the enemy aimed at weakening his will to engage in or to continue hostilities and at reducing his capacity for waging war.

Propaganda, the central component of psychological warfare, is any form of communication in support of national objectives designed to influence the opinions, emotions, attitudes, or behavior of any group in order to benefit the sponsor, either directly or indirectly. See also **black propaganda; grey propaganda; white propaganda.**

Pu-239: An isotope of plutonium produced in reactors through transformation of U-238. The higher the concentration of Pu-239, the greater its suitability for the manufacture of nuclear explosives.

Q

QRA (Quick Reaction Alert): A condition in which specified numbers of aircraft and missiles are readied to deliver designated nuclear strikes on very short notice.

R

Radar: Radio detection and ranging equipment that determines the distance and usually the direction of objects by transmission and return of electromagnetic energy.

Radar Area Correlator Guidance (RADAG): A guidance principle that compares a radar image of terrain along the reentry vehicle flight path with an image of the target area stored in an onboard computer and that makes corrections in the reentry vehicle flight to establish correspondence between the two images to accurately strike the target with the vehicle.

Radiation Dose: The total amount of ionizing radiation absorbed by material or tissues, commonly expressed in rads. Often used in the sense of the exposure dose, expressed in roentgens, that is a measure of the total amount of ionization that the quantity of radiation could produce in the air. Should be distinguished from the absorbed dose, also given in rads, that represents the energy absorbed from the radiation per gram of specified body tissue. Further, the biological dose, in rems, is a measure of the biological effectiveness of the radiation exposure.

Radiation Dose Rate: The radiation dose absorbed per unit of time. A radiation dose rate can be set at some particular unit of time (e.g., H + 1 hour) and would be called H + 1 radiation dose rate.

Radiation Intensity: The radiation dose rate at a given time and place. It may be used coupled with a figure to denote the radiation intensity used at a given number of hours after a nuclear burst; e.g., RI3 is the radiation intensity 3 hours after the time of burst.

Radiation Scattering: The diversion of radiation (thermal, electromagnetic, or nuclear) from its original path as a result of interactions or collisions with atoms, molecules, or larger particles in the atmosphere or other media between the source of radiation (e.g., a nuclear explosion) and a point at some distance away. As a result of scattering, radiation (especially gamma rays and neutrons) will be received at a given point from many directions instead of only from the direction of the source.

Radioactive Cloud: A mass of air and vapor in the atmosphere carrying radioactive debris from a nuclear explosion.

Radioactive Waste: Equipment and materials (from nuclear operations) that are radioactive and for which there is no further use. Wastes are generally classified as high-level (having radioactivity concentrations of hundreds of thousands of curies per gallon or cubic foot), low-level (in the range of one micro-curie per gallon or cubic foot), or intermediate (between these extremes).

Radioactivity: The spontaneous emission of radiation, generally alpha or beta particles, often accompanied by gamma rays, from the nuclei of an unstable isotope. Most natural elements are stable, but almost all elements can exist in unstable forms. The nuclei of these unstable "isotopes," as they are called, are "uncomfortable" with the particular mixture of nuclear particles comprising them, and they decrease this internal stress through the process of radioactive decay. The three basic modes of radioactive decay are the emission of alpha, beta, and gamma radiation:

Alpha: Unstable nuclei frequently emit alpha particles, actually helium nuclei consisting of two protons and two electrons. By far the most massive of the decay particles, it is also the slowest, rarely exceeding one-tenth the velocity of light. As a result, its penetrating power is weak, and it can usually be stopped by a piece of paper. But if alpha emitters like plutonium are incorporated in the body, they pose a serious cancer threat.

Beta: Another form of radioactive decay is the emission of a beta particle, or electron. The beta particle has only about one seven-thousandth the mass of the alpha particle, but its velocity is very much greater, as much as eight-tenths the velocity of light. As a result, beta particles can penetrate far more deeply into bodily tissue and external doses of beta radiation represent a significantly greater threat than the slower, heavier alpha particles. Beta-emitting isotopes are as harmful as alpha emitters if taken up by the body.

Gamma: In some decay processes, the emission is a photon having no mass at all and traveling at the speed of light. Radio waves, visible light, radiant heat, and X-rays are all photons, differing only in the energy level each carries. The gamma ray is similar to the X-ray photon, but far more penetrating (it can traverse several inches of concrete). It is capable of doing great damage in the body.

Common to all three types of nuclear-decay radiation is their ability to ionize (i.e., unbalance electrically) the neutral atoms through which they pass, that is, give them a net electrical charge. The alpha particle, carrying a positive electrical charge, pulls electrons from the atoms through which it passes, while negatively charged beta particles can push electrons out of neutral atoms. If energetic betas pass sufficiently close to atomic nuclei, they can produce X-rays, which themselves can ionize additional neutral atoms. Massless but energetic gamma rays can knock electrons out of neutral atoms in the same fashion as X-rays, leaving them ionized. A single particle of radiation can ionize hundreds of neutral atoms in the tissue in multiple collisions before all its energy is absorbed. This disrupts the chemical bonds for critically important cell structures like the cytoplasm, which carries the cell's genetic blueprints, and also produces chemical constituents that can cause as much damage as the original ionizing radiation.

For convenience, a unit of radiation dose called the "rad" has been adopted. It measures the amount of ionization produced per unit volume by the particles from radioactive decay.

Radiological Defense: Defensive measures taken against the radiation hazard resulting from the employment of nuclear and radiological weapons.

Radiological Operations: Employment of radioactive materials or radiation producing devices to cause casualties or restrict the use of terrain. Includes the intentional employment of fallout from nuclear weapons.

Radius of Action: The maximum distance a ship, aircraft, or vehicle can travel away from its base along a given course with normal combat load and return without refueling, allowing for all safety and operation factors. See also **long-range bomber aircraft; medium bomber**.

Radius of Damage: The distance from ground zero at which there is a 0.50 probability of achieving the desired damage.

Radius of Integration: The distance from ground zero that indicates the area within which the effects of both the nuclear detonation and conventional weapons are to be integrated.

Rapacki Plan: Named after Polish Foreign Minister Adam Rapacki in 1957, the plan called for a nuclear-free zone in the geographical area composed of West Germany, East Germany, Poland, and Czechoslovakia, and a phased reduction of conventional forces in the same area. Aside from other reasons of a political nature, the Western allies rejected the Rapacki Plan because it prevented West Germany from fulfilling its role as a member of NATO.

Rapid Reload Capacity: The ability of a strategic nuclear delivery system to conduct multiple strikes. This characteristic presently is confined to aircraft, but landmobile missiles and hard site ICBMs have the potential. Submarines conceivably could be replenished at sea, but a significantly greater time lag would occur. See also **cold launch**.

Rationalization: Any action that increases the effectiveness of Allied forces through more efficient or effective use of defense resources committed to the NATO alliance. Rationalization includes consolidation, reassignment of national priorities to higher NATO alliance needs, standardization, specialization, mutual support, improved interoperability, or greater cooperation. Rationalization applies to both weapons or materiel resources and non-weapons military matters.

Readiness: The ability of specific armed forces to respond in times allotted to perform assigned missions effectively.

Reallocation of Resources: The provision of logistic resources by the military forces of one nation to the military forces of another nation or nations as directed by the appropriate military authority under the terms incorporated in appropriate NATO or CENTO (Central Treaty Organization) documents.

Reconnaissance: 1. A mission undertaken to obtain, by visual observation or other detection methods, information about the activities and resources of an enemy or potential enemy. 2. To secure data concerning the meteorological, hydrographic, or geographic characteristics of a particular area.

Recycling: The re-use of fissionable material after it has been recovered by chemical processing from spent or depleted reactor fuel, reenriched, and then refabricated into new fuel elements.

Reentry Phase: That portion of the trajectory of a ballistic missile or space vehicle where there is a significant interaction of the vehicle and the earth's atmosphere.

Reentry Vehicle (RV): That portion of a ballistic missile designed to carry a nuclear warhead and to reenter the earth's atmosphere in the terminal portion of the missile trajectory.

Regulus: A surface-to-surface, jet-powered, guided missile. It is equipped with a nuclear warhead, and launched from a surfaced submarine or cruiser.

Reinforcement: Augmenting military capabilities in any given area by introducing locally-available or strategic reserves. See also **strategic reserve**.

Rem (Roentgen Equivalent Mammal): One rem is the quantity of ionizing radiation of any type that, when absorbed by man or another mammal, produces a physiological effect equivalent to that produced by the absorption of one roentgen of X-ray or gamma radiation.

Reprocessing Plant: A facility that separates elements in spent reactor fuel. Plutonium recovered through this process is re-usable as reactor fuel or for the production of nuclear explosives.

Reserve Component: Armed forces not in active service. U.S. Reserve Components include the Army National Guard and Army Reserve; the Naval Reserve; the Marine Corps Reserve; the Air National Guard, and Air Force Reserve.

Residual Forces: Unexpended portions of the remaining U.S. forces that have an immediate combat potential for continued military operations and that have been deliberately withheld from utilization.

Residual Nuclear Radiation: Lingering radiation or radiation emitted by radioactive material remaining after a nuclear explosion; arbitrarily designated as that emitted more than one minute after the explosion.

Residual Radioactivity: Nuclear radiation that results from radioactive sources and persists for longer than one minute. Sources of residual radioactivity created by nuclear explosions include not only fission fragments and radioactive matter created primarily by neutron activation but also by gamma and other radiation activation. Other possible sources of residual radioactivity include radioactive material created and dispersed by means other than nuclear explosions.

Resupply of Europe: The shipping of supplies to Europe during the period from the outbreak of war until the end of such a requirement. These supplies to exclude any materiel already located upon land in Europe, but to include other supplies irrespective of their origin or location.

Retrograde Movement: Any movement of a command to the rear or away from the enemy. It may be forced by the enemy or may be made voluntarily. Such movements may be classified as withdrawal, retirement, or delaying action.

Revolutionary War: Efforts to seize political power by illegitimate or coercive means, destroying existing systems of government and social structures in the process.

Roentgen: A unit of exposure to ionizing radiation. It is that amount of gamma or X-rays required to produce ions carrying one electrostatic unit of electrical charge (either positive or negative) in one cubic centimeter of dry air under standard conditions. See also **rem (roentgen equivalent mammal)**.

Roll Back: The process of progressive destruction or neutralization of the opposing defenses, starting at the periphery and working inward to permit deeper penetration of succeeding defense positions.

S

Sabotage: An act or acts with intent to injure, interfere with, or obstruct the national defense of a country by willfully injuring or destroying, or attempting to injure or destroy, any national defense or war materiel, premises, or utilities, including human and natural resources.

SACEUR (Supreme Allied Commander Europe): The commander is responsible, under the general direction of the Military Committee, for the defense of Allied countries within the command area. In time of war, SACEUR would control all land, sea, and air operations in this area. Internal defense and defense of coastal waters would remain the responsibility of the national authorities concerned, but the supreme commander would have full authority to carry out operations considered necessary for the defense of any part of the area under his command.

SACEUR's peacetime functions include organizing, training, and equipping the North Atlantic forces assigned to the command to ensure that they are knit together into one united force; preparing and finalizing defense plans; and making recommendations to the Military Committee about command forces and any military questions that might affect the ability of SACEUR to carry out assigned responsibilities in peace or war. While receiving direction from the Military Committee, the supreme commander nevertheless has direct access to the chiefs-of-staff of any of the powers and, in certain circumstances, to defense ministers, and heads of government. In addition, all the North Atlantic countries, with the exception of France and Iceland, maintain national military representatives (NMR) at SHAPE (Supreme Headquarters Allied Powers Europe) who are responsible for liaison with their own chief-of-staff. France is represented by a military mission; Iceland has no armed forces. SHAPE, originally located near Paris, now occupies a headquarters complex near Mons, Belgium.

To control the vast areas covered by the Allied Command Europe there are three subordinate commands directly responsible to SACEUR: *The Northern European Command*: Allied Forces North Norway, Allied Forces South Norway, and Allied Forces Baltic Approaches; *The Central European Command*: Northern Army Group, Central Army Group, and Allied Air Forces Central Europe; *The Southern European Command*: Allied Land Forces Southern Europe, Allied Land Forces South Eastern Europe, Allied Air Forces Southern Europe, Allied Naval Forces Southern Europe, and Naval Striking and Support Forces Southern Europe.

In addition, two other commanders are directly subordinate to SACEUR, the Commander Allied Command Europe Mobile Force (Land Component), and the Commander-in-Chief United Kingdom Air Forces.

Safe Burst Height: The height of burst at or above which the level of fallout or damage to ground installations is at a predetermined level acceptable to the military commander.

SALT (Strategic Arms Limitation Talks):

SALT I: The first SALT agreements were signed in May 1972, following two and one-half years of negotiations. The *ABM Treaty* and the supplementary *Protocol of 1974* limit ABM systems to one site on each side, with low limits on the number of permitted ABM/interceptor missiles and radars. This treaty is of unlimited duration, and every five years is subjected to review by the two sides. The first such review took place in 1977. The ABM Treaty reflected a decision on the part of both the United States and the Soviet Union to avoid a massive arms race in ballistic missile defenses that in the end could not prevent destruction of both societies in a nuclear attack. Had the United States and the Soviet Union gone ahead with plans to deploy ABM systems, both nations would also have built more numerous weapons to insure penetration of these defenses, with a consequent reduced stability, heightened political and military tensions, and substantially greater costs.

The *Interim Agreement* on offensive weapons froze for five

years the numbers of ICBM and SLBM launchers to the number operational or under construction at the time of signature of the agreement. The five-year duration of the Interim Agreement expired on October 3, 1977. Given the substantial progress toward a SALT II agreement, and in order to maintain the status quo while the negotiations are being completed, the United States issued a statement indicating its intention not to take any action inconsistent with the provisions of the Interim Agreement or with the goals of the ongoing negotiations. The Soviet Union issued a similar statement expressing the same intentions.

SALT II: The SALT II negotiations began in November 1972. The primary goal of SALT II was the achievement of a comprehensive agreement limiting strategic offensive arms to replace the Interim Agreement. Early discussion between the sides covered a variety of issues, including the systems to be addressed, the means of establishing equality in strategic nuclear forces, as well as specific quantitative and qualitative limits. The positions of the sides differed widely on many of these questions, however, and only limited progress was made.

A major breakthrough occurred at the *Vladivostok meeting* in November 1974 between President Ford and General Secretary Brezhnev when they agreed on basic guidelines for a SALT II agreement. The key elements were: (1) the duration of the new agreement would be through 1985; (2) the sides would be limited to equal aggregate totals of 2,400 strategic nuclear delivery vehicles; (3) the sides would be limited to 1,320 MIRVed (multiple independently targetable reentry vehicles) systems; and (4) forward-based systems (i.e., nuclear-capable U.S. systems based in Europe, such as fighter-bombers) would not be included.

The principle of equal aggregate totals was a major U.S. objective for SALT II and a particularly significant achievement of the Vladivostok accord. The delegations in Geneva resumed negotiations working toward an agreement based on this general framework. During these negotiations, however, it became clear that there were serious disagreements between the two sides on two major issues: the limits on cruise missiles and whether a new Soviet bomber, known as Backfire, was to be considered a strategic heavy bomber and therefore counted in the 2,400 aggregate. While progress was made in other less contentious areas, the negotiations reached a stalemate on these issues. Discussion continued on other issues, including MIRV verification provisions, bans on new strategic weapons, definitions, and missile throw-weight limitations.

Early in 1977, the Carter administration, in its desire to reach significant strategic arms limitations, undertook a detailed interagency review of unresolved SALT issues. On the basis of this review, it was decided to build on the elements agreed to at Vladivostok by adding significant reductions in strategic arms and by emphasizing limits on those elements in strategic arsenals that are most destabilizing. These basic considerations were embodied in the comprehensive proposal that was presented to the Soviets by Secretary of State Vance and Ambassador Warnke in Moscow in March 1978. This proposal called for major cuts in the Vladivostok ceilings, as well as limits on the number of land-based ICBMs equipped with MIRVs and the number of very large, or "heavy" ICBMs. The proposal also called for restrictive limits on the testing and deployment of new types of ICBMs. At this Moscow meeting, the United States also offered an alternative deferral proposal under which the SALT II agreement would be based upon the Vladivostok numbers, with resolution of the Backfire bomber and cruise missile issues to be deferred until SALT III. Both proposals were rejected by the Soviets on the grounds that they were inconsistent with their understanding of what was agreed to at Vladivostok.

SALT II Agreement Framework: In negotiations in May 1978 Secretary of State Vance and Ambassador Warnke reached agreement with Foreign Minister Andrei Gromyko on a general framework for SALT II that accommodated both the Soviet desire for retaining the Vladivostok guidelines and the U.S. desire for more comprehensive limitations. The agreed SALT II framework has three principal elements: (1) a treaty lasting until 1985, based on the Vladivostok guidelines; (2) a protocol that, on an interim basis, would deal with remaining contentious issues not ready for long-term resolution; and (3) a statement of principles for SALT III.

The proposed *SALT II treaty* will establish equal limits for the Soviet Union and the United States on each side's aggregate number of strategic nuclear delivery vehicles—ICBMs, SLBMs, and heavy bombers.

Specifically, the treaty will include the following major provisions: (1) a limit of 2,250 on the total number of strategic launchers; (2) a 1,320 sublimit on MIRVed ICBM and SLBM launchers and aircraft equipped with long-range cruise missiles;

(3) a sublimit of 1,200 on MIRVed ballistic missiles; and (4) a sublimit of 820 MIRVed ICBM launchers; (5) air-launched cruise missiles will be permitted to be deployed on heavy bombers with no limitations on their range. Such aircraft will be counted as heavy bombers within the 2,250 ceiling on strategic systems as well as within a combined ceiling of 1,320 on MIRVed missiles and cruise missile equipped aircraft.

Within the numerical limits set by the treaty, each side may determine its own force structure. In other words, the sides would have "freedom to mix" among these strategic systems. This combination of equal numerical limits, with the freedom to choose the force mix within overall ceilings, resolves the otherwise difficult problem of providing for equivalence given differences in the composition of U.S. and Soviet strategic forces.

The treaty's subceilings on MIRVed ballistic missiles and on ICBMs equipped with MIRVs will place an upper limit on the deployment of the most threatening of the Soviet strategic weapons. In addition, the treaty will include detailed definitions, restrictions on certain new strategic systems, and provisions designed to improve verification. Certain issues not ready for longer term resolution, such as restrictions on new types of ICBMs, cruise missiles, and mobile ICBMs, will be included in the protocol. These issues will be topics for discussion in SALT III.

Specifically, the proposed *SALT II protocol* includes the following provisions:

- A ban on the deployment of all ground-launched and sea-launched cruise missiles with a range greater than 600 km for three years.
- A limitation on the number—ten ICBMs and fourteen SLBMs —of warheads (reentry vehicles) fitted on each new type of MIRVed missile. The number of reentry vehicles fitted on existing missile types are to be frozen at present levels.
- The United States and the Soviet Union will each be limited to the deployment of one new type of land-based ICBM system over the term of the treaty.

The third element of the SALT II package will be a *joint statement of principles for SALT III*. These agreed upon principles will serve as general guide lines for the next stage of SALT. The principles will include commitments to further reductions, more comprehensive qualitative constraints on new systems, and provisions to improve verification.

Salted Weapon: A nuclear weapon that has, in addition to its normal components, certain elements or isotopes that capture neutrons at the time of the explosion and produce radioactive weapon debris. See also **minimum residual radioactivity weapon (MRR weapon)**.

Salvo: 1. In naval gunfire support, a method of fire in which a number of weapons are fired at the same target simultaneously. **2.** In close air support air interdiction operations, a method of delivery in which the release mechanisms are operated to fire all ordnance of a specific type simultaneously.

SAS (Special Ammunition Storage Sites): Storage facilities for nuclear weapons deployed abroad.

Schools of Strategic Thought: *Continental School*: The primacy of the land battle is the focus of this approach. The "land-power proponents" view the "ultimate" object of war as the destruction of enemy armies. Naval and air forces are responsible for logistical support.

Maritime School: Students of Alfred Mahan and Julian S. Corbett fall into this categorization. The maritime proponents view control of the sea lanes and vital strategic choke points as determining the course of the land battle.

Aerospace School: The father of air strategy was Giulio Douhet. The notion that the primary mission of air power is the support of ground forces is rejected here. The tenets of the aerospace school are three: (1) acting independently of ground and naval power, air power is decisive in battle; (2) without constraints, air power renders "protracted wars obsolete," and (3) through control of air space, destruction of enemy counterforce and countervalue targets is facilitated.

Revolutionary School: Such figures as Marx, Ho Chi Minh, and Che Guevara are the central representatives of the revolutionary school. While this approach does not reject the utility of military force, its principal tools are political, social, and psychological.

Scientific and Technical Intelligence: Information or intelligence concerning foreign progress in basic and applied scientific or technical research and development, including engineering research and development, new technology, and weapons systems.

Screen: An arrangement of ships, submarines, or aircraft for the protection of a unit or main body against attack by submarines, aircraft, or missiles.

Sea-Based Nuclear Forces: Sea-based forces capable of delivering nuclear weapons. Currently deployed U.S. forces include submarine-launched ballistic missiles, carrier-based aircraft, surface ship surface-to-air missiles (SAMs), and a variety of antisubmarine warfare weapons. U.S. cruise missiles that could be based on submarines or surface ships are in development. Soviet systems include ballistic and cruise missiles based on diesel and nuclear-powered submarines and cruise missiles based on surface ships and on naval aviation medium bombers. See also **cruise missile; noncentral systems.**

Sea Control: The employment of naval forces, supplemented by land and aerospace forces as appropriate, to destroy enemy naval forces, suppress enemy oceangoing commerce, protect vital shipping lanes, and establish local superiority in areas of naval operations.

Sea Control Operations: The employment of naval forces, supported by land and air forces as appropriate, to achieve military objectives in vital sea areas. Such operations include destruction of enemy naval forces, suppression of enemy sea commerce, protection of vital sea lanes, and establishment of local military superiority in areas of naval operations.

Seafarer: An extremely low frequency (ELF) U.S. Navy communications system for submarines that would allow receipt of messages without the necessity of bringing submarines close to the surface where they are most vulnerable. Presently in the research and development stage, Seafarer could be constructed in the early 1980s.

Sea-Launched Cruise Missile (SLCM): A cruise missile capable of being launched from a submerged or surfaced submarine or from a surface ship. The U.S. SLCM under development is sized for launch from standard submarine torpedo tubes, and thus could be carried by nuclear-powered submarines or attack submarines. The SLCM is to be developed in both strategic and tactical variants, the former being able to carry a nuclear warhead about 1,500 nautical miles. The latter will be designed to be launched from surface ships, aircraft, as well as submarines, primarily as a non-nuclear antiship missile with a range of up to several hundred miles. The SLCM will have a low cruise altitude flight profile and will have a high accuracy. The Soviet Union currently has SLCMs of a shorter range deployed on both nuclear- and diesel-powered submarines and surface ships. See also **cruise missile; Tomahawk cruise missile.**

Sea Superiority: That degree of dominance in a sea battle of one force over another that permits the conduct of operations by the former and its related land, sea, and air forces at a given time and place without prohibitive interference by the opposing force.

Sea Supremacy: That degree of sea superiority wherein the opposing force is incapable of effective interference.

SEATO (Southeast Asia Treaty Organization): A regional military organization established in 1954 to deter aggression in Southeast Asia and to facilitate joint defense planning. Initial participants in this alliance were Australia, Britain, France, New Zealand, Pakistan, Philippines, Thailand, and the United States.

Second Strike: Refers to a retaliatory attack in response to a first strike. A high-confidence second-strike (retaliatory) capability is the primary basis for nuclear deterrence. To provide this capability, U.S. forces have been structured on the basis of well-hedged assumptions regarding force survivability following a first strike and the level of retaliatory destruction needed. Options for a second strike include attacks on cities, industrial facilities, and military installations.

Second-Strike Capability: The ability to survive a first strike with sufficient resources to deliver an effective counterblow. Generally associated with nuclear weapons.

Second-Strike Strategy: The employment of strategic nuclear weapons only in reprisal for a nuclear first strike by the enemy. This strategy implies a capability sufficiently large and invulnerable to sustain an enemy first strike with residual forces available to inflict unacceptable levels of destruction.

Security Countermeasures: Measures designed to impair the effectiveness of an unfriendly or hostile attack upon security.

Seismic Coupling: A measure of the fraction of the total energy released in an underground explosion that is transformed into seismic waves in the earth. The greater the coupling of a particular explosion, the larger will be the seismic waves and the easier will be the detection by seismographs and the determination of the true yield of the explosion.

Selective Mobilization: Expansion of the active armed forces by mobilization of reserve component units or individual reservists, by authority of Congress or the president, to satisfy an emergency requirement; e.g., mobilization for domestic emergencies, such as civil disturbances; to protect life; to protect federal property and functions; or to prevent disruption of federal activities. Selective mobilization differs from partial mobilization in that it would not normally be associated with requirements for contingency plans involving external threats to the national security. See also **mobilization**.

Sergeant: A truck-mounted short-range tactical missile capable of delivering a nuclear weapon against enemy combat forces. Being phased out of the U.S. inventory.

Shell Game: See **M-X**.

Shield: Strategic nuclear weapons that deter a first strike by an opposing nuclear power.

Shielding: 1. Material of suitable thickness and physical characteristics used to protect personnel from radiation during the manufacture, handling, and transportation of fissionable and radioactive materials. **2.** Obstructions that tend to protect personnel or materials from the effects of a nuclear explosion.

Shipping Lane: Indicates the general flow of merchant shipping between two departure or terminal areas.

Shipping Movement Policy: The NATO policy for the conduct of all merchant shipping in the early days of war.

Shock Front: The boundary between the pressure disturbance created by an explosion (in air, water, or earth) and the ambient atmosphere, water, or earth.

Short-Range Attack Missile (SRAM): An air-to-surface missile carried by U.S. FB-11 and B-52 bombers.

Short-Range Ballistic Missile (SRBM): A ballistic missile with a range of up to about 600 nautical miles. The Pershing, Lance, and Sergeant are examples of U.S. SRBMs which are currently deployed. Examples of Soviet SRBMs are the Scud and Scaleboard.

Short Round: 1. The unintentional or inadvertent delivery of ordnance on friendly troops, installations, or civilians by a friendly weapon system. **2.** A defective cartridge in which the projectile has been seated too deeply.

Short Takeoff and Landing (STOL): The ability of an aircraft to clear a 50-foot obstacle within 1,500 feet of commencing takeoff; or in landing, to stop within 1,500 feet after passing over a 50-foot obstacle.

Show of Force: The purposeful exhibition of armed might before an enemy or potential enemy, usually in a crisis situation to reinforce deterrer demands. See also **symbolic attack**.

Shuttle Bombing: Bombing of objectives, utilizing two bases. By this method, a bomber formation bombs its target, flies on to its second base, reloads, and returns to its home base, again bombing a target if required.

Sidewinder: An air-to-air missile that was the second U.S. missile to be chosen for European production by Belgium, Denmark, the Federal Republic of Germany, Greece, the Netherlands, Norway, Portugal, and Turkey. A German firm, Fluggerätewerk, was selected as prime contractor. Production arrangements were approved by NATO in December 1959 and the first missiles were assembled in November 1961. Most of the flight tests were performed in Europe with the assistance of France, who ordered several hundred missiles. Production, which involved a program of the order of 10,000 missiles, was disbanded in December 1966.

Signals Intelligence (SIGINT): The general term for the foreign intelligence mission of the National Security Agency/Central Security Service. SIGINT involves the interception, processing, analysis, and dissemination of information derived from foreign electrical communications and other signals. It is composed of three elements: Communications Intelligence (COMINT), Electronics Intelligence (ELINT), and Telemetry Intelligence (TELINT). Most SIGINT is collected by personnel of the service cryptologic agencies.

Silo: Underground facilities for a hard-site ballistic missile or crew, designed to provide prelaunch protection against nuclear effects.

Single Integrated Operational Plan (SIOP): The strategic nuclear war plan of the United States.

Skip Bombing: A method of aerial bombing in which the bomb is released from such a low altitude that it slides or glances along the surface of the water or ground and strikes the target at or above water level or ground level. See also **minimum altitude bombing**.

Skybolt: A two-stage ballistic missile to be carried by bombers as a stand-off weapon. Would have provided Great Britain nuclear striking power by prolonging the life of her V-bombers. However, the decision by the United States in 1962 to cancel the Skybolt development program meant that Britain had to either abandon plans for a minimum independent nuclear capability, because of lack of an adequate delivery system, or carry on the development independently at exorbitant costs. See **Nassau Agreement; minimum deterrence**.

SLAR: Side-looking airborne radar.

SLBM (Submarine-launched Ballistic Missile): A ballistic missile carried in and launched from a submarine (also called fleet ballistic missiles—FBM).

SLBMs, along with strategic bombers and ICBMs, comprise the basic "triad" structure of the U.S. strategic deterrent force.

Excluded from this category are cruise missiles which, although carried by and launched from submarines, do not fly a ballistic trajectory. Polaris and Poseidon are operational U.S. SLBMs; the Trident I missile is in development. The Soviet SS-N-6 and SS-N-8 are currently deployed Soviet SLBMs.

SLCM (Sea-launched Cruise Missile): See **sea-launched cruise missile (SLCM)**.

Small Arms: All arms, including automatic weapons, up to and including thirty millimeters (1.181 inches).

Soft Missile Base: A launching base that is not protected against a nuclear explosion.

Soft Target: A target not protected against the blast, heat, and radiation produced by nuclear explosions. There are many degrees of softness. Some missiles and aircraft, for example, are built in ways that ward off certain effects, but they are "soft" in comparison with shelters and silos. See also **hardened site; hard targets; overpressure**.

Sortie: 1. A sudden attack made from a defensive position. In this meaning, it is sometimes called a sally. 2. An operational flight by one aircraft. 3. To depart from a port or anchorage with an implication of departure for operations or maneuver. See also **mission**.

Spacetrack: The U.S. Air Force world-wide system for the detection, tracking, and identification of all objects in space. The system is composed of globally situated large radar optical and radio metric sensors. The current Spacetrack optical system is a four-site camera system with sites at San Vito, Italy; Sand Island in the Pacific; Mount John, New Zealand; and Edwards Air Force Base, California.

Spasm War: A brief, cataclysmic conflict in which all available destructive power is employed with scant regard for the consequences. If superpowers are involved, spasmic combat is a form of general war. See also **general war**.

Special Atomic Demolition Munition: A very low yield, man-portable, atomic demolition munition that is detonated by a timer device.

Special Forces: Military personnel with cross training in basic and specialized military skills to conduct unconventional warfare operations, organized into small multiple-purpose detachments with the mission to train, organize, supply, direct, and control indigenous forces in guerrilla warfare and counterinsurgency operations.

Specialization: An arrangement within an alliance wherein a member or group of members most suited by virtue of technical skills, location, or other qualifications assumes greater responsibility for a specific alliance task or a significant portion thereof.

Specified Command: A top-echelon U.S. combatant organization with regional or functional responsibilities that normally is composed of forces from one military service. It has a broad continuing mission and is established by the president through the secretary of defense with the advice and assistance of the Joint Chiefs of Staff. See also **unified command**.

Spent Fuel: Nuclear reactor fuel that has been irradiated (used) to the extent that it can no longer effectively sustain a chain reaction.

Spoiling Attack: A tactical maneuver employed to seriously impair a hostile attack while the enemy is in the process of forming or assembling for an attack. Usually defensively employed by armored units by attacking enemy assembly positions in front of a main line of resistance or battle position.

Spontaneous Fission: Fission that occurs without an external stimulus. The process occurs occasionally in all fissionable materials, including uranium 235.

SS-18: A large Soviet surface-to-surface missile. The largest ICBM in the world, the SS-18 can carry eight to ten megaton-range warheads. Now being deployed, about 300 SS-18s may eventually replace older, single-warhead SS-9s. Smaller SS-19s and SS-17s, both multiple-warhead missiles, are currently replacing older, single-warhead SS-11s.

Staging Base: 1. An advanced naval base for the anchoring, fueling, and refitting of transports and cargo ships and for replenishing mobile service squadrons. 2. A landing and takeoff area with minimum servicing, supply, and shelter provided for the temporary occupancy of military aircraft during the course of movement from one location to another.

Standardization: The process by which member nations achieve the closest practicable cooperation among forces, the most efficient use of research, development, and production resources, and agree to adopt on the broadest possible basis, the use of: (1) common or compatible operational, administrative, and logistic procedures; (2) common or compatible technical procedures and criteria; (3) common compatible, or interchangeable supplies, components, weapons, or equipment; and (4) common or compatible tactical doctrine with corresponding organizational compatibility.

Standardization Agreement: The record of an agreement among

several or all of the member nations to adopt like or similar
military equipment, ammunition, supplies, and stores; and
operational, logistic, and administrative procedures.

Standing Consultative Commission (SCC): A permanent on-going
U.S.-Soviet commission established in December 1972 in accordance with the provisions of the SALT ABM Treaty. Its purpose
is "to promote the objectives and implementation of the provisions" of the treaty and the SALT I agreement. The parties
agreed to use the SCC to: (1) consider questions concerning
compliance with the obligations assumed and related situations
that may be considered ambiguous; (2) provide on a voluntary
basis such information as either party considers necessary to
assure confidence in compliance with the obligations assumed;
(3) consider questions involving unintended interference with
national technical means of verification; (4) consider possible
changes in the strategic situation that have a bearing on the
provisions of the treaty; (5) agree upon procedures and dates for
destruction or dismantling of ABM systems or their components
in cases provided for by the provisions of the treaty; (6) consider,
as appropriate, possible proposals for further increasing the
viability of the treaty, including proposals for amendments in
accordance with the provisions of the treaty; and (7) consider, as
appropriate, proposals for further measures aimed at limiting
strategic arms.

Starfighter: A multipurpose aircraft intended to fulfill a number of
military roles. In December 1960 four European countries
(Belgium, the Federal Republic of Germany, Italy, and the
Netherlands) announced that they had agreed to participate in a
program for the coordinated production in Europe of the American F104-G Starfighter aircraft. In June 1961, NATO set up a
Direction and Control Organization. Production of nearly 1,000
aircraft was completed in 1966 with United States assistance.
Canada, who produced similar aircraft for her own forces, was
closely associated.

Stellar Guidance: A system wherein a guided missile may follow a
predetermined course with reference primarily to the relative
position of the missile and certain preselected celestial bodies.

Stockpile-to-Target Sequence (Nuclear): 1. The order of events
involved in removing a nuclear weapon from storage, assembling, testing, transporting, and delivering it on the target. **2.** A
document that defines the logistical and employment concepts
and related physical environments involved in the delivery of a

nuclear weapon from the stockpile to the target. It may also define the logistical flow involved in moving nuclear weapons to and from the stockpile for quality assurance testing, modification, and retrofit, and the recycling of limited-life components.

Strategic: 1. Relates to a nation's military, economic, or political power and its ability to control the course of military or political events. 2. Intermediate-range or intercontinental means of attack primarily utilizing nuclear capabilities.

Strategic Advantage: The overall relative power relationship of opponents that enables one nation or group of nations to control effectively the course of a military or political situation.

Strategic Airlift: Transport aircraft, both military and civilian, used to move armed forces, equipment, and supplies expeditiously over long distances, especially intercontinentally. See also **tactical airlift**.

Strategic Air Warfare: Air combat and supporting operations designed to effect, through the systematic application of force to a selected series of vital targets, the progressive destruction and disintegration of the enemy's war-making capacity to a point where he no longer retains the ability or the will to wage war. Vital targets may include key manufacturing systems, sources of raw material, critical materiel, stockpiles, power systems, transportation systems, communication facilities, concentrations of uncommitted elements of enemy armed forces, key agricultural areas, and other such target systems.

Strategic Arms Limitation Talks (SALT): See **SALT (Strategic Arms Limitation Talks)**.

Strategic Balance: Some of the indices commonly used in the measurement of the strategic balance are:

- Number of strategic delivery vehicles.
- Total explosive energy yield of strategic nuclear warheads: measured in trillions of joules.
- EMT (equivalent megatonnage): two-thirds power of the explosive energy yield.
- Throw-weight, payload.
- Number of warheads.
- Warhead lethality: two-thirds power of the warhead yield divided by the square of the circular error probability of the delivery system.
- Military expenditures.
- Equivalent weapons: on the basis of certain known targets

and the stock of strategic weapons available, a weighted harmonic mean—an indicator defining EW (equivalent weapons) matches each strategic weapon against "a randomly selected member of the target set"—is used to determine the strategic weapons required to destroy specific targets.

See also **equivalent megatonnage (EMT)**; **payload**; **throwweight**.

Strategic Bomber: A multiengine aircraft with intercontinental range designed specifically to engage targets whose destruction would reduce an enemy's capacity or will to wage war.

Strategic Choke Point: A geographic bottleneck (e.g., straits), through which ships must pass to reach open oceans or seas. Ships passing through choke points are vulnerable to enemy attack.

Strategic Concept: The course of action accepted as the result of the estimate of the strategic situation. It is a statement of what is to be done expressed in broad terms sufficiently flexible to permit its use in framing the basic undertakings resulting from it.

Strategic Coupling: The linking of a lower level conflict; e.g., Soviet and Warsaw Pact military aggression in Europe to the use of U.S. strategic deterrent forces, such as ICBMs, heavy bombers, and SLBMs. With the advent of nuclear parity it has been argued by some that American strategic nuclear forces no longer serve to deter Soviet and Warsaw Pact aggression in Western Europe. This argument rests on the assumption that the U.S. would not risk strategic nuclear warfare in the defense of Western Europe. On the other hand, it has been argued that as long as American troops and nuclear forces remain in Europe, the USSR is likely to perceive a continued linkage between the U.S. forces defending Western Europe and American strategic nuclear power.

Strategic Defense: The strategy and forces designed primarily to protect a nation, its outposts, or its allies from the hazards of general war. It features defense against missiles, both land- and sea-launched, and long-range bombers. See also **strategic offense**.

Strategic Flexibility: The ability to deliver selective nuclear strikes for limited purposes while holding major retaliatory forces in reserve.

Strategic Forces: Commonly refers to U.S. nuclear weapons that can engage targets in the Soviet Union and China, and to Soviet and Chinese weapons that can strike the United States. Also includes actions to defend friends and allies from similar forays by foes.

Strategic Intelligence: Intelligence that is required for the formation of policy and military plans at national and international levels.

Strategic Materiel (Critical): Materiel required for essential uses in a war emergency, the procurement of which is sufficiently uncertain in adequate quantity, quality, or time to require prior provision of the supply.

Strategic Mission: A mission directed against one or more of a selected series of enemy targets with the purpose of progressive destruction and disintegration of the enemy's war-making capacity and his will to make war. Targets include key manufacturing systems, sources of raw material, critical materiel, stockpiles, power systems, transportation system, communication facilities, and other such target systems. As opposed to tactical operations, strategic operations are designed to have a long-range rather than immediate effect on the enemy and his military forces.

Strategic Mobility: The capability to deploy and sustain military forces world-wide in support of national strategy. See also **mobility**.

Strategic Nuclear Sufficiency: A term used by U.S. strategic planners to denote a posture in which the United States possesses a nuclear capability to: (1) maintain an adequate second-strike capability; (2) provide no incentive for the Soviet Union to strike the United States first in a crisis; and (3) prevent the Soviet Union from gaining the ability to cause considerably greater urban and industrial destruction than the United States could inflict on the USSR in a nuclear war.

Strategic Nuclear Weapons Systems: Offensive nuclear weapons systems designed to be employed against enemy targets with the purpose of effecting the destruction of the enemy's political, economic, or military capacity and defensive nuclear weapons systems designed to counteract those systems.

Strategic Offense: The strategy and forces designed primarily to destroy the enemy's war-making capacity during general war or to so degrade it that the opposition collapses. See also **counterforce; general war; strategic defense**.

Strategic Plan: A plan for the overall conduct of a war.

Strategic Psychological Warfare: Actions that pursue long-term and mainly political objectives, in a declared emergency or in war, and that are designed to undermine the enemy's will to fight and to reduce his capacity for waging war. It can be directed against the enemy (the dominating political group, the government and its executive agencies) or towards the population as a whole or particular elements of it. Strategic psychological warfare policy is laid down by the highest authority.

Strategic Reserve: Uncommitted forces of a country or coalition of countries that are intended to support national security interests and objectives, as required. See also **national interests; national objectives; residual forces.**

Strategic Retaliatory: Second-strike strategies and forces designed primarily to destroy the enemy's war-making capacity during general war or to so degrade it that the opposition collapses. See also **combat power; general war; second strike; second-strike capability; strategic offense.**

Strategic Sealift: Naval and merchant ships, together with crews, used to move armed forces, equipment, and supplies over long distances, especially intercontinentally.

Strategic Signal: An act, attitude, or communication that conveys threats or promises intended to influence enemy decisions.

Strategic Stability: Strategic stability encompasses both crisis stability and arms stability, and refers to a relationship in which neither side has an incentive to initiate the use of strategic nuclear forces in a crisis or perceives the necessity to undertake major new arms programs to avoid being placed at a strategic disadvantage. See **arms stability; crisis stability.**

Strategic Sufficiency: A force structure standard that demands capabilities adequate to attain desired ends without undue waste. Superiority thus is essential in some circumstances; parity or essential equivalence suffices under less demanding conditions; and inferiority, qualitative as well as quantitative, is sometimes acceptable. See also **essential equivalence; parity.**

Strategic Vulnerability: The susceptibility of vital elements of a national power to being seriously decreased or adversely changed by the application of actions within the capability of another nation. Strategic vulnerability may pertain to political, geographic, economic, scientific, sociological, or military factors.

Strategic Warning: A notification that enemy-initiated hostilities may be imminent. This notification may be received from minutes, hours, days, or longer prior to the initiation of hostilities.

Strategic Weapons Systems: An offensive or defensive projectile, its means of delivery, and ancillary equipment designed primarily for general war purposes.

Strategy: The art of developing and using political, economic, psychological, and military forces as necessary during peace and war to afford maximum support to policies and in order in war to increase the probabilities and favorable consequences of victory and to lessen the chances of defeat.

Strategy of Ambiguity: A strategy that presents the issue of direct military aggression in unfamiliar terms.

Strategy of Minimum Deterrence: Essentially a countercity strategy that targets a limited number of countervalue targets with a limited number of invulnerable strategic nuclear weapons in the belief that such a threat will be sufficient to deter aggression.

Strategy of Total Withholding: A strategy in which nuclear powers foreswear nuclear retaliation even if a nation's strategic nuclear forces or cities are massively attacked.

Stratosphere: The layer of the atmosphere above the troposphere in which the change of temperature with height is relatively small.

Strike-Back Capability: Nuclear forces that could survive an enemy first strike and then be used against the attacker in a second strike. This second-strike strategy requires the deployment of invulnerable strategic forces.

Strike Configured: Configuration of a delivery system having the necessary hardware and attributes to carry out a strike mission.

Strike Cruiser: A 17,200 ton warship, propelled by nuclear power, armed with antiship, antiair, and antisubmarine systems, and carrying two or more helicopters or vertical take-off and landing (VTOL) planes.

Strip Alert: Fighters or bombers located at the ends of runways that are prepared for takeoff on short notice.

Subkiloton Weapon: A nuclear weapon producing a yield below one kiloton. See also **kiloton weapon; nominal weapon**.

Submarine: A warship designed for operations under the surface of the seas. Nuclear-powered submarines contain the letter designation "N." U.S. nuclear-powered submarines carrying SLBMs are designated "SSBN." The United States has forty-one operational SSBNs with sixteen launch tubes each; the Trident SSBNs will have twenty-four tubes. Comparable submarines include the H, Y, and D classes. Attack submarines, designated "SS" or "SSN," are used to attack enemy surface ships and submarines. Submarines designed for launching cruise missiles are designated "SSGN" or "SSG" and include the Soviet J, W, E, and C class submarines. The United States has no operational cruise missile launching submarines. The Soviet long-range diesel-powered ballistic missile submarines (Golf class) are designated "SSB." The Soviet Union has deployed all of the above types of submarines.

Submarine Barrier: A line (or lines) of attack submarines usually stretching across a **Chokepoint**.

Submarine-launched Ballistic Missile (SLBM): See **SLBM (submarine-launched ballistic missile)**.

Submarine Rocket (Subroc): Submerged, submarine-launched, surface-to-surface rocket with nuclear depth charge or homing torpedo payload, primarily anti-submarine. Designated as UUM-44A.

Submarine Striking Forces: Submarines having guided missile or ballistic missile launching or guidance capabilities to launch offensive nuclear strikes.

Subversion: Actions designed to undermine the military, economic, political, psychological, or moral strength of a nation or entity. It can also apply to an undermining of a person's loyalty to a government or entity.

Superiority: A condition wherein one country or a coalition of countries possesses markedly greater capabilities of certain kinds than the opposition. See also **parity**; **strategic sufficiency**.

Surface Striking Forces: Forces that are organized primarily to do battle with enemy forces or to conduct shore bombardment. Units comprising such a force are normally incorporated in and operate as part of another force but with provisions for their formation into a surface striking force should such action appear likely or desirable.

Surface-to-Air Missile (SAM): A surface-launched missile employed to counter airborne threats. The major U.S. SAM currently under development is SAM-D. Naval systems include the Terrier, Tartar, and Talos. Examples of Soviet systems include the SA-2, low altitude SA-3, and the high altitude SA-5.

Surface-to-Air Missile Envelope: That air space within the kill capabilities of a specific surface-to-air missile system.

Surface-to-Surface Missile (SSM): A surface-launched missile designed to attack targets on the surface. Pershing and Lance are primary examples of U.S. tactical, land-based nuclear SSMs. Their Soviet counterparts are Scud and Frog. Naval SSMs include the U.S. Harpoon (non-nuclear) and the Soviet Styx and Shaddock missiles.

Surge Capability: The ability to generate quickly and sustain a higher than normal rate of military activity.

Surprise Attack: A conventional or nuclear attack taking the victim by surprise.

Survivability: The ability of armed forces and civilian communities to withstand attack and still function effectively. It is derived mainly from passive and active defenses. See also **active defense; passive defense.**

Symbolic Attack: A specialized form of exemplary attack. Nothing need be destroyed. It is only necessary that a weapon be detonated and that it have significance to the opposition. See also **exemplary attack.**

T

Tacit Arms Control Agreement: An arms control course of action in which two or more nations participate without any formal agreement having been made. See also **arms control.**

Tactical: Generally relates to battlefield operations.

Tactical Airlift: Transport aircraft (military only in the United States) used to move armed forces, equipment, and supplies expeditiously within theaters of operation. See also **strategic airlift.**

Tactical Intelligence: Intelligence supporting military plans and operations at the military unit level. Tactical intelligence and strategic intelligence differ only in scope, point of view, and level of employment.

Tactical Nuclear Delivery Vehicles: Nuclear delivery vehicles designed to be employed against enemy targets in a limited conflict. Usually relate to vehicles of shorter range than those that are necessary for the conduct of strategic operations. See **noncentral systems.**

Tactical Nuclear Weapon Employment: The use of nuclear weapons by land, sea, or air forces against opposing powers in defense of installations or facilities, in support of operations that contribute to the accomplishment of a military mission of limited scope, or in support of the military commander's scheme of maneuver, usually limited to the area of military operations.

Tactical Nuclear Weapon Forces or Operations: Nuclear combat power expressly designed for deterrent, offensive, and defensive purposes that contribute to the accomplishments of localized military missions; the threatened or actual application of such power. May be employed in general as well as limited wars. U.S.

tactical nuclear delivery systems are concentrated in general-purpose land and carrier-based fighter or attack aircraft and tube artillery. The Soviets deploy cruise and ballistic missiles, the Backfire bomber being their latest generation tactical aircraft. See also **general war; limited war; strategic defense; strategic offense**.

Tactical Psychological Warfare: Actions designed to bring psychological pressure to bear on enemy forces and civilians in support of tactical military ground, air, or sea operations and in areas where these operations are planned or conducted. Tactical psychological warfare must conform to the overall strategic psychological warfare policy but will be conducted as an integral part of combat operations.

Tactical Troops: Combat troops, together with any service troops required for their direct support, which are organized under one commander to operate as a unit and engage the enemy in combat.

Tactical Unit: An organization of troops, aircraft, or ships that is intended to serve as a single unit in combat. It may include service units required for its direct support.

Tactical Warning: Notification that enemy offensive operations of any kind are in progress. The alert may be received at any time from the moment the attack is launched until its effect is felt. See also **strategic warning**.

Tactical Weapons: Battlefield weapons used in close support of troops and against enemy targets in the battlefield area.

Tactics: Detailed methods used to carry out strategic designs. Military tactics involve the employment of units in combat, including the arrangement and maneuvering of units in relation to each other and to the enemy. See also **military strategy; strategy**.

Talionic Attack: A tit-for-tat exchange. The punishment inflicted by defenders corresponds in kind and degree to the injuries they received.

Talos: A ship-launched anti-aircraft missile system capable of using nuclear or conventional explosives.

Tank, 76-mm Gun: A tracked vehicle providing light armor protection against small arms fire and shell fragments. Primary role of this vehicle is armored reconnaissance. Designated as M41.

Tank, Combat, Full-tracked, 90-mm Gun: A fully armored combat vehicle providing mobile fire power and crew protection for offensive combat, armed with one 90-mm gun, one 50-caliber machine gun, and one 30-caliber machine gun. Designated as M48A2.

Tank, Combat, Full-Tracked, 105-mm Gun: A heavy, fully armored combat vehicle providing mobile fire power and crew protection for offensive combat, armed with one 105-mm gun, one 50-caliber machine gun, and one 30-caliber machine gun. Designated as M60.

Tank, Combat, Full-Tracked, 120-mm Gun: A heavy, fully armored combat vehicle armed with one 120-mm gun, one 30-caliber machine gun, and one 50-caliber machine gun. Designated as M103A1.

Target: Material subjected to particle bombardment or irradiation in order to induce a nuclear reaction; also a nuclide that has been bombarded or irradiated.

Target Acquisition: The detection, identification, and location of a target in sufficient detail to permit the effective employment of weapons.

Target Discrimination: The ability of a surveillance or guidance system to identify or engage any one target when multiple targets are present.

Target List: The listing of targets maintained and promulgated by the senior echelon of command; it contains those targets that are to be engaged by supporting arms, as distinguished from a "list of targets" that may be maintained by any echelon as confirmed, suspect, or possible targets for informational and planning purposes.

Target of Opportunity: 1. A target visible to a surface or air sensor or observer, which is within range of available weapons and against which fire has not been scheduled or requested. 2. A nuclear target observed or detected after an operation begins that has not been previously considered, analyzed, or planned for a nuclear strike. Generally fleeting in nature, it would be attacked as soon as possible within the time limitations imposed for coordination and warning of friendly troops and aircraft.

Target Response: The effect on men, materiel, and equipment of blast, heat, light, and nuclear radiation resulting from the explosion of a nuclear weapon.

Technological Balance: The following items were used in a study by the Library of Congress (*U.S./Soviet Military Balance, A Framework for Congress,* 1976) to compute the Soviet-American technological balance:

General	*Specific*
Commonality of components	Aircraft
Computer technology	Antisubmarine warfare
Ease of maintenance	Armored personnel carriers
Gas turbine engines for ships	Artillery ammunition
Guidance systems	Chemical warfare
Microtechnology	Cold weather equipment
Night vision	Electronic countermeasures
Nuclear-powered ships	Engineer bridging
Optics; acoustics	ICBM "cold launch"
Rockets and ramjets	ICBM payload, yield
Submarine detection	Low-level air defense
Submarine silencing	MIRV reliability
	MARV technology
	Missile accuracy
	Ship size versus firepower
	Short-range surface-to-surface missiles
	Survivable submarines
	Target acquisition

TERCOM (Terrain Contour Matching System): TERCOM guidance is based on the correlation of stored contour map data with changes in the terrain being overflown as measured by a radar altimeter. This data provides fixes along the route to target. Utilizing an inertial guidance system, TERCOM resolves objects on the ground as small as three meters wide and thirty centimeters tall from an altitude of several thousand meters. Developed for the air-launched and sea-launched cruise missiles.

Terminal Guidance: 1. The guidance applied to a guided missile between midcourse guidance and arrival in the vicinity of the target. **2.** Electronic, mechanical, visual, or other assistance given an aircraft pilot to facilitate arrival at, operation within or over, landing upon, or departure from an air-landing or air-drop facility.

Terminal Velocity: 1. Hypothetical maximum speed a body could attain along a specified flight path under given conditions of weight and thrust if diving through an unlimited distance in air of specified uniform density. **2.** Remaining speed of a projectile at the point in its downward path where it is level with the muzzle of the weapon.

Terrier: A ship-launched anti-aircraft missile system capable of using nuclear or conventional explosives.

Th-232: An isotope of thorium that can be substituted for U-238 in nuclear power cycles.

Theater: The geographical area outside continental United States for which a commander of a unified or specified command has been assigned military responsibility. See also **specified command**; **unified command**.

Theater of Operations: A geographical area outside the United States for which a commander of a U.S. unified or specified command has been assigned military responsibility. See also **specified command**; **unified command**.

Thermal Energy: The energy emitted from the fireball produced by a nuclear detonation as thermal radiation. The total amount of thermal energy received per unit area at a specified distance from a nuclear explosion is generally expressed in terms of calories per square centimeter.

Thermal Radiation: Electromagnetic radiation emitted from the fireball produced by a nuclear explosion. Thirty-five percent of the total energy of a nuclear explosion is emitted in the form of thermal radiation, light, ultra-violet and infrared radiation.

Thermal X-Rays: The electromagnetic radiation, mainly in the soft (low-energy) X-ray region, emitted by the extremely hot weapon debris by virtue of its extremely high temperature.

Thermonuclear: An adjective referring to the process (or processes) in which very high temperatures are used to bring about the fusion of light nuclei, with the accompanying liberation of energy. See also **fission**; **fusion**; **thermonuclear weapon**.

Thermonuclear Reaction: A reaction in which very high temperatures bring about the fusion of two light nuclei to form the nucleus of a heavier atom, releasing a large amount of energy. In a hydrogen bomb, the high temperature to initiate the thermonuclear reaction is produced by a preliminary fission reaction.

Thermonuclear Weapon: A weapon in which very high temperatures are used to bring about the fusion of light nuclei such as those of hydrogen isotopes (e.g., deuterium and tritium) with the accompanying release of energy. The high temperatures required are obtained by means of fission. See also **fission**; **fusion**.

Threat: The capabilities, intentions, and actions of actual or potential enemies to prevent or interfere with the successful fulfillment of national security interests or objectives.

Threshold: An intangible and adjustable line between levels and types of conflicts, such as the separation between nuclear and nonnuclear warfare. The greater the reluctance to use nuclear weapons, the higher the threshold. See also **firebreak**.

Threshold Test Ban Treaty: An agreement signed in July 1974 by the United States and the Soviet Union limiting underground nuclear weapons tests to a yield of 150 kilotons each after March 31, 1976. No limitations were placed on underground nuclear tests for peaceful purposes.

Throw-Weight: Ballistic missile throw-weight is the maximum useful weight that has been flight tested on the boost stages of the missile. The useful weight includes weight of the reentry vehicles, penetration aids, dispensing and release mechanisms, reentry shrouds, covers, buses, and propulsion devices with their propellants (but not the final boost stages) that are present at the end of the boost phase.

Time-Sensitive Target: Any counterforce target that is vulnerable only if it can be struck before attack is launched (as with bombers and missiles) or redeployed (as with ground combat troops and ships). See also **counterforce**.

Titan: A liquid-propellant, two-stage, rocket-powered ICBM equipped with a nuclear warhead. Designated as HGM-25, it is guided by radio-inertial guidance. The LCN-25C, an improved version of the HGM-25, is guided by all-inertial guidance and equipped with a higher-yield warhead. The system is for deployment in a hardened and dispersed configuration. See also **ballistic missile; hardened site; ICBM (intercontinental ballistic missile); inertial guidance system; nuclear yields**.

TNT Equivalent: A measure of the energy released from the detonation of a nuclear weapon, or from the explosion of a given quantity of fissionable or fusionable material, in terms of the amount of trinitrotoluene (TNT) that would release the same amount of energy when exploded. See also **kiloton weapon; megaton weapon; yield**.

Tomahawk Cruise Missile: There are two versions of the Tomahawk missile: a shorter-range, conventionally-armed, anti-shipping missile; and a longer-range, nuclear-armed missile to attack land targets. Both versions use the same cylindrical airframe to permit launching from a torpedo tube. This design is also readily adaptable to launching from surface ships, ground platforms, or aircraft. The nuclear-armed Tomahawk is not currently planned to have a strategic nuclear role, except insofar as it would constitute an ultimate strategic nuclear reserve. Rather, it is apparently conceived as a theater nuclear weapon intended for use against targets outside the Soviet Union, such as in Eastern Europe and as such would not require the launching ships to be continuously available to deliver nuclear strikes thus not impairing their conventional operations.

The only strategic nuclear application for Tomahawk that is currently contemplated is the possibility of an air-launched version (Tomahawk air-launched cruise missile or TALCM). Because Tomahawk is a longer-range missile than the Air Force ALCM (air-launched cruise missile) and has an airframe not designed for the SRAM (short-range attack missile) rotary rack, the use of a TALCM on the B-52 would require at least a modification or replacement of the SRAM launcher and, in some plans, a shortening of the missile as well. (The Air Force ALCM is designed to be interchangeable on a one-for-one basis with SRAMs carried both internally and externally on the B-52 intercontinental bomber. However, deployment of the 154-inch TALCM in a B-52 incurs a reduction by at least one of the aircraft's internal missile capacity. While eight Air Force ALCMs can be carried onboard the B-52, seven at most of the Navy TALCMs can be deployed on a one-for-one basis with the SRAMs.) These changes would limit the flexibility of the B-52 to carry mixed loads of gravity bombs, SRAM, and cruise missiles. While the TALCM is the only version of the Tomahawk currently envisaged for a strategic role, sea- or land-launched versions of this weapon could be adapted to strategic nuclear missions if desired. The sea-launched nuclear-capable Tomahawk is twenty-feet long and twenty-one inches in diameter and fits into standard submarine torpedo tubes. See also **air-launched cruise missile (ALCM)**; **cruise missile**; **noncentral systems**.

Tooth-to-Tail Ratio: The proportion of combat forces to administrative or logistics support in a nation's armed forces and in specific military organizations, such as divisions, air wings, and fleets.

Toss Bombing: A method of bombing where an aircraft flies on a line towards the target, pulls up in a vertical plane, releasing the bomb at an angle that will compensate for the effect of gravity drop on the bomb.

Total Mobilization: Expansion of the active armed forces or generation of additional units or personnel beyond the existing approved active and reserve structures to respond to a national emergency or preparation for war, including mobilization of all national resources needed to create and sustain such forces. See also **mobilization**.

TOW: Tubular-launched, optically-tracked, wire-guided missile.

An Army anti-tank guided missile.

Transporter-Erector-Launcher (TEL): A surface vehicle in which land-mobile ballistic missiles can be moved into position, prepared for launch, and fired.

Treason: Violation of the allegiance owed to one's sovereign or state; betrayal of one's country.

Triad: The term used in referring to the basic structure of the U.S. strategic deterrent force. It is comprised of land-based ICBMs, the strategic bomber force, and the Polaris and Poseidon submarine fleet. The U.S. Triad of forces evolved from an allocation of national resources and priorities in order to meet certain strategic objectives, the most important of which was the capability to deter nuclear conflict. Each element of the Triad relies on somewhat different means for survival; hence, an enemy's potential for a successful first-strike attack is severely complicated. Bombers rely on warning, fast reaction, and ground or airborne dispersal for survival; ICBMs are placed in individual hardened silos for survivability; SLBMs depend on the uncertainty of location of the submarine to enhance survivability.

Triage: The process of determining which casualties (from a large number of persons exposed to heavy radiation) need urgent treatment, which ones are well enough to go untreated, and which ones are beyond hope of benefit from treatment.

Trident: A submarine and missile program intended to be the successor to the current ballistic missile submarine fleet. The Trident submarine is larger than current Polaris and Poseidon vessels and carries twenty-four missiles. The submarine is designed for more quiet, less detectable operation than current ballistic missile submarines. It has considerable growth space for more capable missiles and for possible countermeasures to hedge against Soviet antisubmarine warfare (ASW) advances. The first five Trident submarines are currently in various stages of construction, with subsequent ships to be built at the rate of three every two years. The first Trident will begin deployment in 1979. The current Navy plan envisages eventual replacement of the current SLBM force with the Trident or a follow-on system. The first ten Trident submarines will operate from the Trident base at Bangor, Washington, now under construction; a base location to serve additional submarines has not yet been determined, although a site at King's Bay, Georgia, appears to be the leading candidate.

The Trident I (C-4) missile is designed to have a range of about

4,000 nautical miles with a full payload of higher yield warheads and accuracy equal to that of Poseidon. This extended range increases the ocean area available for patrol by between ten and twenty times. It greatly complicates the Soviet ASW task and significantly enhances the future survivability of the SLBM force. The MK-500 Evader maneuvering reentry vehicle (MARV) has been deployed and demonstrated for possible deployment on the Trident C-4 missile. MARV would provide a capability to frustrate any Soviet antiballistic missile (ABM) system deployment.

The Navy also plans to arm some of the older Poseidon submarines with Trident C-4 missiles. As U.S. ballistic missile submarines are withdrawn from the base in Rota, Spain, this Trident backfit program will enable these vessels to come within range of their targets more promptly when operating from a U.S. port and will expand the target coverage available to these vessels. It will also permit the United States to achieve a Trident deployment in the Atlantic Ocean at an early date without requiring an acceleration of Trident submarine construction, and will complicate Soviet ASW efforts in two oceans.

Also included in the Trident program is a research and development effort for the Trident II (D-5) SLBM. This missile is intended to have significantly increased range and payload over the Trident C-4 missile, and the Navy expects each of its warheads to have sufficient accuracy and yield to offer a very good capability against hardened targets. The Navy would expect to have this missile available in the mid- to late-1980s, depending upon congressional action.

Tripwire: A largely symbolic force positioned on an ally's soil to advertise the owner's commitment to a particular country or coalition of countries. Attacks against the token force would trigger a massive response. U.S. forces in Europe have been said to have been serving a "tripwire" function.

Truman Doctrine: The provision of American military and economic aid to those nations (initially Greece) resisting Soviet aggression and expansion. The foundation for the American containment policy. See also **containment**.

TSP (Tactical Strike Program): A plan for conducting nuclear strikes against targets in the **Nuclear Operations Plan (NOP)** other than **PSP (Priority Strike Program)** targets.

Tube Artillery: Howitzers and guns, as opposed to rockets and guided missiles. May be towed or self-propelled.

Two-Man Rule: A system designed to prohibit access by one individual to nuclear weapons and certain designated components by requiring the presence at all times of at least two authorized persons, each capable of detecting incorrect or unauthorized procedures with respect to the task to be performed.

Types of Burst: See **high airburst; low airburst; nuclear airburst; nuclear exoatmospheric burst; nuclear surface burst; nuclear underground burst; nuclear underwater burst.**

U

U-233: An isotope of uranium not found in significant amounts in nature. The isotope is produced in reactors containing thorium and is suitable for nuclear explosives.

U-235: An isotope of uranium found at a concentration of 0.7 percent in natural uranium. Through enrichment, this concentration of U-235 is used for fuel in American reactors and is usable for nuclear explosives if enriched to a concentration of at least ninety percent.

U-238: Not suitable for nuclear explosives, this isotope of uranium exists in a concentration greater than ninety-nine percent in natural uranium.

Unacceptable Damage: Degree of destruction anticipated from an enemy second strike that is sufficient to deter a nuclear power from launching a first strike. The degree of damage that will deter a first strike is a function, in part, of national value preferences and economic considerations and is therefore difficult or impossible to predict.

Unconventional Warfare: A broad spectrum of military and paramilitary operations conducted in enemy held, enemy denied, or politically sensitive territory. Unconventional warfare includes, but is not limited to, the interrelated fields of guerrilla warfare, evasion and escape, subversion, sabotage, direct action missions, and other operations of a low visibility, covert, or clandestine nature. These interrelated aspects of unconventional warfare may be prosecuted singly or collectively by predominantly indigenous personnel, usually supported and directed in varying degrees by external sources during all conditions of war or peace.

Unconventional Warfare Forces: United States forces having an existing unconventional warfare capability consisting of Army special forces and such Navy, Air Force, and Marine units as are assigned for these operations.

Unified Command: A top-echelon U.S. combatant organization with regional or functional responsibilities that normally is composed of forces from two or more military services. It has a broad, continuing mission and is established by the president through the secretary of defense with the advice and assistance of the Joint Chiefs of Staff (JCS). When authorized by the JCS, commanders of unified commands established by the president may form one or more subordinate unified commands within their jurisdictions.

Unilateral Arms Control Measure: An arms control course of action taken by a nation without any compensating concession being required of other nations.

Unwarned Exposed: The troop safety status of friendly forces with respect to nuclear weapon effects. In this status personnel are assumed to be standing in the open when the flash of the nuclear blast is sensed, at which time they drop to the prone position immediately, prior to the arrival of the shock wave. They are assumed to be wearing uniforms that will not shield the skin of the hands and face from direct thermal radiation.

V

Variability: 1. The manner in which the probability of damage to a specific target decreases with the distance from ground zero. 2. In damage assessment, a mathematical factor introduced to average the effects of orientation, minor shielding, and uncertainty of target response to the effects considered.

Verification: The process of determining the degree to which parties to an agreement are complying with provisions of the agreement. The verification of arms control may be said to have three distinct purposes: 1. Verification serves to detect violations of an agreement (or to provide evidence that violations may have occurred) and hence to furnish, as far as possible, timely warning of any threat to the nation's security arising under a treaty regime. 2. By increasing the risk of detection and complicating any scheme of evasion, verification helps to deter violations of an agreement. The deterrent value of verification depends to a considerable extent on a potential violator being ignorant of the exact capability of the intelligence techniques used to monitor his compliance with an agreement—a fact that helps to explain the importance of secrecy regarding many of these techniques. 3. Verification serves to build domestic and international confidence in the viability of an arms control agreement. By providing evidence that the parties to an agreement are in fact fulfilling the obligations they have assumed, verification contributes to mutual trust among the parties and helps to create a political environment necessary for further progress in arms control. At the same time, it provides an important safeguard against wishful illusions and against possible manipulation of an atmosphere of trust in the pursuit of unilateral advantage.

Verification Panel: The senior group (in the National Security Council structure) responsible for the examination of U.S. strategic arms limitations policies; a panel chaired by the assistant to the president for national security affairs. Includes the director of the **Arms Control and Disarmament Agency (ACDA)**, the deputy secretary of state, the deputy secretary of defense, the director of the Central Intelligence Agency (CIA), and the chairman of the Joint Chiefs of Staff. The vice-president has responsibility for the overall analyses of issues of strategic arms limitations (**SALT**) negotiations. A Verification Panel Working Group (VPWG) acts under the guidance of the Verification Panel and has the delegated responsibility for the preparation and coordination of detailed analyses of specific SALT issues.

Vertical Take-Off and Landing: The capability of an aircraft to take off and land vertically and to transfer to or from forward motion at heights required to clear surrounding obstacles.

Vulnerability: 1. The susceptibility of a nation or military force to any action by any means through which its war potential or combat effectiveness may be reduced or its will to fight diminished. 2. The characteristics of a system that cause it to suffer a definite degradation (incapability to perform the designated mission) as a result of having been subjected to a certain level of effects in an unnatural (manmade) hostile environment.

W

War Fighting: Combat actions, as opposed to deterrence (which is designed to prevent, rather than prosecute, wars).

War-Fighting Strategy: A strategy designed primarily to fight any kind of war at any level in the conflict spectrum, (as opposed to deterrence strategies, which are designed to prevent wars).

War Game: A simulation, by whatever means, of a military operation involving two or more opposing forces, using rules, data, and procedures designed to depict an actual or assumed real-life situation.

Warhead: That part of a missile, projectile, torpedo, rocket, or other munition that contains either the nuclear or thermonuclear system, high-explosive system, chemical or biological agents, or inert materials intended to inflict damage.

Warhead Lethality: A measure of the capability to destroy hard targets. The lethality of a warhead is computed as two-thirds of its yield divided by the square of the **circular error probability (CEP)** of the delivery system. See also **strategic balance.**

Warhead Mating: The act of attaching a warhead section to the rocket, or missile body, torpedo, airframe, motor, or guidance section.

War Reserves: War reserves are stocks of materiel amassed in peacetime to meet the increase in military requirements consequent upon an outbreak of war. War reserves are intended to provide the interim support essential to sustain operations until resupply can be effected.

Warsaw Treaty Organization (WTO): An East European military organization. Members of the Warsaw Pact include Bulgaria, Czechoslovakia, East Germany, Hungary, Poland, Romania, and the Soviet Union. The WTO established a unified military command for the armed forces of the participating states and represented a codification of the East-West military balance.

Weapon Debris: The residue of a nuclear weapon after it has exploded; that is, materials used for the casing and other components of the weapon, plus unexpended plutonium or uranium together with fission products.

Weapons of Mass Destruction: In arms control usage, weapons that are capable of a high order of destruction or of being used in such a manner as to destroy large numbers of people. Can be nuclear, chemical, biological, or radiological weapons, but excludes the means of transporting or propelling the weapon where such means is a separable and divisible part of the weapon.

White Propaganda: Propaganda disseminated and acknowledged by the sponsor or by an accredited agency.

Wild Weasel: An Air Force air defense suppression aircraft.

Wooden Bomb: A concept that pictures a weapon as being completely reliable and having an infinite shelf life while at the same time requiring no special handling, storage, or surveillance.

X

XM-I: A new Army medium tank built by Chrysler to U.S. Army specifications. The XM-I and Germany's Leopard II tank will be the main battle tanks for NATO (North Atlantic Treaty Organization) into the 1990s.

Y

Yield: The force of a nuclear explosion expressed in terms of the number of tons of TNT that would have to be exploded to produce the same energy. See **nuclear yields**.

Part 2
Policy Concepts

1. Strategic Nuclear Forces

U.S. strategic nuclear forces are charged with the mission of deterring a Soviet nuclear attack on the United States. Since defenses against a nuclear attack are both difficult and limited by the Antiballistic Missile Treaty between the United States and the Soviet Union, the United States relies upon the ability of its strategic forces to carry out a devastating retaliatory strike against Soviet cities to deter a Soviet attack. U.S. forces are designed to be capable of carrying out this "assured destruction" mission after having absorbed a well-coordinated surprise Soviet strike against them.

In order to hedge against the failure or destruction of one part of its nuclear force, the United States maintains a mixed force of long-range bombers, land-based intercontinental ballistic missiles (ICBMs), and submarine-launched ballistic missiles (SLBMs), known collectively as the Triad. By diversifying the force among three parts, each of which has different vulnerabilities, a Soviet nuclear attack on U.S. strategic forces, usually referred to as a "counterforce" attack, is made more difficult.

In recent years, however, concern has grown that one element of the U.S. strategic Triad, land-based ICBMs, may become vulnerable to a disarming first strike by an increasingly capable Soviet force. Using a fraction of their ICBM force, the postulated Soviet attack would destroy large portions of U.S. missiles in their hardened silos. Simultaneous attacks on U.S. Strategic Air Command (SAC) bases and submarine ports would destroy bombers not on alert and missile-carrying nuclear submarines (SSBNs) not at sea. At the same time, the existence of a large Soviet reserve force capable of destroying U.S. cities would deter a U.S. counterstrike against Soviet cities and thus leave U.S. leaders with few attractive retaliatory options.

Reprinted from the Congress of the United States, Congressional Budget Office. *Counterforce Issues for the U.S. Strategic Nuclear Forces.* Background Paper, January 1978, pp. 1-8.

Considerable controversy has surrounded both the issue of U.S. vulnerability to a Soviet counterforce attack and the question of what the Soviets might hope to gain from such an attack. Many observers believe that the United States faces a significant, and growing, Soviet counterforce threat and that a deterrence doctrine that relies upon retaliation against Soviet cities would provide American leaders with few credible responses to such an attack. They believe that to deter a Soviet counterforce attack U.S. strategic forces must be able to carry out a counterattack against the Soviet ICBM force, since the threat to retaliate against Soviet cities might not be credible as long as U.S. cities remain intact.

On the other side are critics of any U.S. attempt to plan and build forces for counterforce wars, those confined to each side's nuclear forces. These critics believe that a Soviet nuclear attack confined to strikes against U.S. strategic forces would inflict so much damage on U.S. cities and population that the United States would be expected to respond with its surviving SLBMs and alert bombers and that this expectation should deter any but the most desperate Soviet leadership from attempting such a strike. Furthermore, many believe that U.S. preparations to fight counterforce battles only make nuclear war more likely to occur because U.S. weapons capable of counterattacking against Soviet ICBMs might appear to pose a first-strike threat to Soviet strategic forces and thus cause a Soviet leadership facing a serious international crisis to launch a preemptive attack.

Over the next several years the Congress will face a number of important force procurement issues that depend critically on judgments about the degree and significance of U.S. strategic vulnerability to Soviet counterforce capability and the proper response to such a development. By the mid-1980s, when U.S. silo-based missiles will probably become increasingly vulnerable to Soviet attack, Trident nuclear submarines and Trident I submarine-launched missiles will be entering the force, and cruise missiles will be deployed on B-52 bombers. Although these systems will probably be sufficient for retaliation against Soviet industry, leadership targets, and general purpose military forces, many analysts have expressed concern about the possibility that improved Soviet ICBMs will enable the Soviet Union to launch a counterforce strike against U.S. silo-based ICBMs, while the United States could not respond in kind. If the Congress wishes to maintain strategic forces capable of carrying out a second-strike counterforce attack against Soviet ICBMs, the procurement of new and more sophisticated weapons would be required.

Judgments about the significance of Soviet counterforce capability and the need for a similar U.S. capability will, to a great extent, determine the pace of development and magnitude of procurement of M-X mobile missiles, Trident submarines, Trident II missiles, cruise missiles, and cruise missile carriers beyond the existing B-52 force.

The M-X missile, a more accurate, more powerful, and potentially mobile ICBM now in the research and development (R&D) stage and available for deployment by the mid-1980s, will provide a future option to reduce the vulnerability of land-based missiles, and at the same time substantially upgrade the counterforce potential of the U.S. nuclear arsenal.

The large missile tubes of the Trident submarines now under construction will be capable of housing a larger and more accurate Trident II missile. This missile, which could be developed by the mid- to late-1980s, offers an alternative means of developing a capability to attack Soviet ICBM silos in a second strike. Since the assignment of submarine-launched missiles to the counterforce role would, however, require the procurement of additional submarines beyond those needed for retaliation against Soviet cities, the present Trident building rate of three submarines every two years would have to be accelerated in the near future.

The U.S. cruise missile, guided to its target by a terrain-matching guidance system that is asserted to be extremely accurate, will provide another means to enhance the counterforce capability of U.S. strategic forces. If the Congress decided to procure extra cruise missiles for the counterforce task, additional carriers, such as wide-bodied aircraft, would be required.

Decisions about these programs to augment and modernize U.S. strategic nuclear forces in the mid- to late-1980s will depend upon several basic questions:

- Under what circumstances might the Soviets be tempted to strike one vulnerable element of the U.S. Triad, knowing that a large retaliatory force would survive?
- Should the United States develop the capability to retaliate against Soviet ICBMs?
- Is the best response to increasing ICBM vulnerability a shift to more survivable basing systems or the development of a similar threat to Soviet ICBMs?
- How might the Soviet Union react to a threat to their ICBMs, and would this reaction be desirable or undesirable?

2. Counterforce Strategies

In any discussion of counterforce exchanges it should always be remembered that a major nuclear war would be a catastrophe of unprecedented proportions; starting or risking such a war would be a desperate act undertaken only under great stress and in the face of a perceived threat to very important values. Even a war confined strictly to attacks on nuclear forces would likely cause millions of deaths and great damage and disruption on both sides. In addition, neither side could be certain that a limited nuclear exchange would remain limited and not eventually escalate to all-out attacks that would cause the deaths of tens of millions. In fact, it is difficult to imagine the circumstances in which initiating a nuclear war would be the least miserable option facing national leaders. Precisely because a nuclear war would be such a catastrophe, however, prudence demands that the factors that might contribute to its occurrence be carefully considered.

In general, there are at least three Soviet counterforce strategies that have been postulated. They are:

- An attack on the U.S. ICBM force designed to reduce U.S. options in a limited nuclear war.
- An attack on U.S. strategic forces designed to shift decisively the balance of nuclear power in favor of the Soviet Union.
- An attack on U.S. strategic forces designed to limit damage to the Soviet Union in an all-out nuclear war.

In recent years the Department of Defense (DOD) has concentrated on the first of these strategies, expressing concern that a successful Soviet counterforce strike against land-based missiles would endanger the ability of the United States to execute flexible options short of all-out retaliation. The superior accuracy and command and control capability inherent in a land-based system, capabilities that might be important for strikes against Soviet military forces involved in a war in Europe or other areas of U.S. treaty commitments, would be lost in such an event. Leaving aside the controversy surrounding the issue of limited nuclear options and the desirability of maintaining forces designed for such contingencies, there are several questions that can be raised about the scenario postulated by the Defense Department.

For one thing, it is unclear that the United States would remain interested in the execution of flexible and controlled responses after having absorbed a large-scale nuclear attack on U.S. ICBMs that killed millions of Americans. In any case, given the existence of thousands of nuclear weapons in surviving ICBMs, bombers, and submarines, as well as tactical missiles and aircraft, the United States would retain many retaliatory options, since surviving forces would be capable of carrying out strikes against Soviet conventional forces or important isolated economic targets. Many analysts believe, however, that U.S. forces should be capable of carrying out a counterattack against Soviet ICBM silos. A requirement that U.S. strategic forces be able to perform such a second-strike counterforce mission might call for the procurement of additional, and more sophisticated, U.S. nuclear weapons.

Others have suggested that the Soviet Union might be motivated to strike U.S. strategic forces in order to shift decisively the balance of power in their favor. A counterforce attack with this goal in mind would be designed to destroy such a large portion of U.S. forces with such a small expenditure of Soviet force that the Soviets would gain strategic superiority so massive that the extreme asymmetry in the destruction that the two sides could inflict on one another would deter the United States from using its inferior force in retaliation. In this case, American leaders might be left with few response options, and U.S. forces might fail to deter a Soviet first strike. To deter a Soviet counterforce attack designed to shift the balance of nuclear power, many analysts believe that the United States must maintain survivable forces large enough to prevent a massive Soviet advantage in the ability to inflict damage. Others believe that the U.S. forces should be capable of counterattacking against Soviet strategic forces remaining after a counterforce strike against the United States. In this way, the United States might be able to redress an imbalance of power resulting from a Soviet first strike.

A third possible Soviet counterforce strategy would involve attacks on U.S. nuclear forces for the purpose of limiting the damage that the

United States could inflict on the Soviet Union in an all-out nuclear war. Obviously, a Soviet leadership considering such an attack would have to be convinced that circumstances were so desperate that nuclear war was imminent. In this case, by striking first, the Soviets might be able to destroy a large percentage of the U.S. nuclear force, thus making the outcome of a nuclear war less catastrophic for the Soviet Union than it otherwise would have been. Deterrence of a damage-limiting strike requires that U.S. nuclear forces must be able to survive a Soviet counterforce attack against them and then carry out a devastating retaliatory attack against Soviet cities. U.S. forces capable of retaliating against Soviet nuclear forces would not be required in this case.

Those who believe that the Soviet Union might be tempted to attack U.S. strategic forces for the purpose of reducing American options or shifting the balance of power suggest that deterrence requires not only forces capable of destroying Soviet cities but also weapons designed to counterattack against Soviet nuclear forces. Opponents of such a second-strike counterforce policy suggest that there is a dilemma involved in the procurement of U.S. counterforce weapons. They believe that a U.S. force large enough to retaliate against Soviet nuclear forces in a second strike would, by definition, pose a significant first-strike threat to the Soviet Union. Furthermore, this threat might dangerously destabilize the strategic balance and provide an incentive for a Soviet first strike.

3. Force Requirements for Alternative Deterrent Postures

FORCE REQUIREMENTS FOR ALTERNATIVE DETERRENT POSTURES

A. Current Policy

Strategy	Desired Force Characteristics	Illustrative Force
Be prepared to launch a major retaliatory strike against civilian and military targets, designed to reduce the national power and influence of the Soviet Union and prevent their recovery.	Highly survivable forces capable of destroying large numbers of hardened targets, but not threatening surprise attack.	B-52 bombers armed with cruise missiles.
	ICBM force able to destroy many targets, some of which are hardened, but not large enough to threaten Soviet strategic forces.	200-400 M-X missiles; 350-550 Minuteman III; 450 Minuteman II; 54 Titan II.
OR		
Be prepared to destroy Soviet land-based strategic forces after a counterforce attack on United States.	Secure force for retaliation against civilian targets.	Trident submarines (numbers undetermined).
Also be prepared to launch a subsequent strike against civilian targets.	Forces for flexible use in either strategic or tactical situations.	Sea-launched cruise missiles, ICBMs, and bombers.
In both strategies be prepared to engage in limited nuclear operations.		

Reprinted from the Congress of the United States, Congressional Budget Office. *U.S. Strategic Nuclear Forces: Deterrent Policies and Procurement Issues.* Budget Issue Paper, April 1977, pages 7-32.

B. A Policy of Finite Deterrence

Strategy	Desired Force Characteristics	Illustrative Force
Be prepared to launch a major retaliatory strike against civilian targets in response to any nuclear provocation.	Secure force capable of destroying civilian targets.	20 Trident submarines.
	Multiple warhead ICBM force to supplement primary retaliatory force.	550 Minuteman IIIs.
	Bombers able to attack civilian targets not heavily defended.	B-52s or FB-111s, armed with cruise missiles and other weapons.
	Secure, hardened system for communicating with submarines.	ELF (extremely low frequency) communication system.

C. A Policy of Limited Nuclear Options

Strategy	Desired Force Characteristics	Illustrative Force
Be prepared to launch a major retaliatory strike against civilian targets. Also be prepared to carry on limited nuclear operations.	Secure force capable of destroying civilian targets.	20 Trident submarines.
	Multiple warhead ICBM force to supplement primary retaliatory force.	550 Minuteman III.
	Single warhead ICBM force principally for limited employment.	450 Minuteman II, ultimately replaced by improved single warhead missile.
	Bombers capable of destroying civilian targets or making limited strikes outside USSR.	B-52s and FB-111s armed with cruise missiles.
	Forces for flexible limited use.	Sea-launched cruise missiles.
	Secure, hardened systems for communicating with submarines.	ELF system.
	Forces to prevent coercive use of Soviet bomber force.	Advanced interceptor aircraft and air defense system.
	Systems providing information on nature and progress of limited operations.	Improved warning, surveillance, and communication systems.

D. A Policy of Essential Equivalence

Strategy	Desired Force Characteristics	Illustrative Force
Make U.S. strategic forces unambiguously equal or superior to Soviet strategic forces.	Forces that increase mega-tonnage delivered by U.S. forces.	B-52 bomber force armed with cruise missiles.
	Increased emphasis on size and capabilities of U.S. ICBM force.	600 M-X missiles; 450 Minuteman II; 54 Titan II
	Larger SLBM force.	30 Trident submarines built on accelerated schedule.
	Forces that Soviets cannot easily duplicate.	Air- and sea-launched cruise missiles.
	Improved defensive systems.	Advanced interceptor air-craft, expanded civil defense programs, accelerated missile defense programs.

4. NATO Theater Nuclear Forces: Purposes, Capabilities, and Employment Concepts

Purposes of NATO Theater Nuclear Weapons

The United States, in cooperation with its NATO allies, currently maintains theater nuclear weapons in Europe to contribute, along with conventional and strategic nuclear forces, to deterring Warsaw Pact initiation of a European conflict or coercion of the NATO allies. NATO theater nuclear forces are intended to deter two types of Soviet action:

- Soviet first use of tactical nuclear weapons, and
- Soviet launching of an overwhelming conventional attack against Western Europe.

For theater nuclear forces to deter these Soviet actions effectively, at least two conditions must be met:

- NATO must be seen to have the capability and determination to use these forces if necessary, and
- Enough NATO theater nuclear weapons must be able to survive a Soviet attack on them, and be able to threaten an appropriate response.

Consequently, the United States has formulated a twofold requirement for theater nuclear forces:

- Warsaw Pact must appreciate that NATO has an assured capability to execute its theater-wide nuclear war options in

Reprinted from the Congress of the United States, Congressional Budget Office. *Planning U.S. General Purpose Forces: The Theater Nuclear Forces.* Budget Issue Paper, January 1977, pp. 5-20.

the event of a surprise nuclear attack, and
- NATO must be capable of executing effective nuclear attacks against Warsaw Pact military forces, with discrimination and limited collateral damage, in response to a major conventional or limited nuclear attack.

It is fairly clear that the threat of theater nuclear response is intended to restrain the Soviet Union from a nuclear first strike or from mounting an overwhelming conventional attack. However, it is not equally clear how the execution of NATO's theater-wide nuclear war options would improve NATO's combat position in the event of a Soviet surprise nuclear attack. Nor is it clear precisely how NATO execution of limited tactical nuclear attacks would save NATO forces from defeat by an overwhelming Soviet conventional attack without provoking devastating Soviet nuclear retaliation. It is possible that these uncertainties may undermine the credibility of the theater nuclear deterrent.

The contribution of theater nuclear forces to the deterrence of a European conflict rests partly on the additional capability they potentially offer in support of conventional defenses and partly on the "linkage" they are thought to provide between the conventional and strategic nuclear forces. The precise nature of this linkage has not been satisfactorily explained. However, the basic idea is that a strategic nuclear response to a Soviet aggression would be intuitively more plausible if theater nuclear weapons had already been used and had failed to halt the Soviet attack. This basic idea is reinforced by the fact that the Nuclear Operations Plan (NOP) for theater nuclear forces is integrated with the Single Integrated Operational Plan (SIOP) for U.S. strategic forces so that the two may be executed together. Thus, the execution of certain theater nuclear strikes might signal the willingness of the United States to escalate to general nuclear war.

This perception of U.S. willingness to employ strategic nuclear weapons on behalf of Europe is very important to the NATO allies. They evidently believe that the Soviet Union will be deterred from an attack on Western Europe only if such an attack would be likely to result in the destruction of the USSR. The continued presence of theater nuclear weapons in Europe remains important because the possibility of their use raises the possibility of further escalation.

In addition to their deterrent and combat functions, NATO theater nuclear forces serve an important political function. These forces provide an opportunity for the United States' NATO allies to participate to some extent in the alliance's nuclear deterrent, and so reduce whatever need some allies might feel to develop independent nuclear capabilities.

The Relationship between Conventional and Theater Nuclear Forces

Although theater nuclear forces are intended to support the conventional forces in the event of a breakdown of deterrence, they are not considered to be a substitute for conventional forces. It has generally been accepted that a reduction of NATO's conventional forces would increase the probability that NATO would face a choice between defeat or resort to nuclear weapons. However, it is important to note that use of nuclear weapons in such a case would by no means assure turning defeat into victory. Rather it might provoke a large-scale response from formidable Soviet nuclear forces.

If the objective is to maintain a constant level of security against both the conventional and nuclear capabilities of the Soviet Union and its allies, an increase in NATO theater nuclear strength does not permit a reduction in conventional forces. A Soviet theater nuclear deterrent now exists. Consequently, any reduction in NATO conventional forces, whether or not accompanied by increases in NATO theater nuclear forces, simply lowers the conventional deterrent threshold. Conventional forces, however increased, do not provide the same deterrent against Soviet attack as do NATO theater nuclear weapons. Thus, conventional forces are not regarded as a substitute for theater nuclear forces.

Since theater nuclear forces and conventional forces are not, in principle, substitutes for each other, the most important issue does not appear to be that of achieving conventional force reductions through improvements in theater nuclear forces. Rather, the most significant issue is the extent to which projected improvements in theater nuclear forces will enhance their ability to deter a Soviet first use of tactical nuclear weapons.

Composition of the NATO Theater Nuclear Forces

As of August 5, 1974, the effective date of the Defense Authorization Act of 1974, the United States had about 7,000 nuclear warheads deployed in Europe. The great majority of these weapons are intended for use by NATO air and ground forces on the continent. NATO is also supported by aircraft carriers with additional tactical nuclear bombs and by other naval forces with submarine-launched ballistic missiles (SLBM), nuclear antisubmarine warfare (ASW) weapons and nuclear air defense weapons: A substantial proportion of the U.S. warheads in Europe are deployed under Programs of Cooperation (POCs) and stockpile agreements. These are formal bilateral agreements between the United States and other nations that involve the transfer of delivery vehicles capable of nuclear delivery or deployment of nuclear weapons for use by the host nation under the direction of SACEUR or SACLANT. Host nations provide support for U.S. weapons and weapons provided for their use. The nuclear warheads remain in U.S. custody until release by the U.S. president in time of war.

The NATO theater nuclear weapons maintained in Europe are stored in over 100 Special Ammunition Storage sites (SAS). These sites consist of storage magazines, called igloos, as well as ancillary and security structures. The installations are commonly set in a clearing and are surrounded by a double perimeter security fence that is floodlit at night. Thus, in its peacetime deployment, the NATO theater nuclear stockpile, together with the delivery systems maintained at fixed bases, constitute a limited number of readily identifiable, high value targets for Warsaw Pact attack. The locations of these targets are assumed to be known to the Soviet Union.

NATO currently maintains nuclear-capable artillery, surface-to-surface missiles (SSM), nuclear-capable aircraft, Nike-Hercules air defense weapons, Poseidon submarine-launched ballistic missiles (SLBM), and atomic demolition munitions (ADM) for possible use in Europe.

NATO nuclear-capable artillery consists of eight inch and 155 mm artillery pieces, which are able to fire relatively small nuclear weapons over distances of several miles. The principal advantages of nuclear-capable artillery are said to be their high accuracy, relatively low yields, and short delivery ranges. These characteristics are thought to reduce the danger of nuclear escalation arising from a local defensive use of nuclear weapons. Currently, the U.S. forces possess most of the eight inch artillery pieces in Europe; the much more numerous 155 mm artillery pieces are more evenly distributed among NATO forces.

There are currently three NATO surface-to-surface missiles: Honest John, Lance, and Pershing. Each of these missiles can deliver a single nuclear weapon at distances of tens or hundreds of miles. Although Lance has replaced Honest John and Sergeant SSM in the U.S. forces, a few Honest John launchers are retained by NATO allies. Honest John is an older, unguided tactical support rocket whose low rate of fire, low accuracy and high yields are seen as inappropriate to its mission. Lance, also a tactical support weapon, has greater mobility and accuracy than its predecessors. Pershing is a longer range SSM, maintained by U.S. and West German forces and intended for use largely against fixed interdiction-type targets on Warsaw Pact territory. Some Pershing missiles are maintained on peacetime Quick Reaction Alert (QRA) at fixed sites for possible employment against "specific (Warsaw Pact) high priority, time sensitive targets."

The NATO allies maintain a large number—at one time estimated at roughly 1,000—of nuclear-capable tactical aircraft on land, with additional carrier-based aircraft at sea. These aircraft are capable of dropping nuclear weapons on designated enemy targets. A small number of U.S. and allied land-based aircraft are maintained on peacetime QRA. These are probably also designated for fixed, high priority, time sensitive targets. More aircraft would presumably be put on alert in time of crisis, though this would reduce the numbers of aircraft available for conventional missions.

Fixed-based, nuclear-capable Nike-Hercules surface-to-air missiles (SAM) are useful for deterring and countering massed, high-altitude Warsaw Pact air attacks. These weapons can be used for operation in a surface-to-surface mode.

A portion of the U.S. Poseidon SLBM force, as well as the whole United Kingdom's Polaris SLBM force, are currently committed to the NATO nuclear deterrent force. They are presumably intended for employment against fixed soft targets in Warsaw Pact territory. These are the least vulnerable elements of the NATO theater nuclear forces. Because the Poseidon is commonly regarded as an element of the U.S. strategic nuclear forces, its tactical use in a European conflict would be ambiguous. The USSR would not immediately know whether its target was in the European theater or in the Soviet Union.

Atomic Demolition Munitions (ADMs) are nuclear devices that must be manually emplaced and mechanically or electronically detonated. They are used to create barriers to retard and force the concentration of attacking enemy forces. Because these weapons require suitable terrain features for optimal effectiveness, and because they must be set in place before the arrival of enemy troops, there are definite territorial and temporal limits to their usefulness in combat.

All U.S. nuclear weapons deployed in Europe are fitted with Permissive Action Links (PAL), coded devices designed to impede unauthorized use. Further, all weapons are maintained at all times under positive control by at least two U.S. military personnel, so that one person, acting alone, cannot arm or fire the weapon.

The Employment Concept for NATO Theater Nuclear Forces

In the event that NATO forces were to fail to deter the Warsaw Pact from initiating a European conflict, the United States and its NATO allies would confront a vital decision as to whether to prepare all of the theater nuclear forces for possible use.

Preparing for and ordering the employment of NATO theater nuclear forces requires that a number of activities must be completed: many of the weapons must be moved from peacetime storage sites to using units; higher political authorities must determine the circumstances that warrant the use of nuclear weapons; suitable targets for nuclear weapons must be located; the use of weapons against these targets must be authorized by the political authorities; and the designated nuclear strikes must be carried out. The authorization to use nuclear weapons must be guided by previously established military or political objectives if the strikes are to make some contribution to NATO's defense.

If NATO were seen to be likely to experience difficulty in carrying out any of the essential steps, the credibility of the U.S. threat to use these weapons would be partially undermined, and the deterrent effect of this threat would presumably be reduced, though never completely eliminated.

In the event of a war in Europe, NATO theater nuclear weapons would have to be moved from their peacetime storage sites to the vicinity of the using units if the weapons were ever to be used. This would also reduce the risk of their destruction by Soviet military action.

The theater commander can decide to disperse weapons from the SAS at any time before or during the conflict. Removing the weapons from the SAS prior to the outbreak of war would require either "early and persuasive warning of an imminent (conventional or nuclear) attack" or a period of unprecedentedly high crisis. The successful evacuation of the SAS after the outbreak of war would require that there be an initial conventional phase of combat, since early Soviet use of nuclear weapons would probably be directed toward the destruction of NATO's theater nuclear assets.

Finally, the dispersal of NATO theater nuclear weapons, either before or after the outbreak of war, would require the presence of adequate transport. This would compete to some extent with the transportation requirements for conventional operations.

Assuming that NATO theater nuclear weapons were effectively dispersed, a determination would have to be made as to what circumstances might necessitate the use of these weapons. The decision to employ theater nuclear weapons can only be made by the National Command Authority (NCA), in consultation with the NATO allies if time permits. There appear to be no particular circumstances that constitute a necessary or sufficient condition for their use without NCA authorization. However, it is possible to identify some conditions or criteria that might make a decision to employ theater nuclear weapons more likely, such as when:

- the Warsaw Pact had initiated the use of nuclear weapons;
- an unacceptably large amount of NATO territory had been lost, perhaps with further losses imminent;
- a significant portion of NATO's nuclear assets had been, or were in danger of being destroyed, so as to seriously erode the potential effectiveness of a nuclear response;
- NATO defensive positions were in imminent danger of being breached by a Warsaw Pact offensive and reserves were unavailable or inadequate to contain the attack.

These situations are only hypothetical and illustrative, however, and the NCA would not be constrained to use nuclear weapons in these or any other situations.

While it is possible to identify circumstances that might occasion the use of theater nuclear weapons, there are some situations in which the use of nuclear weapons by the NATO defenders would be unlikely to improve their situation. This would be the case if NATO defenses had been breached and Warsaw Pact forces were moving rapidly through NATO territory. In such an instance, the extreme difficulty of quickly locating enemy units and directing nuclear strikes on them would minimize the effectiveness of any battlefield nuclear weapons used. It is not clear that the use of longer-range nuclear strikes against Warsaw Pact territory would affect the operations of attacking forces. Therefore, NATO theater nuclear weapons would have the greatest effect on the battle if they were used while sufficient conventional forces remained to hold defensive positions or to retake lost territory.

In the event that the use of theater nuclear weapons should be authorized, the current NATO objective in employing these weapons would be to cause significant loss to the attacker, including damage to his allies, cause him to reconsider his actions by demonstrating

NATO resolve and altering his assessment of early victory, and allow NATO to militarily exploit the use of nuclear weapons in order to bring about a termination/settlement of the conflict on terms that are advantageous to NATO. The actual employment of theater nuclear weapons has traditionally been divided into two types: selective use and general nuclear response.

The current concept for selective use involves the preplanning of "packages" of nuclear weapons for use against advancing Warsaw Pact troops or selected rear area targets of immediate military significance. "A package is a group of nuclear weapons of *specific yields*, for employment in a *specified area*, within a *limited timeframe* to support a *tactical contingency*." The numbers and yields of weapons and the spatial limitations included in a package are determined by the collateral damage constraints imposed by political guidance. The objective in employing a package of nuclear weapons is to quickly and decisively influence the immediate military situation by destroying enemy military forces.

Apparently, both long-range and short-range NATO theater nuclear delivery systems can be used in planning various types of employment packages. Such packages could range from a relatively few tactical nuclear bombs or longer-range missile warheads to perhaps 150 shorter-range nuclear weapons. Preplanning the use of weapons in specified areas streamlines the procedure for requesting authorization for nuclear employment, and reduces the sensitivity of targeting to a time delay in securing authorization.

NATO general nuclear response involves the launching of large numbers of longer-range nuclear delivery systems, such as SLBM, Pershing, and tactical aircraft, against targets in Warsaw Pact territory under the NOP. Within the NOP is the Priority Strike Program (PSP), which comprises the highest priority targets of concern to SACEUR and against which the QRA systems are targeted, as well as the Tactical Strike Program (TSP). The magnitude of the full NOP strike would probably be such that it could only be intended to inflict retaliatory punishment on the Warsaw Pact. The plan is so constructed that the execution of selective use options against targets in the NOP will not impair NATO's capability to attack the remaining NOP targets. However, the general nuclear response (i.e., the execution of the entire NOP) would apparently occur with the simultaneous execution of the SIOP.

Regardless of the circumstances under which the NOP might be executed, it is clear that it requires a capability that is survivable against a possible Soviet attack in order to pose a credible deterrent. However, if some NATO assets for executing the NOP are vulnerable to Soviet nuclear attack, and if "NATO has an assured capability to execute its theater-wide nuclear war options in the event of a surprise nuclear attack" then it must be inferred that this capability resides largely in the NATO-committed SLBM forces, and perhaps to a lesser extent in Pershing. If NATO-committed Poseidon reentry vehicles, perhaps in conjunction with the U.K. Polaris force, are adequate to perform the NOP mission, then one could question the need for other relatively more vulnerable assets, such as tactical aircraft or Pershing, to perform this same mission.

5. Soviet Theater Nuclear Capabilities and Doctrine

It is necessary to examine Soviet capabilities and doctrine for the use of nuclear weapons in a European conflict to evaluate the appropriateness of NATO's current theater nuclear posture and the prospective improvements in it. This is so because, apart from their contribution to the deterrence of any Soviet aggression, the most important function of NATO's theater nuclear forces is to deter Soviet use of nuclear weapons to coerce or to attack the United States' European allies. Conventional forces, however adequate, cannot provide this same deterrence against a Soviet nuclear threat to Europe. Moreover, it is widely thought that U.S. strategic nuclear forces could not fully and credibly deter this threat without theater nuclear forces that can provide more limited, local responses to a Soviet attack.

Soviet Theater Nuclear Capabilities

The Soviet Union possesses a very large array of capabilities for delivering nuclear weapons against NATO military forces and territory. The Soviets have emphasized the development of "operational tactical missiles" as the principal means of delivering nuclear strikes to support ground operations. This emphasis has led to the Soviet deployment of large numbers of the unguided Frog tactical rocket, the short-range (85-160 nautical miles) Scud tactical ballistic missile, and the longer-range Scaleboard surface-to-surface missile. In 1972, the number of these tactical missile launchers was given at 850, but this may well have increased in the years since. The Soviets

Reprinted from the Congress of the United States, Congressional Budget Office. *Planning U.S. General Purpose Forces: The Theater Nuclear Forces.* Budget Issue Paper, January 1977, pp. 21-27.

may possibly have nuclear-capable field artillery, though the status and scope of this development have not been disclosed. Most of the Soviet tactical aircraft—an estimated 1,100 in 1972—are said to be capable of nuclear delivery. In addition to these tactical nuclear capabilities against Western Europe, the Soviets are also said to deploy a variety of nuclear cruise missiles and surface-to-air missiles, nuclear-capable naval artillery, and nuclear torpedoes and depth bombs.

Elements of the Soviet strategic nuclear forces also pose a serious threat to the European allies. The Soviet Union's medium and intermediate range ballistic missiles (M/IRBMs), currently estimated to number 600 launchers and perhaps 1,000 missiles when refires are included, are capable of attacking targets throughout Western Europe with nuclear warheads. The current Soviet MRBM and IRBM are older systems, dating from the late 1950s and early 1960s. However, the Soviets have been testing a new, mobile IRBM—the SS-20—that is said to be ready for deployment at any time, and that is capable of carrying multiple independently-targetable reentry vehicles (MIRV). Although it is not clear whether the SS-20 will replace or augment the current Soviet M/IRBM force, this new MIRV capability represents a significant increase in Soviet strategic delivery potential against Western Europe. The USSR has also maintained a number of dual-purpose, variable-range SS-11 intercontinental ballistic missiles (ICBMs), which were credited with a capability against European targets.

Finally, the nuclear-capable aircraft of the Soviet Long Range Aviation, numbered at 700 in 1972, and Soviet Naval Aviation, numbered at 500 in 1972, could also be employed for nuclear missions against Western Europe. The recent Soviet deployment of the Backfire bomber for such peripheral attack missions will significantly augment the nuclear delivery capability of both of these Soviet air arms.

It is the use of these large nuclear delivery capabilities against Western Europe that NATO theater nuclear forces, in conjunction with U.S. strategic forces, are to deter.

Soviet Theater Nuclear Doctrine

The Soviet portrayal of their post-war military doctrine can generally be characterized as offensively oriented. Although a NATO aggression is postulated for the beginning of a European war, Soviet doctrine emphasizes the assumption of the offensive at the earliest feasible moment, with the objective of not only recapturing supposedly lost territory but of destroying NATO military forces in detail. Soviet military writings portray this offensive as beginning with a massed nuclear strike, followed by the rapid advance of Soviet maneuver units through the breaches in enemy defenses opened by the nuclear strikes.

Because NATO theater nuclear forces pose a strong threat to Soviet forces massed for the offensive, the paramount objective of Soviet nuclear strikes would be the destruction of NATO theater nuclear forces. The Soviets stress that these forces must be destroyed without delay, as soon as their presence is detected, to minimize their threat to Soviet troops. The Soviets emphasize two principles to improve the effectiveness of their attempts to neutralize NATO theater nuclear forces: surprise, in the sense of misleading NATO as to Soviet intentions so as to forestall nuclear weapons dispersal, as well as tactical surprise in the delivery of nuclear strikes; and anticipation and preemption of NATO nuclear employment. Still, Soviet writers do not expect that all NATO nuclear weapons will be destroyed with one nuclear strike, and anticipate the need for follow-on strikes to destroy additional nuclear delivery units as they are detected. Soviet efforts to neutralize NATO theater nuclear forces would not be confined to nuclear strikes, but would include conventional artillery and aviation barrages, airborne assaults, and perhaps other non-nuclear military operations. These could also take place in an early, conventional phase of the war, before nuclear use by either side.

In addition to its stress on destroying enemy means of nuclear attack, Soviet doctrine calls for very high rates of advance by ground forces in exploiting breaches in enemy defenses, penetrating into enemy rear areas, encircling and destroying enemy troops, and seizing territory. A prime motive for achieving such rapid rates of advance is to complicate the delivery of enemy nuclear strikes on fast-moving Soviet troop formations and so minimize exposure to this risk. Soviet troops are said to be better trained and equipped than their NATO counterparts for operations in a radiological environment created by either Soviet or NATO nuclear strikes.

In summary, Soviet doctrine attempts to deal with the NATO theater nuclear threat to a successful offensive in two ways: nuclear strikes and conventional attacks to neutralize NATO theater nuclear forces, and high rates of advance to minimize the exposure of Warsaw Pact troops to strikes by surviving NATO nuclear weapons.

Limitations of Soviet Doctrine as a Guide to U.S. Policy

Although Soviet military writings proceed on the assumption that Soviet military capabilities are fully adequate for the missions identified in their doctrine, there may be serious questions as to whether the Soviets could actually muster the required resources and capabilities. Similarly, though many Soviet military writings place heavy emphasis on early use of nuclear weapons and assume that political authorization for this would be received, there are great uncertainties over whether Soviet leaders would authorize such early nuclear use. Political leaders are certainly not constrained to follow established military doctrine in time of war. Given the tremendous significance and the unforeseeable consequences of a Soviet decision to use nuclear weapons, it is certainly possible that the Soviet leaders would not resort to their early use.

However, it can also be argued that if the Soviet leaders ever began or allowed themselves to be dragged into a European war, knowing that it would involve a direct conflict with the United States, then they would have had to recognize and accept the risks of nuclear conflict associated with such a course of action. If, by this line of reasoning, Soviet conduct of a war in Europe would imply acceptance of the risk of nuclear warfare, the Soviet leaders might well elect to use nuclear weapons first to degrade NATO theater nuclear capabilities.

In summary, the arguments about the intentions of Soviet leaders are inconclusive. But given that Soviet forces are equipped, trained, and postured for the type of warfare described in their doctrine, it seems prudent that the United States seriously consider the possibility of a Soviet first use of nuclear weapons.

It is possible that the Soviets would not elect to begin a war in Europe with nuclear weapons; there have been indications of interest in such a possibility in Soviet military writings. In such a situation, NATO would be better situated to use nuclear weapons first in the event that conventional defenses should fail. Nevertheless, the dangers of preemptive or retaliatory Soviet nuclear strikes would remain.

Because NATO theater nuclear forces would pose a threat to the success of a Soviet conventional offensive, the Soviets would probably attempt to destroy them by conventional means, especially before they were dispersed. The effectiveness of direct Soviet conventional attacks is limited by formidable NATO air defenses and conventional bombing inaccuracies. However, the vulnerability of NATO theater nuclear forces to such conventional operations as airborne assault may be substantial. Moreover, the seriousness of a Soviet conventional threat to NATO theater nuclear forces will probably be increased with the eventual Soviet acquisition of conventional precision guided munitions (PGM) capabilities. Soviet acquisition of such conventional PGM capabilities would not only pose an independent threat to the survivability of NATO's nuclear means in the early stages of a postulated conventional conflict, but would supplement Soviet nuclear means of attack.

Implications for NATO Theater Nuclear Forces

From an examination of Soviet capabilities and doctrine for the use of nuclear weapons in a European conflict, at least three important conclusions relevant to NATO theater nuclear force structure can be drawn:

- The United States and its NATO allies may very well not be the first to employ nuclear weapons in a European conflict. Therefore, a theater nuclear force posture predicated upon a Soviet conventional aggression to which NATO, at some point, might respond with theater nuclear weapons may be an inappropriate scenario for planning U.S. theater nuclear forces.
- To constitute an effective deterrent to Soviet attack in Europe directed at the destruction of NATO's nuclear assets, NATO theater nuclear forces should be sufficiently survivable to be able to deliver theater nuclear responses consistent with stated U.S. objectives. They must be able to survive both a Soviet theater nuclear and conventional PGM attack.
- The United States and its NATO allies should have a carefully thought out doctrine and objectives for employment of theater nuclear attack in response to a Soviet theater nuclear attack.

The translation of such general conclusions into specific force structure and posture changes is clearly very difficult. However, such conclusions may be useful as a point of departure in evaluating the appropriateness of various proposed changes in the NATO theater nuclear force structure, discussed above.

6. History of NATO/Warsaw Pact Balance Assessments

Official U.S. perceptions of the NATO and Warsaw Pact conventional force balance have gone through three major phases. Outright pessimism regarding NATO's conventional capabilities—in the form of perceived Soviet conventional superiority—dominated U.S. and European views in the 1940s and 1950s. In the 1960s, however, the official U.S. view shifted toward optimism as the balance between NATO and Warsaw Pact forces was seen to have become about even. In the last few years, commentary on the balance has resumed a more pessimistic tone.

Actual changes in the opposing forces have prompted most of this evolution. But the shifting official view of the balance can also be linked to changes in the concerns of policymakers and to changes in analytical perspective.

The Era of Perceived Soviet Conventional Superiority

From the close of World War II to the early 1960s, Western analysts agreed that the Soviet Union had overwhelming superiority in conventional forces in Europe. Soviet ground forces throughout this era were estimated to number 2.5 million men with 175 or more well-equipped divisions. Western forces, at the outset a handful of units doing occupation duty in Germany, grew over the period to between 16 and 20 divisions—each larger than its Soviet counterpart—in the central region. Despite this improvement, nuclear weapons were seen as the principal Western response to the Soviet army during this era.

This policy was challenged briefly in the United States following

Reprinted from the Congress of the United States, Congressional Budget Office. *Assessing the NATO/Warsaw Pact Military Balance.* Budget Issue Paper for Fiscal Year 1979, December 1977, pp. 39-46.

the victory of Communist forces in China and the explosion of the first Soviet atomic device in 1949. These events led to one of the most famous policy reviews of the last thirty years. Known as NSC-68, it predicted a long, intense competition between the Soviet Union and the United States in military, political, and economic fields. In the military realm, it forecast the creation of Soviet nuclear forces as a deterrent to U.S. power, and argued that failure to build strong conventional forces would leave an exploitable gap in Western defenses.

For the next three years, coinciding with the Korean War, the United States not only spent more for conventional forces, but also for an accelerated buildup of strategic forces to deter Soviet nuclear attacks. Additional U.S. divisions were deployed to Europe, and the NATO integrated command structure was created. However, in the early 1950s, efforts to reach a conventional balance with the Soviets in Europe seemed to be beyond the economic reach of NATO.

Thus, beginning in 1954, the United States returned to an emphasis on nuclear deterrence and retaliation, a policy to be supplemented by the tactical use of nuclear weapons in Europe. By 1957, NATO's force goals for the central region had been scaled down to thirty nuclear-armed divisions; actual forces reached less than two-thirds of this goal.

Toward the end of the 1950s, the launch of Sputnik and the rapid growth in Soviet nuclear forces for the European theater both signaled the need to reconsider this doctrine. By the end of the decade, a number of analysts held the view that nuclear deterrence had become a two-way street. Reviving the position taken in NSC-68, they argued that with weak conventional forces, NATO in a crisis would be faced with a choice between nuclear suicide or conventional defeat. But the major hurdle to achieving an adequate conventional defense capability remained the perception of Soviet conventional dominance in Europe.

The Growth of the Perception of Rough Parity

In the next half-dozen years, the official U.S. view of the balance changed dramatically. By the mid-1960s it appeared to Defense Secretary Robert S. McNamara and his staff that NATO and the Warsaw Pact had approximate equality on the ground in central Europe as well as approximately equal abilities to reinforce.

This new perception had two sources. The first was a major increase in NATO's general purpose forces capabilities. Following the Berlin crisis of 1961, U.S. general purpose forces were strengthened in a variety of ways. Procurement for the general purpose forces between 1962 and 1969, for example, was forty percent higher than it had been from 1954 to 1961, even excluding funds for Southeast Asia operations. Procurement for mobility forces doubled. The allies also provided additional forces. Thus, by 1965 NATO could count more than twenty-nine divisions available in the central region on M-day—an improvement of as much as eighty percent since 1960.

The second source of the change in perception was major revisions in estimates of Soviet military capability. These reflected both actual changes in Soviet forces and a closer look at the conventional wisdom on the size, strength, and readiness of the Soviet army. Beginning in the late 1950s, the Soviet Union undertook a large reduction in military manpower. Meanwhile, the Kennedy administration, in an effort to define with more precision the requirements for a conventional option in Europe, began a reassessment of the threat to NATO. When the review was completed, the estimated size of the Soviet army had been scaled back from 2.5 million men and 175 well-equipped, ready divisions to about 2 million men and between 140 and 150 divisions of lesser individual capability than NATO's larger divisions, and maintained at varying levels of readiness. Thus, instead of crediting the Warsaw Pact with a capability of assembling over 125 divisions against NATO in a matter of weeks, the new assessments held that the Pact was unlikely to deploy more than eighty to ninety divisions in the central region over a period of several months.

By 1967, the NATO allies were persuaded of the feasibility of at least an initial defense of NATO with conventional forces. Formal NATO doctrine was altered to reflect this capability, under the label of "flexible response."

But the withdrawal of France from the NATO command structure and the Soviet invasion of Czechoslovakia combined to darken the tone of assessments after 1968.

The Swing Back toward Pessimism

The 1970s have seen the emergence of a new concern with NATO's conventional defense capabilities in central Europe. This concern has focused on two issues: uncertainty about NATO's capability to defend against a surprise attack, and uncertainty about the speed, size, and capabilities of Soviet reinforcements.

Although the surprise attack problem surfaced as early as 1965, concern with it increased after 1968, when the Soviet Union moved five divisions from its territory to Czechoslovakia, and still more in the mid-1970s, following evidence of gains in the firepower, mobility, and air support of Soviet forces in Europe.

Concern with the mobilization and reinforcement capabilities of the Warsaw Pact surfaced in a series of assessments performed in the early years of the Nixon administration. Although some of these reinforced the assessments of the 1960s that a conventional defense of NATO was feasible for as long as three months or more, others found NATO unlikely to hold against a determined Pact attack for more than about two weeks.

Thus, within the last several years, the official view of the balance seems to have shifted towards the pessimistic end of the scale. Defense Secretary Rumsfeld's statement on the fiscal year 1978 defense budget, for example, said that:

> At present, the United States and its allies in NATO have sufficient active forces to maintain an acceptable ratio of defense-to-offense against either type of attack. However, it would be a mistake to conclude that, because of an acceptable ratio, we have high confidence of conducting a successful forward defense in all instances.... Contrary to conventional wisdom, NATO may have enough manpower to stem both the short-warning and the full-scale attack, but without prompt remedial action, the alliance may lack the necessary firepower and mobility to do its job.

The view that the balance may be shifting toward the Warsaw Pact but is not yet hopeless also seems to be the view of the Carter administration. Reporting on the results of the most recent milestone in balance assessments, Presidential Review Memorandum (PRM) 10, Defense Secretary Brown declared that force improvements continue to be needed in NATO's initial combat capabilities and rapid reinforcing capabilities.

7. NATO/Warsaw Pact Military Balance: How To Make the Balance Look Good/Bad

The previous section (6) illustrated some of the differences various assumptions can make in portraying the military balance. This section combines many of these assumptions into two separate groupings that result, on the one hand, in a pessimistic view of the balance and, on the other, a more optimistic view. Each construct is internally consistent, and while few of the many balance assessments may conform fully to one or the other of these frameworks, we believe each is fairly typical of one of the two general classes of balance assessments.

Pessimistic Assessments

Pessimistic assessments of the NATO/Pact balance tend to see the Warsaw Pact as efficient because its command structure is hierarchical and dominated by a single nation, the USSR.

Implicit in statements like this is the view that the decision-making process in the Warsaw Pact—less subject to outside scrutiny, delay, compromise and the influence of domestic or nationalistic concerns—can make decisions on strategy faster. And once they are made, it is believed the hierarchical rigidity of the communist system allows the decisions to be carried out with speed, facility, and vigor. In this view, the Pact has an advantage over the NATO system where decisions are made by committee and are implemented through a process of negotiation, compromise, and consensus. Thus, relative unity and speed characterize the Pact's military behavior; delay and disarray are typical of NATO's behavior.

Reprinted from the Congress of the United States, Congressional Budget Office. *Assessing the NATO/Warsaw Pact Military Balance.* Budget Issue Paper for Fiscal Year 1979, December 1977, pp. 27-37.

Another characteristic of pessimistic assessments is the belief that it is better to err by giving the Pact the benefit of the doubt in the absence of information than to underestimate Pact strength. A primary focus on wartime fighting rather than deterrence also tends to support such a conservative bias regarding uncertain Pact capabilities.

Pessimistic assessments tend toward symmetrical counting, but not toward symmetrical assumptions regarding the military behavior of the Pact and NATO. That is, they tend to compare totals of like things—manpower strengths, units, weapons systems—rather than evaluate how well each side can pursue its differing strategies. As a result, the categories of comparison are relatively limited; these assessments tend to exclude elements of strength on both sides that are not easily comparable. And when such unlike elements are included in pessimistic assessments, the analyst chooses those techniques for comparison that give greater weight to the relative strengths of the Pact.

Pessimistic assessments also tend to include more elements of Pact strength in their calculations of the balance than do optimistic assessments. They will often include forces from the Soviet strategic reserve and from Soviet deployments outside the central front area in discussions of the central front balance, count authorized rather than actual strengths, and sometimes include paramilitary forces—border and security troops—in Pact totals.

In contrast, pessimistic assessments normally disregard French forces in their tallies of NATO strength, or include only those based in Germany. Danish forces are usually included only in terms of the NATO/Pact balance on the northern front, not the central front. And non-NATO members of Western Europe are generally ignored in these assessments. More importantly, forces such as the German Territorial Army may be disregarded.

Pessimistic assessments are often tied to a short-warning scenario. This is due in part to the commitment to see the balance in terms of NATO's problems in fighting a war and a consequent fascination with those points in a scenario where the disparity in forces is greatest. It is also a function in part of the tendency to give the Pact the benefit of the doubt in areas where, one way or the other, evidence is lacking. These assessments tend to disregard command and control difficulties in moving large ground force units and to assume relatively high levels of readiness on the part of Pact forces.

It is important to note how some of the characteristics of pessimistic assessments reinforce each other. The assumption that the Pact political system facilitates military decisions and their efficient implementation, for example, supports the assumption of a short-warning attack. Efficiency, in this view, can be translated into a greater capability to carry out a well disciplined and concealed movement of large forces, a necessary condition of the short-warning attack assumption. The assumption of a short-warning attack, in turn, reinforces the assumptions that French forces would not be involved on the NATO side and that German territorial forces would not play a significant role. (The shorter the warning, the more difficult it would be to reintegrate the French back into a NATO command structure and to turn the German territorial forces into an integral part of NATO's defense.) It would also make it more difficult for NATO to adjust its forces along the Front to bolster any local areas of weakness. This, in turn, could mean that the Pact could build a local force edge of up to 12:1 in areas like the north German plain, where NATO's forces are relatively weak. Thus, the assumption of Pact efficiency, because it supports the assumption of a short-warning attack, tends to reinforce the assumptions that French forces and German territorial forces should not be counted. In short, pessimistic analysts develop an internally consistent chain of logic, rooted in judgments on the military effectiveness of the Pact political system.

Optimistic Assessments

Optimistic assessments judge the Pact political system very differently. They tend to view its hierarchical rigidity not as a source of military efficiency, but as inhibiting individual and lower-level initiatives, incapable of rectifying errors in data of judgment, and because of internal secrecy and distrust, more cumbersome than the negotiation and consensus associated with NATO. Optimistic analysts do not equate Soviet domination of the Warsaw Pact with effective use of its military resources. Instead, the Soviet-Pact relationship is seen as fundamentally insecure. Soviet forces are seen not as partners in a military alliance, but in part as occupation troops, repressing nationalistic tendencies of the rest of the Pact.

One implication is a reluctance to grant the Pact the benefit of the doubt in areas of uncertainty. Where pessimistic assessments note the dangers of NATO's need for consensus and envy the military simplicity of the Pact's unified political system, optimistic ones tend to see the command problems as the same in both alliances—but dealt with less efficiently by the Pact. That difference in judgment is a major reason why the calculations of the military balance in optimistic assessments do not usually grant the Pact the benefit of the doubt in areas of uncertainty.

In contrast to pessimistic assessments, optimistic assessments typically tend toward asymmetrical counting. That is, they tend to avoid one-on-one comparisons of like entities and attempt instead to assess the capability of NATO to carry out its strategy of defense against the capability of the Pact to carry out a strategy of aggression. This tendency introduces more complexity to the comparative effort. It is in optimistic assessments that greater efforts are found to introduce the contribution of air and naval forces to the ground force balance, and comparisons move away from numbers of entities toward numerical expressions of capability.

Optimistic assessments generally include forces on the NATO side of the equation that are left out by pessimistic assessments. Thus, French forces are added to NATO's totals; West German territorial forces are included, as are small, but incrementally important contributions from non-NATO West Europeans, and Danish forces are seen in terms of their contributions to the critical central front balance, not in terms of being limited to the flanks.

Optimistic assessments also tend to discount large drawdowns from Soviet strategic reserve forces or from the forces deployed along the flanks or the Sino-Soviet border in their calculations of the central front balance. They also tend to discount contributions by Polish and Czech forces. Some assessments degrade the level of Soviet forces in these countries on the grounds that some of them would be oriented toward rear security. Nearly all optimistic assessments disregard potential contributions made by Pact paramilitary forces—border and security troops—in their calculations.

Optimistic analysts tend to discount surprise or short-warning Pact attacks. If the Pact launched an attack without warning, they believe, the strength of the attack would necessarily be limited. The Pact could not build to a clearly predominant level of force, in this view, in a short time, and the effort could not be done without alerting NATO. This tradeoff is premised on a series of assumptions that stress the command and control difficulties associated with moving Pact forces and preparing them for an attack. Optimistic analysts do not question the physical capacity of the road and rail networks to accommodate the movements required. They do discount the human capabilities to manage the movement and establish the necessary command and control structures.

As in the case of pessimistic assessments, optimistic ones have their internal logic and consistency. The view that the Pact is limited by distrust and repression, for example, supports arguments against including non-Soviet Pact forces in strength tallies, justifies not counting border or security troops as part of an attacking force, and suggests that even some regular Soviet forces might be charged with rear security missions in the event of conflict. Given the kind of conservative biases these assessments associate with Soviet decision-makers, the probability that the Soviets would risk redeployments from the flanks logically declines. Thus, judgments regarding the Pact's political system support the view that it would take the Pact relatively long to assemble and prepare a large attack. And given the deduction that a Pact build-up would be obvious and long, it becomes logically more consistent to assume a reintegration of French forces to the NATO command structure and to count them on the NATO side of the balance. It also makes it logical to assume that NATO would have more opportunity to adjust its forces along the front to correct any weaknesses in its current posture.

Illustrative Underlying Assumptions in NATO/Warsaw Pact Balance Assessment

Pessimistic	Optimistic
Major aim is to defeat Pact forces in event of war. Valid therefore to hedge against not having enough military resources.	Major problem is to deter Pact attack. Implies level of capacity that may not be as high as necessary to defeat Pact forces.
Authoritarian/hierarchical system allows Pact nations to carry out military plans effectively and quickly.	Pact concern with control and secrecy degrades efficiency. Inhibits lower unit initiatives. Leads to internal distrust.
Better to err on the side of over-estimates of Pact military strength.	Not advisable to give Pact forces benefit of the doubt in absence of data. Pact forces likely to have at least as much difficulty in command and control as NATO's.

Illustrative NATO/Warsaw Pact Balance Comparisons: Central Front Ground Forces

A. *Pessimistic Views*

Military Personnel		*Rationale*
NATO	Pact	Includes active U.S./NATO divisions only; Soviet Category III divisions at full strength on assumption that these forces would not be involved directly in conflict with Pact.
1.045 million	1.216 million	

Tanks		
NATO	Pact	Tanks viewed as a valid measure because of Soviet doctrine; data include prepositioned stocks for two U.S. divisions; estimated stocks in storage for USSR.
6,615	16,000	

Divisions		
NATO	Pact	Includes all active divisions in NATO center region less French, which are not under NATO control; Category I divisions in East Germany, Czechoslovakia, and Poland; excludes separate brigades and regiments.
24	51	

Size of Pact Threat After 30 Days Mobilization	*Pact/NATO Force Ratio at:*			
	M-Day	*M+14*	*M+30*	Assumes rapid reinforcement of Central Front by Soviet forces elsewhere; delayed entrance of French forces. Does not count West German territorial forces.
85 Divisions	1.5	2.1	1.6	
128 Divisions	1.5	2.4	2.4	

B. *Optimistic Views*

Military Personnel		*Rationale*
NATO	Pact	Includes active duty German territorial forces and forward deployed French and Danish forces on assumption they would be involved; includes Category II and III divisions at less than authorized strength.
1.096 million	1.124 million	

Numbers of tanks not included because one-on-one comparisons considered misleading.

Divisions		*Rationale*
NATO	Pact	Includes separate brigades and regiments aggregated as division equivalents; includes five French divisions on assumption that French would be involved in event of conflict.
32	51	

Size of Pact Threat After 30 Days Mobilization	*Pact/NATO Force Ratio at:*			*Rationale*
	M-Day	*M+14*	*M+30*	Assumes delays in Soviet reinforcements; early entrance by French forces; counts West German territorial forces.
85 Divisions	1.4	1.6	1.4	

Illustrative NATO/Warsaw Pact Balance Comparisons: Central Front Air Forces

---

A. *Pessimistic Views*

Combat Aircraft		*Rationale*
NATO	Pact	Data refer to aircraft in Central Europe on argument that this is best comparative basis; excludes French, U.S. carrier-based
1,810	2,500	and U.S. dual-based aircraft.
		Generally does not seek additional comparative measures.

B. *Optimistic Views*

Combat Aircraft		*Rationale*
NATO	Pact	Data refer to resources that can supplement aircraft already in place. Includes U.S. dual-based and French aircraft and naval air from two carrier wings, plus some rapid deploying
3,462	3,680	reserves.
NATO/Pact Ratio of Bomb Tonnage Drop Capability at Equi-distances		Accounts for variation in aircraft capabilities and missions and allows easier integration to ground force balance.
100 nm.	200 nm.	
3:1	7:1	

---

8. NATO/Warsaw Pact Military Balance: Modes of Analysis

"Bean Counting"

Nearly all assessments of military balances compare numerical factors on one side with those on another. Even assessments that assume that nonquantifiable factors are really what count in military relationships (e.g., will, leadership, loyalty, etc.) generally begin with tallies of what is easier to count. These tallies may be adjusted or discounted by applying some formula that introduces less quantifiable elements, but any such construct still requires a count of people and things.

There are two general approaches to counting that run through the various assessments. The first, and most prevalent, bases its conclusions on tallies of the same or very similar entities on both sides of the balance. The second approach counts different things on each side. For purposes of discussion, the two approaches can be characterized as symmetrical and asymmetrical counting.

Symmetrical Counting

Symmetrical counting is a comparative exercise in which the same genre of entities is addressed. The approach recognizes that there may be differences among and between the things that are tallied on each side, but assumes that meaningful comparisons can be made so long as what is counted can reasonably be related to combat strength, are essentially the same things, and are counted accurately.

These criteria can, however, pose analytic difficulties in practice. For while there are weapons systems on both sides of the NATO/

Reprinted from the Congress of the United States, Congressional Budget Office. *Assessing the NATO/Warsaw Pact Military Balance.* Budget Issue Paper for Fiscal Year 1979, December 1977, pp. 53-63.

Warsaw Pact balance that are clearly comparable in terms of either physical characteristics or combat role, there are other items on each side that possess significant combat potency, but for which there is no clear counterpart on the other side. The analytic problem is complicated by these kinds of important but singular entities, and counts that stress symmetry in their tallies must often either stretch the categories of comparison to account for dissimilarities in major items of equipment or exclude such items from the comparisons. In short, the prices of symmetrical counting are often a lack of comprehensiveness or a diffusion brought about by very broad categories of comparison.

The accuracy of symmetrical counting is inhibited by the efforts of both sides to conceal major components of military strength. The greatest efforts at deception may be associated with those items that bean counts are most interested in.

Even with these inherent difficulties, symmetrical counting profoundly influences perceptions of military balances. Counts of the same things on both sides of a military equation provide the quickest, apparently least complicated overview of the actual balance. For these reasons, symmetrical counts are prominent in public discussions. They appeal to people who seek to mobilize support for or against decisions. They lend themselves to dramatic presentation and can be politically potent.

Asymmetrical Counting

While symmetrical counting concentrates on the same or similar things, the asymmetrical approach begins on the assumption that each side of a military equation is best measured against its objective.

Many of the same data that form the heart of symmetrical counting exercises are also important to the asymmetrical approach. But the arrangement of these data may be very different. For while a symmetrical approach expresses a balance by tallying, say, the tanks on each side, an asymmetrical approach would be more interested in comparing tanks on one side to antitank weapons on the other. This avoids the tendency to stretch categories of comparison in order to fit unlike systems into a bean count.

But asymmetrical counting introduces a new order of complexity and the risk of double-counting. Many major items of equipment, for example, possess the capability of countering more than one component of military power on the other side. This poses problems of presentation. No matter how realistic it may be to count, say, fighter-attack aircraft against different targets, presenting such data simply looks very much like double-counting. While asymmetrical counting provides what many believe to be analytic rigor, the price paid in presentation may be great.

Compensating for Differences

Nearly all assessments share the assumption that, at base, the military balance is a function of people (manpower), technology (weaponry), and organization. The first two elements in this relationship are most susceptible to counting; the organizational aspects are more difficult; and the interrelationships between manpower, weaponry, and organization are the most difficult to capture in the assessment. Most assessments, then, include counts of people and weapons, but differ in how they handle the manner in which manpower and technology is merged and organized.

A basic analytical difficulty in comparing ground forces is the need to reflect adequately the large differences in organization between NATO, with a small number of large divisions and large support forces, and the Pact, with a large number of small divisions and relatively small support forces.

Firepower as a Common Denominator

The most prominent methods of comparing unlike forces have focused on firepower capabilities.

A crude way of doing this is to simply add the numbers of major items of equipment in opposing units, establish a ratio on the basis of these sums, and then rank the units accordingly. By this kind of measure, for example, an American mechanized division is about ten percent "superior" to a Soviet mechanized rifle division and a U.S. armored division is roughly thirty-five percent superior to a Soviet armored division. Running divisional units on both sides through this kind of a calculation and doing the same thing with aggregates of independent, smaller units (e.g., creating divisional equivalents—three separate brigades equal one division, etc.) provides one means of dealing analytically with variations in size and structure on both sides of the balance.

A more sophisticated approach, however, is to try to account for all the firepower capability in different units, in effect comparing unlike systems to each other. Some analyses use "judgmental" firepower scores, associated with the terms Weapons Effectiveness Indices and Weapon Unit Value (WEI/WUV).

Judgmental Firepower Scores. Judgmental firepower scores are produced by experienced military officers who estimate the relative effectiveness in combat of various weapons in the course of systematic discussions. These dialogues result in conclusions that, say, a mortar has forty times the casualty-producing capability of a rifle or that, in a tank-to-tank engagement, a U.S. tank is about 1.2 times more effective than a Soviet tank. Where possible, these judgments are tested against historical data and refined through a delphi technique (a systematic process of narrowing differences between participants). This process produces a series of index numbers that, in effect, can reduce any given weapon to an "equivalent" of rifles, tanks, etc. These numbers, referred to as Weapons Effectiveness Indices (WEIs), provide the common denominators for comparing units. Any given unit can then be assigned a number, referred to as a Weighted Unit Value (WUV), by counting the various weapons it has, multiplying each type by a WEI, and adding the results. This process is the basis for the balance assessments provided in many of the Executive Branch's national security study memoranda over the last decade and the recent PRM-10.

Quality

The incorporation of considerations of quality in balance assessments can be deceptively simple, particularly in those assessments that use index numbers to reduce different forces to a common comparative basis. Once this has been done, for example, it is a simple mathematical task to multiply the index number by another numerical factor that adjusts for variations in quality of the force. The derivation of the quality factor is, however, quite debatable. There have been at least two ways in which it has been attempted, neither of which is fully satisfactory.

One means of adjusting for quality is to seek some objective standard against which the judgment of quality can be applied. A prominent example is in the designation of different readiness categories for Soviet divisions, categories that are based on the levels of manning and equipment maintained by the various divisions in the Soviet force structure. Here, judgments as to the relative quality of a division are consciously tied to objective evidence. Another means is behavioral or historical. An example is the Arab-Israeli military balance, where the "balance," as portrayed by manpower, unit comparisons, or firepower scores has nearly always favored the Arabs yet has not reflected the outcome of the last three confrontations between the two sides. Analysis reveals that the ratio in favor of Arab manpower or firepower potential has been remarkably stable, hovering around about 4:1 in the Arab favor prior to each Arab-Israeli war over the last two decades. The fact that the Israelis did not "lose" in any of these confrontations has led some analysts to suggest that while manpower or firepower favor the Arabs, discipline, leadership, and training have favored the Israelis. They argue that the Israeli edge in these areas can be reflected in balance assessments by multiplying the Israeli side of the equation by some number that reflects the Israeli ability to compensate for relative deficiencies in manpower and firepower vis-à-vis the Arabs.

Unfortunately for analysis—but fortunately for the world—there has been no historical pattern of NATO/Warsaw Pact confrontations that could generate a similar quality factor applicable to the balance in Europe. Explicit efforts to adjust the balance to reflect quality considerations have therefore been restricted primarily to those of the first approach.

Implicitly, however, considerations of relative quality enter balance assessments in several ways. One is via the manner in which firepower scores are generated, particularly those that have previously been described as judgmental firepower scores. Here, subjective evaluation of the quality of different weapons systems in combat enters the derivation of the firepower score directly. And even in the laboratory-derived firepower scores there is leeway for subjective evaluation of the quality both of weapons and of the manner in which they are used to enter the equation. The difficulty is not so much that firepower scores carry implicit considerations on non-quantifiable elements, but that these considerations are seldom made explicit and clear.

Strategy

Variations of strategy are usually dealt with in balance assessments by adjusting the numerical comparisons according to whether one side or another is attacking or defending. One common method is to apply certain "threshold" force ratios (based on firepower scores, manpower, or other comparisons) below which an attack is likely to be unsuccessful. These ratios are based on traditional military rules of thumb for which historical evidence is inconclusive. Typical threshold attacker/defender ratios used in many current assessments include:

- A "breakthrough" ratio (5:1)
- An "offensive" ratio (3:1)
- A "prepared defense" ratio (1.7:1—one defender for every 1.7 attackers)
- A "hasty defense" ratio (1.4:1)

It is important to recognize that these ratios—which clearly favor

Firepower Index for Various Units
(91-100 Percent Strength)

Type of Unit	Offense	Defense
Mechanized Division	25	20
Armored Division	30	15
Armored Cavalry Regiment	3	6
Artillery Group	3	4

the defense—are meant to apply to localized situations, not across a theater front (as in central Europe) or even at the army group or corps level. Thus, it is possible for an attacker to achieve a breakthrough against a numerically superior opponent (as German forces did in 1940 and 1941) by concentrating his forces and employing surprise and speed—provided the defense fails to react appropriately. On the other hand, a defender may be able to frustrate a numerically superior attack even when the initial force ratios are highly unfavorable, if the defender can send more reinforcements to the sector more rapidly than the attacker can increase his effort. Many analysts argue that outcomes depend as critically on such factors as how forces are distributed, intelligence, mobility, and the preparation of defensive lines as they do on theater-wide force ratios.

Adjustments for strategy or tactical mode can also enter assessments of the balance at other points. Some firepower scores, for example, include consideration of different tactical modes, as suggested by the following table, which illustrates the way in which these judgments can enter analysis.

As the table shows, both the mechanized and armored divisions are viewed as relatively more effective in an offensive mode than in a defensive mode. In contrast, the effectiveness implied for artillery units is higher in the defensive mode than it is in an offensive context. These are, of course, judgments. There is a logical rationale for them—assigning a higher potency to artillery in a defensive mode, for example, takes account of the fact that a defensive posture usually permits better knowledge about one's position and reference points and therefore allows better shooting. But once introduced to the calculations, they can generate very different balance assessments depending on the overall strategy portrayed for one side or the other.

Two general cautions regarding adjustments made for strategy are worth noting. First, the derivation of the factors used to adjust the assessment one way or another are generally unclear. Historical example runs through most of them, and it is quite debatable whether history is an accurate guide to a future conflict. Second, since adjustments for strategy can enter at several different points in an analysis, there is the danger that they may be introduced repeatedly. Thus, any assessment that claims to have dealt with the impact of strategy should be looked at carefully to assure that it has not done so too often.

Static and Dynamic Analyses

So far, this discussion has concentrated on what is known as static analysis and has outlined the manner in which numerical factors are arrayed on both sides of a military equation for any given point in time. This is the essence of static analysis—a snap shot, not a moving picture. Time can be dealt with in static analyses by constructing the numerical comparisons for several points during each side's mobilization or for different periods during a postulated confrontation. But static analyses are not constructed to portray the process of conflict, nor do they usually deal with conflict situations as opposed to the pre-conflict period or periods of mobilization.

Static analyses go beyond simple order-of-battle intelligence in several ways. For one thing, they often convert information on both sides to a common comparative basis, providing some greater depth in comparisons. For another, static analyses can be coupled with assumptions or judgments on the effect of different strategies or of qualitative elements such as leadership or discipline. In short, although any static analysis has inherent restrictions on the extent to which it can advance understanding of a military relationship, it has an appealing flexibility. And in going beyond simple order-of-battle comparisons between increasingly disparate force structures, static analyses do provide insights to the actual military balance not offered by earlier modes of comparison.

Dynamic analysis supplements and expands the vista offered by static analyses by portraying processes and by concentrating on the course of a postulated conflict as opposed to the preconflict period. Dynamic analysis is the generic name for a wide range of military models, simulations, and games. All these devices share the common effort to provide a moving picture of the course of a confrontation between opposing sides.

Dynamic analysis rests on data the same as, or similar to, those used in static analyses. It takes such data and "fights a war" by using computers, human players, or some combination of men and machines. In all cases, however, the structure of the model—its equations or computational routines—transforms numerical inputs into numerical assertions describing outcomes, most commonly expressed in terms of casualties on both sides or in terms of changes in the front line between two ground forces.

The war-fighting aspects of dynamic analysis make it a more complete and comprehensive mode of analysis than static analysis. It extends the analytic capability to evaluate various arrays of forces on both sides of a balance. And, if done correctly, a dynamic assessment allows detailed criticism because it provides a documented record of the criteria and judgments made in reaching conclusions on the significance of the balance between two forces.

On the other hand, dynamic analysis usually involves an additional order of assumptions and calculations. Apart from the burdens of reducing different force structures to a common base for comparisons, dynamic analysis generally requires a vast number of assumptions about what happens when two sides of a military operation actually engage in conflict with each other. Few, if any, analysts claim that they have successfully modeled all the vagaries of war. Many argue that while dynamic analysis can provide insights to the relationship between two contending military forces, confidence in any specific results of the approach should be carefully weighed against the complexity that this mode of analysis inherently entails. The analysts argue that a dynamic approach is most valuable not in trying to answer questions about which side would win in an actual confrontation, but in testing the relative impact of varying inputs to the analysis. That is, dynamic analysis is particularly well suited to assessing how differences in force availability, reinforcements, weapons, or ammunition supply affect the potential of one side to fight, not in forecasting actual outcomes in the event the two sides go to war.

9. Planning the General Purpose Forces

The general purpose forces are of use in a range of contingencies, from terrorist attack or civil disorder to major war. Because of the diversity of capabilities the forces embody, it is impossible to predict how, where, or against what adversary they might next be employed. Recent experience demonstrates the variety of uses to which they might be put. In the past five years, general purpose force elements engaged in major ground and air combat in Vietnam, Laos, and Cambodia. Military Airlift Command aircraft flew supplies to Israel during the Yom Kippur War in 1973, while elements of the Sixth Fleet and other military units demonstrated U.S. support. Air Force, Navy, and Marine units evacuated Americans and other civilians from Southeast Asian cities and rescued the crew of the Mayaguez. Air Force and Navy units were deployed to Korea and adjacent waters after the murder of U.S. soldiers in Panmunjom. In each case, U.S. forces were engaged or could have been engaged in combat. None of these uses for the forces could have been predicted far in advance.

The president and secretary of defense have to provide clear and explicit guidance to the armed services in order for them to plan forces. The guidance cannot be simply to plan forces for use anywhere, against any adversary, in any numbers. Some arbitrary selection of criteria for force planning is required, and possible scenarios have to be specified. The selection of a scenario is not equivalent to a prediction that U.S. forces will certainly be used in the place and manner specified; a scenario is principally a device to impose order on the planning of forces, logistics and manpower, and to give content to debates and decisions about such issues. Forces

Reprinted from the Congress of the United States, Congressional Budget Office. *Planning U.S. General Purpose Forces: Overview.* Budget Issue Paper, January 1977, pp. 7-11.

planned for one set of circumstances may have great capability in other, unanticipated events. Planning for a small number of scenarios, however, does carry a risk that some force components that are appropriate hedges against unforeseen threats will be eliminated.

Planning Scenarios and Our Strategic Concept

Thus, the Department of Defense (DOD) makes detailed assumptions in order to plan future forces systematically. These assumptions take the form of a small number of scenarios or situations for which the conventional forces are planned and in terms of which force plans are justified to the Congress by the Department of Defense. Underlying these scenarios is a "strategic concept," as described in the current Annual Defense Department Report. The concept derives from four main principles:

- That we support two main centers of strength—in Western Europe and in Northeast Asia;
- That we have the non-nuclear capability, in conjunction with our allies, to deal simultaneously with one major contingency and one minor contingency;
- That we have the ability to keep open the lines of communication by sea between Western Europe and Northeast Asia and the United States;
- That we allocate our resources in such a way that our active forces provide an initial defense capability and our reserve forces supplement the more costly active units; the reserves also provide a hedge against non-nuclear campaigns of substantial duration.

Following these principles the primary emphasis in planning of specific forces is on a hypothetical NATO conflict. As the Annual Defense Department Report states:

> Since the centerpiece of our strategic concept is to have the ability, in conjunction with our allies, to manage one major contingency, we believe that the most prudent way to arrive at the specific requirement for general purpose forces is to consider what we would need to establish and maintain a forward defense in Central Europe.

The European contingency is viewed as a suitably realistic and severe test case because of (1) the importance of Europe in U.S. international interests; (2) the existence of a concrete military threat deployed in Eastern Europe that could be reinforced by other Warsaw Pact forces; and (3) the belief that if our forces are adequate for NATO, they will also be adequate for other contingencies.

Although this strategic concept concentrates on conflict in Europe, it assumes as well that there would be combat or a threat of combat in Northeast Asia at the same time. The Soviet Union maintains significant numbers of submarines and surface warships on its eastern coast, and these fleet units could threaten shipping in the Pacific and preclude movement of parts of the U.S. fleet to European or Atlantic waters. Thus, U.S. forces deployed in the Pacific may have a direct role to play in worldwide conflict with the USSR. In addition, some forces may be required for the "minor contingency" specified above. It is unlikely that significant forces would be withheld from a major European war to deal with hypothetical minor contingencies elsewhere; however, U.S. forces are intended to be able to deal with a minor contingency without substantially reducing their capability to deal with a NATO war that breaks out during—or as a consequence of—that minor conflict.

The NATO Scenario

The NATO scenario assumes a large-scale attack on NATO's central region (mainly on Germany). Canada and all U.S. allies in Europe, including France, are assumed to participate. The Soviet Navy is assumed to attack shipping and naval forces in the Atlantic and Mediterranean. Since a European conflict could become worldwide, U.S. and allied forces hold a defensive position in Northeast Asia and defend lines of communication to that area. Less intense naval conflict is assumed in the Pacific.

Should the war described in the planning scenario actually occur, it would cause enormous casualties, widespread destruction, and profound disruption and confusion. All of the options open to the United States would be miserable alternatives, and all of the choices would have uncertain outcomes.

NATO policy stresses forward defense as far east in Germany as possible. The aim is to hold loss of NATO territory to a minimum. This emphasis arises out of political considerations in Europe and out of the military fact that it requires more force to recover territory once it is lost than to hold it in the first place. Because Soviet doctrine and structure of force emphasize rapid offensive movement, "blitz-krieg" tactics, the United States also views the initial stages of a war in Europe as particularly critical. Accordingly, planning emphasizes initial combat capability of active forces.

Except for four reserve brigades associated with active divisions and selected units that provide combat service support to active forces, reserve ground units cannot contribute significantly to combat capability soon after mobilization. The main purpose of these forces is to provide a hedge against the possibility that a NATO war could draw out over a period of months or even years. Recent evidence of improvement in Soviet capability to fight a longer war has reinforced U.S. concern with this possibility.

The roles of the U.S. armed services in a NATO war are as follows:

- The primary role of the Army is to fight the land war in Europe. Nearly all Army forces are devoted to this, although it takes up to six months after mobilization for the Army reserves to be ready to fight.
- The Marines provide amphibious capability in case it is needed on NATO's southern or northern flanks, and help in the land war.
- The Air Force's missions are to secure air superiority, provide close air support for the land battle, make interdiction attacks, and carry out airlift to Europe.
- The Navy's job is to defend shipping, defeat the Soviet Navy, and possibly to project airpower ashore on NATO's flanks from its aircraft carriers.

Although those are the roles of the U.S. armed forces, it is important to realize that they might not be successful. The balance of forces between NATO and the Warsaw Pact is such that neither can be sure of a successful military outcome. The United States is probably unable to buy general purpose forces large enough to guarantee a NATO victory in such a situation. An attempt to acquire such large forces might simply provoke an offsetting Soviet buildup. Thus, in a major war with the Soviet Union, the outcome would be uncertain because the United States and its allies are not likely to have the overwhelming predominance of force required to reduce to zero the role of generalship, circumstances, morale, and luck. Either side can undertake programs that might shift the odds, but there is no way for either in the near term to acquire an overwhelming advantage.

10. Chronology of Arms Control and Disarmament Agreements

Geneva Protocol
Protocol for the Prohibition of the Use in War of Asphyxiating, Poisonous or Other Gases, and of Bacteriological Methods of Warfare.
Signed in 1925.
Entered into force, 1928.

The Antarctic Treaty
Prohibits Any Military Use of the Region.
Signed, December 1959.
Ratified by U.S., August 18, 1960.
Entered into force, June 1961.

"Hotline" Agreement
Established a direct communications link between the U.S. and the USSR.
Signed and entered into force, June 1963.

Limited Test Ban Treaty
Bans nuclear weapons tests in the atmosphere, in outer space, and under water.
Entered into force, October 1963.

Outer Space Treaty
Governs the activities of states in the exploration and use of outer space, including the moon and other celestial bodies.
Signed, January 1967.
Entered into force, October 1967.

Treaty For the Prohibition of Nuclear Weapons in Latin America
Signed at Tlatelolco, Mexico February 1967.
Entered into force, April 1968.
Additions to the Tlatelolco Treaty were signed by the United States in
    April 1968; ratified with understandings and declarations by the
    United States, May 1971.

Nonproliferation Treaty
Treaty on the nonproliferation of nuclear weapons.
Signed, July 1968.
Entered into force through U.S. ratification, March 1970.

Seabed Arms Control Treaty
Treaty on the prohibition of the emplacement of nuclear weapons
    and other weapons of mass destruction on the seabed and the ocean
    floor and its subsoil.
Signed, February 1971.
Entered into force through U.S. ratification, May 1972.

"Accidents Measures" Agreement
Agreement to reduce the risk of outbreak of nuclear war between the
    United States and the Soviet Union.
Entered into force, September 30, 1971.

"Hotline" Modernization Agreement
Agreement between the United States and the Soviet Union on
    measures to improve the U.S.-USSR Direct Communications
    Link.
Entered into force, September 30, 1971.

Biological Weapons Convention
Convention prohibiting the development, production, and stock-
    piling of bacteriological (biological) and toxin weapons.
Signed at Washington, London, and Moscow, April 10, 1972.

ABM Treaty
Treaty between the United States and the Soviet Union on the
    limitation of antiballistic missile systems.
Signed at Moscow, May 26, 1972.
Entered into force through U.S. ratification, October 3, 1972.

Interim Agreement (SALT I)
Interim agreement between the United States and the Soviet Union
   on limitation of strategic offensive arms.
Signed at Moscow, May 26, 1972.
Entered into force through U.S. ratification, October 3, 1972.

ABM Protocol
Protocol to the treaty between the United States and the Soviet Union
   on the limitation of antiballistic missile systems.
Signed at Moscow, July 3, 1974.
Entered into force, May 24, 1976.

Prevention of Nuclear War
Agreement between the United States and the Soviet Union relating
   to cooperative relations.
Entered into force, June 22, 1973.

Threshold Test Ban and Protocol
Treaty between the United States and the Soviet Union and Protocol
   to the Treaty on Underground Nuclear Explosions for Peaceful
   Purposes.
Signed at Moscow, July 3, 1974.

Underground PNE Ban and Protocol
Treaty between the United States and the Soviet Union and Protocol
   to the Treaty on Underground Nuclear Explosions for Peaceful
   Purposes.
Signed in Washington and Moscow on May 28, 1976.

Environmental Modification Ban
Convention banning hostile use of environmental modification
   techniques.
Signed in Geneva, May 18, 1977.

Part 3
Statistical Information

TABLE 1

U.S. STRATEGIC NUCLEAR FORCES: PRESENT FORCE

Launcher	Number	Warheads per Launcher	Total Warheads	Yield in Megatons	Total Megatons	Equivalent Megatons	Reliability	Circular Error Probable
Minuteman II	450	1	450	1.0	450.0	450	0.80	1,800 ft.
Minuteman III	550	3	1,650	0.17	280.5	512	0.80	700 ft.
Titan II	54	1	54	9.0	486.0	232	0.75	3,000 ft.
Total ICBMs	1,054		2,154		1,216.5	1,194		
Polaris	160	1	160	0.6	96	163	0.80	3,000 ft.
Poseidon	496	10	4,960	0.04	198	595	0.80	1,500 ft.
Total SLBMs	656		5,120		294	758		
B-52 G/H	255	4 SRAM	1,020	0.2	204	347		
B-52D	75	4 Bombs	1,020	1.0	1,020	1,020		
		4 Bombs	300	1.0	300	300		
		2 SRAM	120	0.2	24	41		
FB-111	60	2 Bombs	120	1.0	120	120		
Total Bombers	390		2,580		1,668	1,828		
Grand Total	2,100		9,854		3,178.5	3,780		

Source: Congress of the United States, Congressional Budget Office, *Counterforce Issues for the U.S. Strategic Nuclear Forces.* Background Paper, January 1978, pp. 16-19.

TABLE 2

U.S. STRATEGIC NUCLEAR FORCES: MID-1980s PROJECTIONS

Launcher	Number	Warheads per Launcher	Total Warheads	Yield in Megatons	Total Megatons	Equivalent Megatons	Reliability	Circular Error Probable
Minuteman II	450	1	450	1.0	450.0	450	0.80	1,800 ft.
Minuteman III	550	3	1,650	0.17	280.5	512	0.80	700 ft.
(with MK-12A)	(550)	(3)	(1,650)	(0.35)	(572.5)	(825)	(0.80)	(600 ft.)
Titan II	54	1	54	9.0	486.0	232	0.75	3,000 ft.
Total ICBMs	1,054		2,154		1,216.5 (1,508.5)	1,194 (1,507)		
Poseidon	336	10	3,360	0.04	134	403	0.80	1,500 ft.
Poseidon C-4	160	8	1,280	0.10	128	282	0.80	1,500 ft.
Trident I	240	8	1,920	0.10	192	422	0.80	1,500 ft.
Total SLBMs	736		6,560		454	1,107		
B-52 G/H	165	6 SRAM	990	0.2	198	337		
B-52CM	165	4 Bombs / 20 ALCM / 2 SRAM	660 / 3,300 / 120	1.0 / 0.2 / 0.2	660 / 660 / 24	660 / 1,122 / 41		300 ft.
FB-111	60	2 Bombs	120	1.0	120	120		
Total Bombers	390		5,190		1,662	2,280		
Grand Total	2,180		13,904		3,332.5 (3,629.5)	4,581 (4,894)		

Source: Congress of the United States, Congressional Budget Office, Counterforce Issues for the U.S. Strategic Nuclear Forces. Background Paper, January 1978, pp. 16-19.

TABLE 3

ESTIMATED SOVIET STRATEGIC NUCLEAR FORCES, 1985

Launcher	Number	Warheads per Launcher	Total Warheads	Yield in Megatons	Total Megatons	Equivalent Megatons	Reliability	Circular Error Probable
SS-11	330	1	330	1.5	495	432	0.70	3,000 ft.
SS-17	200	4	800	0.6	480	560	0.75	1,500 ft.
SS-18	308	8	2,464	1.5	3,696	3,228	0.75	to
SS-19	500	6	3,000	0.8	2,400	2,580	0.75	1,200 ft.
SS-16	60	1	60	1.0	60	60	0.75	
Total ICBMs	1,398		6,654		7,131	6,860		
SS-N-6 SS-N-8	600	1	600	1.0	600	600	0.70	6,000 ft.
SS-N-17 SS-N-18	300	3	900	0.2	180	306	0.70	3,000 ft.
Total SLBMs	900		1,500		780	906		
Bear	100	1	100	20	2,000	740		
Bison	40	1	40	5	200	116		
(Backfire)	(250)	(2)	(500)	(0.2)	(100)	(170)		
Total Bombers	140 (390)		140 (640)		2,200 (2,300)	856 (1,026)		
Grand Total	2,438 (2,688)		8,294 (8,794)		10,111 (10,211)	8,622 (8,792)		

Source: Congress of the United States, Congressional Budget Office, Counterforce Issues for the U.S. Strategic Nuclear Forces. Background Paper, January 1978, pp. 16-19.

TABLE 4

U.S. STRATEGIC BALLISTIC MISSILES

System	Class	In Service	Fuel	Length/ Diameter	Range	Guidance	Weight/ Throw Weight	Warhead	Launch Platform
Polaris	SLBM	1964	Solid	31.3 ft./ 4.5 ft.	2500nm	Inertial	35000 lbs./ 1000 lbs.	3x200KT MIRV	1,2,3 *
Poseidon	SLBM	1971	Solid	34.1 ft./ 6.2 ft.	2500nm	Inertial	64000 lbs./ 2000 lbs.	6 to 14 MIRV	3,4,5 *
Trident I	SLBM	1979	Solid	34.1 ft./ 6.2 ft.	4000nm	Inertial/ equipped with digital computer	70000 lbs./ 3000+ lbs.	10 MK-4 MIRV	5,6 *
Trident II	SLBM	mid= 1980	Solid	45.8 ft./ 6.2 ft.	6000nm	Inertial/ equipped with digital computer	126000 lbs./ 5000+ lbs.	Unofficial, 17 MIRV's	6 *
Titan II	Heavy ICBM	1963	Liquid	103.0 ft./ 10.0 ft.	6296nm	Inertial	330000 lbs./ 8000 lbs.	MK-6 over 5 MT	Fixed Site
Minuteman II	Light ICBM	1965	Solid	57.6 ft./ 6.0 ft.	6080nm	Inertial	70000 lbs./ 2500 lbs.	MK-11B/ MK-11C	Fixed Site
Minuteman III	Light ICBM	1970	Solid	59.9 ft./ 6.0 ft.	6950nm	Inertial	76000 lbs./ 2500 lbs.	MK-12	Fixed Site

Source: Library of Congress, Congressional Research Service. Projected Strategic Offensive Weapons Inventories of the U.S. and USSR. An Unclassified Estimate. 1977, pp. 141-172.

*Sea-based Launch Platforms, Submarine Class: 1-George Washington, 2-Ethan Allen, 3-Lafayette, 4-James Madison, 5-Benjamin Franklin, 6-Ohio.

TABLE 5

U.S. NON-STRATEGIC MISSILES

SYSTEM	ROLE	GUIDANCE	PROPELLANT	WARHEAD	LAUNCH WEIGHT/ LENGTH	SPEED/ RANGE
Nike-Hercules Air-defense Missile	Surface to air guided missile	Command	Solid	Nuclear or HE	4858 kg/ 12.1 m	super-sonic/ 140 km
Tomahawk Sea-Launched Cruise Missile (Strategic variant)		Inertial plus active radar homing	Solid	454 kg HE Bullpup B	-- 6.25 m	880 km/h --
Harpoon RGM-84A	Anti-ship tactical cruise missile	Pre-programmed references, radar altimeter, electromechanical control active radar; terminal guidance	Solid	HE penetrating	667 kg/ 4.57 m	-- 90 km+
U.S. Navy Tomahawk (Tactical variant)	Cruise missile	Command; TERCOM	Solid	HE directed blast	80 kg/ 2.89 m	Mach 1.2/ 3000 m
Lance MGM-52C	Mobile surface-to-surface tactical guided missile	Inertial	Liquid	Nuclear or HE	1527 kg/ 6.14 m	Mach 3/ 120 km

204

TABLE 5 (Cont.)

SYSTEM	ROLE	GUIDANCE	PROPELLANT	WARHEAD	LAUNCH WEIGHT/ LENGTH	SPEED/ RANGE
Pershing Battlefield Support Missile MGM-31A	Land mobile air-transportable surface-to-surface tactical ballistic missile	Inertial	Solid	Nuclear	4600 kg/ 10.5 m	Mach 8/ 740 km
Sergeant Battlefield Support Missile MGM-29A	Surface-to-surface tactical guided missile	Inertial	Solid	Nuclear or HE	4536 kg/ 10.5 m	Super-sonic/ 140 km
Hound Dog (AGM-28B)	Air-to-ground missile	Inertial	Pratt and Whitney J52-P-3 turbojet	Nuclear	4500 kg/ 13 m	Mach 2+/ 960 km
Walleye	Air-to-surface missile					
I		Television	none	Conventional HE	499 kg/ 344 cm	-- --
II		Television	none	Conventional HE	1061 kg/ 404 cm	-- --
III		Television	none	SEE WALLEYE II		
Shrike (AGM-45A)	Air-to-surface missile	Passive radar homing	Solid	HE fragmentation	177 kg/ 304.8 cm	Mach 2/ 12-16 km
SRAM (AGM-69A)	Short-range attack missile	Inertial	Solid	Nuclear	1000 kg/ 425 cm	Mach 3/ 60-160 km
Maverick (AGM-65A)	Air-to-surface missile	TV-homing system	Solid	HE-conical shaped charge	209 kg/ 246 cm	-- --
(AGM-65C) Laser Maverick		Laser Designation				
(AGM-65D) Infra-red Maverick		IIR-Imaging Infra-red;				

ALCM (AGM-86)	Air-launched cruise missile	TERCOM	Williams F107-WR-100 turbofan	Nuclear	900 kg/ 4.26 m	high sub-sonic/ 1300 km
ASLAM	Advanced Strategic Air launched cruise missile	Inertial; TERCOM	Ramjet with sustainer	Nuclear	900 kg/ 4.26 m	-- 1300 km+
Bullpup A (AGM-12)	Air-to-surface tactical missile	Radio Command; optical tracking to target	Liquid	Conventional HE or nuclear	258 kg/ 3.2 m	app. Mach 2/ 11 km
Bullpup B					812 kg/ 4.07 m	-- 17 km
Standard (RIM 66 and RIM 67) (Successors to Terrier and Talos)	Shipborne Surface-to-air missile					
SM-1		conical-scan semi-active radar homing	Solid	Conventional HE	590 kg/ 4.57 m	Mach 2+/ 18 km+
SM-2		Inertial	Solid	Conventional HE	1060 kg/ 8.23 m	Mach 2.5+/ 55 km+
Talos	Surface-to-air missile	Semi-active radar homing	Solid w/ liquid sustainer	HE and Nuclear	-- 9.53 m	Mach 2.5/ 120 km+
Tartar	Medium-range surface-to-air Shipboard guided missile	Semi-active radar homing	Solid	HE	-- 4.6 m	Mach 2/ 16 km+

TABLE 5 (Cont.)

SYSTEM	ROLE	GUIDANCE	PROPELLANT	WARHEAD	LAUNCH WEIGHT/ LENGTH	SPEED/ RANGE
Terrier	Surface-to-air anti-aircraft missile	Semi-active radar homing	Solid	HE	1400 kg/ 8. m	Mach 2.5/ 35 km
Dragon Anti-tank Assault Weapon M-47	Anti-tank Guided missile	Wire-guided; Command to line of sight	Solid	Shaped charge	12.25 kg/ --	--/ 1 km
Shillelagh Close support Weapon	Land mobile Surface-to surface guided weapon system	Infra-red	Solid	Shaped charge	27 kg/ 1.14 m	--/ 4500 m+
TOW	Heavy anti-tank guided weapon system	Wire-guided optically tracked	Solid	HE shaped charge, armor piercing	18 kg/ 117 cm	1000 km/h / 3500 m
Chaparral (M-48	Ground-to-air heat-seeking missile	Infra-red homing; optical aiming	Solid	HE	84 kg/ 2.91 m	Super-sonic/ --
Hawk MIM-23A and 23B	Surface-to-air missile	Semi-active homing	Solid	HE fragmentation	580 kg/ 5.12 m	Super-sonic/ --
Patriot	Land-mobile surface-to-air guided weapon	Command w/ semi-active radar homing	Solid	Nuclear or HE	--/ 5.2 m	Super-sonic
Redeye	Shoulder-fired guided missile system	Optical aiming; infra-red homing	Solid	HE	13 kg/ 1.22 m	Super-sonic/ --
Stinger (Successor to Redeye)	Man-portable anti-aircraft missile	Passive infra-red homing	Solid		--/ 152. cm	
TGSM (Terminally Guided Sub-Missile)	Unpowered missile-launched guided anti-armor missile	Passive infra-red homing	Provided by delivery system	HE	16 kg/ 89. cm	--/ with Lance 160 km

	Cannon-launched guided projectile	Terminal	Launched from Conventional Howitzers	Shaped Charge	warhead weight	
Copperhead M712	Cannon-launched guided projectile				22.5 kg/137.2 cm	--/20 km
Standard ARM (AGM-76)	Anti-radiation missile	Passive radar homing	Solid dual thrust	HE	635 kg/4.5 m	Super-sonic/25 km+
HARM (AGM-88A)	High-speed anti-radiation missile	Passive radar homing	Solid	HE	354 kg/4.17 m	Super-sonic
Hellfire	Tactical air-to-surface missile	Laser-seeking; RF/IR seekers	--	--	43 kg/178 mm	--/--
Brazo	Air-to-air anti-radiation missile	Passive radar homing	--	--	--/--	--/--
Falcon (AIM-4D)	Air-to-air missile	Infra-red homing	Solid	HE	60 kg/198 cm	Mach 4/--
Super Falcon (AIM 4E/F)	Air-to-air missile	Semi-active radar homing	Solid	HE	E-63.5 kg, F-68 kg/218.4 cm	Mach 3/--
AIM 4G	Air-to-air missile	Infra-red homing	Solid	HE	65.7 kg/105.7 cm	Mach 3/--
Falcon (AIM 26 A/B)	Air-to-air missile	Radar homing	Solid	HE	90. kg/213.4 cm	--/--
Genie (AIR-2A)	Air-to-air missile	None	Solid	Nuclear	370. kg/274. cm	Mach 3/9.6 km
Phoenix (AIM-59A)	Air-to-air missile	Semi-active radar homing	Solid	--	380 kg/396 cm	110-165 km
Sidewinder (AIM 9)	Air-to-air missile	Infra-red homing	Solid	HE	75 kg/284 cm	Mach 2/1700 m
Sparrow (AIM 7E/F)	Air-to-air missile	Semi-active radar guidance	Solid	HE	200 kg/3.65 m	--/25 km

TABLE 6

U.S. STRATEGIC BOMBERS

SYSTEM	IN SERVICE	WING SPAN/ LENGTH	POWERPLANT/ SERVICE CEILING	MAXIMUM SPEED AT ALTITUDE	RANGE/ WEIGHT	WEAPONS LOADING AND ARMAMENT
FB-111A Medium Bomber, Intermediate Range	1969	WS: Fully spread-63 ft. Fully swept-31.11 ft. L: 73.5 ft.	Two Pratt and Whitney TF 30-P-7 Turbofans, each rated at 20,350 lbs. thrust with after burning. SC: over 60,000 ft.	2.5 Mach at sea level, 1.2 Mach	R: (with max. internal) over 3300 nm. Wt.(Max T.O.): 91,500 lbs.	Up to 35,000 lbs.; four AGM-69A Short Range Attack Missiles (SRAM) on external pylons, plus 2 in the weapons bay.
B-52 G/H	1959	WS: 185 ft. L: 157.7 ft.	Eight Pratt and Whitney J57-P-43W Turbofans, rated at 17,000 lbs. thrust for G series; Eight Pratt and Whitney TF 33 Turbo-fans, each rated at 17,000 lbs. thrust for H series. SC: over 50,000 ft.	over 565 knots	R: 8684 nm. Wt.(Max T.O.): 488,000 lbs.	G and H series can carry 20 AGM-69A Short-Range Attack Missiles (SRAM's) under each wing and eight in the bomb bay, or an equal number of ALCM's. For H series, Vulcan multi-barrel tail guns.
B-1 Heavy Bomber, Long Range	----	WS: Fully spread-136.7 ft. Fully swept-78.2 ft. L: 150.2 ft.	---	1.6 Mach	R: Approx. 5300+ nm. (unrefueled) WT.(Gross T.O.): 395	Three internal weapons bays, accommodating a total of 24 SRAM's on three rotary dispensers, or 75,000 lbs. of free fall bombs. Provision for 8 more SRAM's or 40,000 lbs. of free fall weapons externally.

TABLE 7

U.S. BALLISTIC MISSILE SUBMARINES

CLASS	IN SERVICE	DISPLACEMENT	LENGTH	MAIN PROPULSION MACHINERY	SPEED	MISSILE LAUNCHERS/ TYPE	TORPEDO TUBES/ SIZE/ LOCATION
GEORGE WASHINGTON SSBN	1960	5900 tons/surface 6700 tons/sub- merged	381.7 ft	Nuclear reactor; pressurized, water- cooled; 2 geared tur- bines 15,000 shp; one shaft	20 knots/ surface; 30 knots/ submerged	16 tubes/ Polaris A-3	6/21 inch forward
ETHAN ALLEN SSBN	1961	6900 tons/surface 7900 tons/sub- merged	410.5 ft	Nuclear reactor; pressurized, water- cooled; 2 geared tur- bines; 15,000 shp; one shaft	20 knots/ surface; 30 knots/ submerged	16 tubes/ Polaris A-3	4/21 inch forward
LAFAYETTE MADISON FRANKLIN SSBN's	1963 (for Lafayette)	6650 tons/ light surfaced 7320 tons standard on surface 8250 tons submerged	425 ft	Nuclear reactor; pressurized, water- cooled; 2 geared tur- bines; 15,000 shp; one shaft	20 knots/ surface; 30 knots/ submerged	16 tubes/ Polaris A-3 on some La- fayette class, Posei- don C-3 on all others	4/21 inch forward
OHIO SSBN's	1979	1200 tons/ surface; 18700 tons/ submerged	560 ft	Nuclear reactor; pressurized, water-cooled; geared turbines, ? shp; one shaft	?	24 tubes/ Trident I or Trident II	4/?/ forward

TABLE 8

UNITED STATES AIRCRAFT

AIRCRAFT SYSTEM	IN SERVICE	ROLE	POWERPLANT	SPEED/ RANGE	WEIGHT	WING SPAN/ LENGTH	ARMAMENT
T-34-C (Turbo Mentor)	1976	Navy 2-seat turbine powered trainer	1-533 hp. Pratt and Whitney PT6A-25 turboprop engine	288 mph/ 749 miles	4742 lb.	WS: 33.3 7/8 ft. L: 28.8½ ft.	none
T-42A (Cochise)	1976	Army trainer	2-260 hp. Continental IO-470-L flat-six engines.	236 mph/ 1085 miles	5100 lb.	WS: 37.10 ft. L: 28. ft.	none
VC-6B (USAF) T-44A (Army)	1976	Trainer	2-550 hp. Pratt and Whitney PT6A-21 turboprop engines	(Cruising) 256 mph/ 1384 miles	9650 lb.	WS: 50.3 ft. L: 35.6 ft.	none
U-21F (Army)	1971	Utility aircraft	2-680 hp. Pratt and Whitney PT6A-28 turboprop engines.	(Cruising) 285 mph/ 1089 miles	11,800 lb.	WS: 45.10½ ft. L: 39.11 3/8 ft.	none
C-12A (USAF, Army) RU-21J	mid-1970's	Transport	2-805 hp. Pratt and Whitney PT6A-41 turboprop engines. C-12-A-2 PT6A-38 engines.	333 mph/ 2023 miles	12,500 lb.	WS: 54.6 ft. L: 43.10 ft.	none
UH-1D/H-Bell (Army)	1963	General Purpose helicopter	1-1400 hp. Lycoming T53-L-13 turboshaft	127 mph/ 318 miles	9,500 lb.	(Rotor diameter): 48. ft. L:57.1 ft.	none
OH-58-Bell (Army)	1969	Observation helicopter	1-317 hp. Allison T63-A-700 turboshaft engine	138 mph/ 305 miles	3,000 lb.	(Rotor diameter): 35.4 ft. L: 40.11 3/4 ft.	none

	Year	Type	Engine	Speed/Range	Weight	Dimensions	Armament
AH-1G (Huey Cobra) (Army)	1967	Attack helicopter	1-1400 hp Lycoming T53-L-13 turboshaft engine	219 mph/ 357 miles	9,500 lb.	(Rotor diameter): 44 ft. L: 52.11½ ft.	XM-28-mounting either 2 mini-guns with 4000 rounds each; 2 XM-129 40 mm. grenade launchers, each with 300 rounds; or one minigun and one grenade launcher •four external stores under stub wings accommodate seventy-six 2.75 rockets in 4 packs; 28 rockets in four packs or 2 minigun pods. •XM-35 20mm cannon is available.
AH-1J (Sea Cobra) (USMC)	1974	Attack helicopter	1-1800 hp Pratt and Whitney T400-CP-400 coupled free-turbine turbo-shaft engine	207 mph/ 359 miles	10,000 lb.	(Rotor diameter): 44 ft. L: 53.4 ft.	Electrically driven 20mm turret system houses an XM-197 three barrel weapon. •four external attachment stores under stub wings accommodate stores including 7.62 mm minigun pod as well as 2.75 rockets.

TABLE 8 (Cont.)

AIRCRAFT SYSTEM	IN SERVICE	ROLE	POWERPLANT	SPEED/ RANGE	WEIGHT	WING SPAN/ LENGTH	ARMAMENT
AH-1T (Sea Cobra) (USMC)	1976-77	Attack helicopter	1-1970 hp Pratt and Whitney T400-WV-402 free-turbine turboshaft engine	-- --	14,000 lb.	(Rotor diameter): 48 ft. L: 56.11 ft.	none
UH-1N (Navy, USMC USAF)	1970	General purpose helicopter	2-Pratt and Whitney PT6 turbo-shaft engines, each 1800 hp	126 mph/ --	11,200 lb.	(Rotor diameter): 48.2¼ ft. L: 57.3¾ ft.	none
XV-15 (Army)	late 1970's	Tilt-rotor research aircraft	2-Lycoming T53 turboshaft engines, each 1800 hp	(Cruising) 380 mph/ --	15,000 lb.	WS: 32.2 ft. (Rotor diameter): 25 ft. L: 41.1¼ ft.	none
YAH-63 (Army)	proto-type	Advanced attack helicopter	2-1536 hp General electric T700-GE-700 turboshaft engines	(Forward speed) 163.5 mph	15,940 lb.	WS: 17.2 2/5 ft. (Rotor diameter): 51 ft. L: 60.8 4/5 ft.	XM-188 3-barrel 30mm cannon, mounted in turret FLIR Technology •Four underwing pylons, carry up to 16 TOW or 76-2.75 rockets or combinations.
VC-137 (USAF)	mid-1950's	Tanker/ Transport	4-Pratt and Whitney JT3D-7 turbofan engines, each 19,000 lb. thrust	627 mph/ 7475 miles	330,600 lb.	WS: 145.9 ft. L: 152.11 ft.	none
T-43A (USAF)	1967	Short-range transport	2-Pratt and Whitney JT8D turbofan engines	586 mph/ 2530 miles	129,000 lb.	WS: 93 ft. L: 100 ft.	none

Aircraft	Type	Date	Engines	Speed/Range	Weight	Dimensions	Armament
E-3A (USAF)	AWACS Aircraft	mid-1970's	4-Pratt and Whitney TF33-P-7 turbofans each 21,000 lb. thrust	see VC-137	see VC-137	see VC-137	none
E-4 (USAF)	Advanced airborne command post	late 1970's early 1980's	4-Pratt and Whitney JT9D engines	--	--	WS: 195.8 ft. L: 231.4 ft.	none
YC-14 (USAF)	Advanced STOL transport	late 1970's	2-General Electric CF6-50D two-shaft high bypass ratio turbofan engines, each 51,000 lb. thrust	504 mph/ ferry range, 3190 miles	STOL Wt.: 170,000 lb. Max. T.O.Wt. 237,000 lb.	WS: 129 ft. L: 131.8 ft.	none
CH-47C (Chinook) (Army)	Medium transport helicopter	1961	2-3750 hp 755-L-11C Lycoming turboshaft engines	178 mph/ (Mission radius): 115 miles	38,500 lb.	(Rotor diameter): 60 ft. L: 99 ft.	none
YUH-61A (Army)	Transport	late 1970's	2-1500 hp General Electric T700-GE-700 turboshaft engines	178 mph/ 370 miles	15,157 lb.	(Rotor diameter): 49 ft. L: 60.8 2/5 ft.	none
U-3 (USAF)	Five or Six-seat monoplane	mid 1950's	2-285 hp Continental IO-520M flat-six engines	283 mph/ 569 miles	5,500 lb.	WS: 36.11 ft. L: 31.11½ ft.	none

TABLE 8 (Cont.)

AIRCRAFT SYSTEM	IN SERVICE	ROLE	POWERPLANT	SPEED/ RANGE	WEIGHT	WING SPAN/ LENGTH	ARMAMENT
T-37B (USAF)	1959	Two-seat Jet trainer	2-Continental J69-T-25 turbojets, 1025 lb. thrust	402 mph/ 943 miles	7,500 lb.	WS: 33.9½ ft. L: 29.3 ft.	Provision for 2-250 lb. bombs or 4-Sidewinder missiles
A-37B (USAF)	late 1960's	2-seat light strike aircraft	2-General Electric J85-GE-17A turbojets	524 mph/ 460 miles	14,000 lb.	WS: 35.10½ ft. L: 28.3¼ ft.	•7.62mm mini-gun in forward fuselage •each wing has four pylons-2 inner pylons carrying 870 lb. each, inter-mediate pylon carrying 600 lb. and outer pylon carrying 500 lb.
O-2A (USAF)	1967	Air control aircraft	2-210 hp Continental IO-360-C flat-six engines	206 mph/ 1140 miles	4,360 lb.	WS: 38.2 ft. L: 29.9 ft.	Four underwing pylons for external stores of rockets, flares or other light ordnance.
AU-23A (USAF) (Peacemaker) -license from Switzerland-	1966- 67	Counter-insurgency aircraft	1-650 hp Garrett TPE 331-1-101F engine	174 mph/ 558 miles	6,100 lb.	WS: 49.8 ft. L: 36.10 ft.	Under-fuselage hard point capable of carrying 600 lb. ordnance store and 4 under-wing hardpoints, in-board pair carries 575 lb. each and outboard pair carries 350 lb. each

Aircraft	Date	Role	Engines	Speed / Range	Weight	Dimensions	Armament
A-10A (USAF)	mid-1970's	Single-seat close support aircraft	2-General Electric TF-34-GE-100 high bypass ratio turbofans, each 9065 lb. thrust	518 mph/(ferry range): 2647 miles	47,400 lb.	WS: 57.6 ft. L: 53.4 ft.	•Avenger 30mm seven-barrel cannon; 4 pylons under each wing, one inboard, three outboard and three under fuselage for maximum external load of 16000 lb.
F-111A	mid-1960's	Tactical fighter bomber	2-Pratt and Whitney TF30-P-1 turbofan engines	Mach 2.2/3165 miles	91,500 lb.	WS: 63 ft. L: 73.6 ft.	One M61 multi-barrel 20mm gun or two 750 lb. bombs in internal weapons bay •four external pylons under each wing.
F-16A	1974	Single-seat light-weight air combat aircraft	1-Pratt and Whitney F100-PW-100 turbofan engine, rated 25000 lb. thrust	Mach 2.0/(ferry range): 2303 miles	27,000 lb.	WS: 32.10 ft. L: 47.7 2/3 ft.	•M-61A1 gun; mounting for an infra-red air-to-air missile on each wingtip, one under fuselage hardpoint and six underwing hardpoints for additional stores. Typical load includes Sidewinder missiles.
E-2C (Hawkeye)	1975	Air-borne early warning aircraft	2-4591 hp Allison T56-A-422/425 turboprop engines	374 mph/(ferry range): 1605 miles	51,569 lb.	WS: 80.7 ft. L: 57.7 ft.	none

216

TABLE 8 (Cont.)

AIRCRAFT SYSTEM	IN SERVICE	ROLE	POWERPLANT	SPEED/ RANGE	WEIGHT	WING SPAN/ LENGTH	ARMAMENT
A-6E (Intruder)	late 1970's	Two-seat carrier-based attack bomber	2-Pratt and Whitney J52-P-8A turbojet engines 9300 lb. thrust each	793 mph/ 1924 miles	58,600 lb. (Catapult)	WS: 53 ft. L: 54.7 ft.	•Five weapons attachment points each carry 3600 lb. load. Typical load, 30-500 lb. bombs, in clusters of six.
F-14A (Tomcat)	early 1970's	Two-seat carrier-based multi-role fighter	2-Pratt and Whitney TF30-P-412A turbofan engines, 20,900 lb. thrust with after-burning	Mach 2.4 --	74,348 lb.	WS: 64.1½ ft. L: 61.10½ ft.	1-M-61A1 Vulcan 20mm gun; 4 Sparrow air-to-air missiles mounted under fuselage; 2 wing pylons, one under each fixed wing section carry 4 Sidewinder missiles or a mix of Sparrow, Phoenix and Sidewinder missiles.
TH-55A (Osage) (Army)	1961	Light helicopter	1-180 hp Lycoming HIO-360-A1A flat-four engine	87 mph/ 300 miles	1,670 lb.	(Rotor diameter): 25.3½ ft. L: 28.10 3/4 ft.	none
OH-6 (Cayuse) (Army)	late 1960's	Army light observation helicopter	1-317 hp Allison T63-A-5A turboshaft engine	150 mph/ 380 miles	2,400 lb.	(Rotor diameter): 26.4 ft. L: 30.3 3/4 ft.	Provision for armament on port side of fuselage, to include, XM-27 7.62 mm machine gun or XM-75 grenade launcher.

Name	Date	Type	Engines	Performance	Weight	Dimensions	Armament/Features
YAH-64 (Army)	late 1970's	Advanced attack helicopter	2-1536 hp General Electric T700-GE-700 turboshaft engines	191 mph/ 359 miles	17,400 lb.	(Rotor diameter): 48 ft. L: 49.4½ ft.	• XM-230, 30mm chain; four underwing hardpoints which carry 16 TOW anti-tank missiles or up to 76 2.75 mm rockets in launchers or a combination thereof.
SH-2F (Seasprite) (Navy)	1973	ASW and anti-missile defense helicopter	2-1350 hp General Electric T58-GE-8F turboshaft engines	165 mph/ 422 miles	12,800 lb.	(Rotor diameter): 44 ft. L: 52.7 ft.	• Active and passive sonobuoys, electric support measures; ASW homing torpedos
P-3C (Orion) (Navy)	early 1970's	ASW turboprop aircraft	4-4910 hp Allison T56-A-14 turboprop engines	473 mph/ max. mission radius, 2383 miles	135,000 lb.	WS: 99.8 ft. L: 116.10 ft.	• Bombay to accommodate a 20000 lb. mine, 3-1000 lb. mines, 3 Mk57 depth bombs, eight Mk-54 depth bombs and eight torpedos; ten underwing pylons for additional stores.

TABLE 8 (Cont.)

AIRCRAFT SYSTEM	IN SERVICE	ROLE	POWERPLANT	SPEED/ RANGE	WEIGHT	WING SPAN/ LENGTH	ARMAMENT
S-3A (Viking)	1974	Carrier-borne ASW aircraft	2-General Electric TF34-GE-2 turbofan engines, each 9275 lb. thrust	518 mph/ combat range, 2303 miles	52,539 lb.	WS: 68.8 ft. L: 53.4 ft.	•Split weapons bay equipped with bomb rack assemblies to carry 4 Mk-36 destructors, 4-Mk-46 torpedos, 4-Mk-82 bombs, two Mk-57 depth bombs or four Mk-54 bombs. •Bombracks on wing pylons carry flare launchers, mines and cluster bombs.
C-130H (USAF) (Hercules)	1964	Medium- long range combat trans- port	4-4508 hp. Al- lison.T56-A-15 turboprop engines	(Cruising) 386 mph/ 5135 miles	175,000 lb.	WS: 132.7 ft. L: 106.4 ft.	none
C-141 (USAF) (Starlifter)		Medium- long range logistical and combat transport	4-Pratt and Whitney TF33- P-7 turbofan engines	505 mph	325,000 lb.	WS: 160 ft. L: 145 ft.	none
C-5A (USAF) (Galaxy)	early 1970's	Long-range logistical transport	4-General Electric TF39-GE-1 turbofan engines, each 41,000 lb. thrust	571 mph/ 3749 miles	220,000 lb; with payload, 769,000 lb.	WS: 222.8½ ft. L: 247.10 ft.	none

F-4B (Navy, Marine Corps)		Two-seat all-weather fighter	2-General Electric J79-GE-8 turbojet engines each 17,000 lb. thrust /w/ afterburning	over Mach 2/ combat radius, over 1000 miles	54,600 lb.	WS: 38.5 ft. L: 58.3 ft.	•Six Sparrow III or 4 Sparrow III and four Sidewinder air-to-air missiles on four mountings, under fuselage and two underwing mountings; provision for alternate loads of nuclear and conventional bombs and missiles (16,000 lb)
F-15A (Eagle)	1976	Single-seat air superiority fighter	2-Pratt and Whitney F100-PW-100 turbofan engines	Mach 2.5/ (ferry range): 3450 miles	41,500 lb.	WS: 42.9 3/4 ft. L: 63.9 ft.	•Twin under-fuselage gun racks for 20mm cannon; single 1000 lb. stores on fuselage centerline; three stores under each wing, outer wing store carries Sidewinder missile.
AV-8B (Advanced Harrier)	in development	V/STOL aircraft	1-Rolls-Royce Bristol Pegasus 11 Vectored-thrust turbofan engine	-- vertical TO, 115 miles short TO, 748 miles	30,000 lb.	WS: 30.3½ ft. L: 42.10 3/4 ft.	•Twin under-fuselage gun racks for 20 mm cannon; single 1000 lb. stores on fuselage centerline; three stores under each wing, outer wing store carries Sidewinder.

TABLE 8 (Cont.)

AIRCRAFT SYSTEM	IN SERVICE	ROLE	POWERPLANT	SPEED/ RANGE	WEIGHT	WING SPAN/ LENGTH	ARMAMENT
F-18	early 1980's	Single-seat carrier-based air-combat fighter	2-General Electric F404-GE-400 low bypass turbojet engines, each 16000 lb. thrust	Mach 1.8/ combat radius, 460 miles	44,000 lb.	WS: 37.6 ft. L: 55.7 ft.	•Nine weapons stations, combined weapons load of 13,000 lb. of ordnance. including station for Sidewinder and Sparrow missiles.
C-9A (USAF)	1965	Short-medium range aircraft, transport	2-Pratt and Whitney JT8D turbofan engines	(Cruising) 564 mph/ 1831 miles, (ferry range): 2199 miles	77,000 lb.	WS: 89.5 ft. L: 104.4 3/4 ft.	none
C-9B (Skytrain) (Navy)	1973	Short-medium range transport aircraft	2-Pratt and Whitney JT8D turbofan engines	(Cruising) 576 mph/ 2923 miles	110,000 lb.	WS: 93.5 ft. L: 119.3½ ft.	none
A-4M (Navy)	1970	Single-seat attack bomber	1-11,200 lb. thrust Pratt and Whitney J52-P-408 turbojet engine	646 mph/ (ferry range): 2000 miles	24,000 lb.	WS: 27.6 ft. L: 40.4 ft.	3500 lb. weapons capacity; armament includes nuclear or HE bombs, Sidewinder and Bullpup bombs.
F-5A (USAF)	early 1960's	Light tactical fighter and reconnaissance	2-General Electric J85-GE-13 turbojets each 4080 lb. thrust	Mach 1.4/ 1387 miles	20,677 lb.	WS: 25.3 ft. L: 47.2 ft.	•Two Sidewinder missiles on wing-tip launchers and 2-20mm guns in fuselage nose. •five pylons, one under fuselage, two under each wing.

Aircraft	Year	Type	Engines	Performance	Weight	Dimensions	Armament
F-5E (USAF)	1973	Single-seat light tactical fighter	2-General Electric J85-GE-21 turbojet engines, each 5000 lb. thrust	Mach 1.63/1595 miles /w/ tanks	24,675 lb.	WS: 26.8 ft. L: 48.2 ft.	2 Sidewinder missiles on wingtip launchers; 2-20mm cannons in fuselage nose; up to 7000 lb. mixed ordnance.
YF-17	proto-type	Single-seat light-weight fighter	2-General Electric YJ101-GE-100 turbojet engines, each 14000 lb. thrust	above Mach 2/ (Radius of action): 576 miles	--	WS: 35 ft. L: 56 ft.	1-M61 20mm gun in fuselage nose; one Sidewinder missile on each wingtip.
T-2C (Navy)	late 1960's	General Purpose Jet Trainer	2-2950 lb. thrust General Electric J85-GE-4 turbojet engines	522 mph/ 1047 miles	13,179 lb.	WS: 38.1¼ ft. L: 38.3½ ft.	•Guns, practice bombs, practice bomb clusters, rocket launchers, carried in two store stations.
OV-10A	1968-69	2-Seat Multi-purpose counter insurgency aircraft	2-715 hp Ai-Research T76-G-416/417 turbo-props	(without weapons), 281 mph/ (combat radius), 228 miles	9908 lb.	WS: 40 ft. L: 41.7 ft.	•2 weapons attachment points each with 600 lb. weapons capacity under each wing; additional attachment points under fuselage, 1200 lb. capacity.
XFV-12A (Navy)	Proto-type, flown 1976	Single-seat all-weather V/STOL fighter/ attack aircraft	1-Pratt and Whitney F401-PW-400 afterburning engine, 30,000 lb. thrust	greater than Mach 2 --	Vertical TO-19,500 lb. Short TO-24,250 lb.	WS: 28.6¼ ft. L: 43.11 ft.	•Carries air-to-air and air-to-ground missiles and inner gun in fuselage.

TABLE 8 (Cont.)

AIRCRAFT SYSTEM	IN SERVICE	ROLE	POWERPLANT	SPEED/ RANGE	WEIGHT	WING SPAN/ LENGTH	ARMAMENT
Sh-3D (Seaking) (Navy)	1966	Amphibious all-weather ASW helicopter	2-1400 hp General Electric T58-GE-10 turboshaft engines	166 mph/ 625 miles	18,626 lb.	(Rotor diameter): 62 ft. L: 72.8 ft.	•Provision for 840 lb. of weapons including homing torpedos.
CH-3E (USAF)	late 1960's	Amphibious transport helicopter	2-1500 hp General Electric T58-GE-5 turboshaft engines	162 mph/ 465 miles	22.050 lb.	(Rotor diameter): 62 ft. L: 73 ft.	none
CH-54B Tahre (Skycrane) (Army)	late 1960's	Heavy-flying crane helicopter	2-Pratt and Whitney T73-P-1 turboshaft engines	126 mph/ 230 miles	42,000 lb.	(Rotor diameter): 72 ft. L: 88.6 ft.	none
CH-53A (Sea Stallion) (Navy)	1966	Heavy assault transport helicopter	2-2850 hp General Electric T64-GE-6 turboshaft engines	-- --	app. 37,000 lb.	(Rotor diameter): 72.3 ft. L: 88.3 ft.	none
RH-53D (Navy)	early 1970's	Mine-countermeasure helicopter	2-General Electric T64-GE-413A 7560 hp turboshaft engines	-- --	50,000 lb.	see CH-53A	•Two 0.50 machine guns to detonate surface mines.

XH-59A (Army)	Proto-type	Research helicopter	1-Pratt and Whitney PT6T-3 Turbo-Twin; Provision for 2 Pratt and Whitney J60 turbojet engines	-- / --	--	(Rotor diameter): 36 ft. L: 41.5 ft.	none
YUH-60A (Army)	Proto-type	Combat assault squad transport helicopter	2-1536 hp General Electric T700-GE-700 turboshaft engines	198 mph/ --	21,400 lb.	(Rotor diameter): 53.8 ft. L: 16.5 ft.	• Side-firing machine gun.
A-7 (Corsair)	1968	Subsonic tactical fighter	1-Allison TF-41-A-1 non-after-burning engine	646 mph/ (ferry range) 2871 miles	42,000 lb.	WS: 38.9 ft. L: 46.1½ ft.	• Total ordnance weight of 15,000 lb. carried on six underwing pylons and two fuselage stations.

TABLE 9

USSR STRATEGIC BALLISTIC MISSILES

SYSTEM	CLASS	IN SERVICE	FUEL	LENGTH/DIAMETER	RANGE	GUIDANCE	WEIGHT/THROW WEIGHT	WARHEAD	LAUNCH PLATFORM
SS-N-5	Medium-Range SLBM	1963	Solid	32.8 ft/4.9 ft	700 nm	Inertial	36000 lb/2000 lb	Single RV	HOTEL II-class SSBN
SS-N-6	Medium-Range SLBM	MOD I-1968, MOD II-1974, MOD III-1974	Liquid	42.5 ft/5.9 ft	MOD I 1300 nm, MOD II/III 1600 nm	Inertial	400000 lb/2000 lb	MOD I/II-Single RV, MOD III-Carries 2-3 MRV's	YANKEE-class SSBN
SS-N-8	Long-Range SLBM	1973	Liquid	?/5.9 ft	4200 nm	Inertial	400000+ lb/2000 lb	Single RV	DELTA-class SSBN
SS-7	Medium ICBM	MOD I/II 1962, MOD III 1963	Liquid	98-115 ft/9.8 ft	6000 nm	Probably inertial	?/8000 lb	Single RV	Fixed Site
SS-8	Medium ICBM	1963	Liquid	82.0 ft/9.0 ft	6000 nm	Inertial	140000 lb/8000 lb	Single RV	Fixed Site
SS-9	Heavy ICBM	MOD I 1967, MOD II 1966, MOD III 1969, MOD IV 1971	Liquid	114.8 ft/9.8 ft	6500+ nm	Inertial	?/10-15000 lb	*1	Fixed Site
SS-11	Light ICBM	MOD I 1966, MOD II/III 1973	Liquid	65.6 ft/8.2 ft	5600+ nm	Probably Inertial	?/2000 lb	*2	Fixed Site
SS-13	Light ICBM	1969	Solid	65.7 ft/ 1st stage-67 in. 2nd stage-55 in. 3rd stage-39 in.	4300+ nm	Inertial	80000 lb/2000 lb	Single RV	Fixed Site

Designation	Type	Year/MOD	Propellant	Length/Diameter	Range	Guidance	Weight	Reentry Vehicle	Basing
SS-16 (replaces SS-13)	Light ICBM	?	Solid	65.6 ft/8.2 ft	5000+ nm	Advanced Inertial	? 2000 lb	Single RV	Fixed Site
SS-17 (Replaces SS-11)	Medium ICBM	1965	Liquid	78.7 ft/8.2 ft	5000 nm	Probably Inertial	? 5000 lb	4-6 MIRV	Fixed Site
SS-18 (Replaces SS-9)	Heavy ICBM	MOD I 1974 MOD II/III ?	Liquid	121.4 ft/9.8 ft	5500+ nm	Inertial, plus onboard digital computer	? 15000 lb	*3	Fixed Site
SS-19 (Replaces SS-11)	Medium ICBM	1974	Liquid	65.6 ft/8.2 ft	5000+ nm	Inertial	? 7000 lb	4-6 MIRV	Fixed Site

*1 - SS-9 MOD I   Single Reentry Vehicle
SS-9 MOD II   Single Reentry Vehicle
SS-9 MOD III Depressed trajectory and FOBS test vehicle; not operational.
SS-9 MOD IV   Test vehicle for Soviet research on MIRV's carries 3 MRV's.

*2   SS-11 MOD I   Single Reentry Vehicle
SS-11 MOD II   Single Reentry Vehicle; has been tested with aids designed to assist penetration of ABM system
SS-11 MOD III 3 MRV warheads.

*3- SS-18 MOD I   Single Reentry Vehicle
SS-18 MOD II   Carries 5-8 MIRV's.
SS-18 MOD III Single Reentry Vehicle But with more accuracy and lighter than MOD I.

TABLE 10

USSR NON-STRATEGIC MISSILES

SYSTEM	ROLE	GUIDANCE	PROPELLANT	WARHEAD	LAUNCH WEIGHT/ LENGTH	SPEED/ RANGE
AT-1 (Snapper)	Surface-to-surface anti-tank missile	Wire-guided; command to line of sight	Solid	Hollow charge	22.25 kg./ 1.13 m	320 km/ph / 500-2300 m
AT-2 (Swatter)	Surface-to surface and air-to-sur-face guided anti-tank missile	Radio—com-mand to line of sight	Solid	HE-armor piercing	26.6 kg/ 1.12 m	-- 600-2500 m
AT-3 (Sagger)	Surface-to-surface guided anti-tank missile	Wire-guided; command to line of sight	Solid	Hollow charge	11.3 kg/ 86 cm	-- 500-3000 m
Hamlet Cruise Missile	Surface-to-surface jet-powered cruise missile	Command	Turbojet motor	Nuclear or conventional	-- 7.0 m	Mach 0.8-0.9/ 200 km
SS-N-1 (Scrubber)	Shipborne surface-to-surface missile	Possibly infra-red homing	Solid boosters	HE	-- 7.6 m	Sub-sonic/ 185 km
SS-N-2 (Styx)	Shipborne surface-to-surface missile	Command and infra-red homing	Booster and intern-al motor	HE	-- --	Mach 0.9/ 40 km
SS-N-3 (Shaddock)	Shipborne surface-to-surface missile	Command and infra-red homing	--	Kiloton Nuclear	-- --	Mach 0.9 --

Designation	Type	Guidance	Propulsion			Speed/Range
SS-N-7	Submarine launched cruise missile	Autopilot command /w homing system	Solid	--	-- / --	-- / 45-55 km
SS-N-9 (Siren)	Shipborne surface-to-surface missile	Mid-course by cooperating aircraft /w autopilot and active radar homing	Solid	--	-- / --	Mach 1.4 / 275 km
SS-N-10	Shipborne surface-to-surface missile	Command /w infra-red homing	Solid	--	-- / --	Mach 1.+ / 55 km
SS-N-11	Shipborne surface-to-surface missile	--	Solid	--	-- / --	Mach 0.9+ / 30 miles
SA-N-1 (Goa)	Shipborne surface-to-air missile	--	Solid	--	5.9 m	-- / 15 km
SA-N-2 (Guideline)	Shipborne surface-to-air missile	--	Solid; liquid sustainer	--	-- / --	-- / --
SA-N-3 (Goblet)	Shipborne surface-to-air-missile					
SA-N-4	Shipborne surface-to-air missile					

TABLE 10 (Cont.)

SYSTEM	ROLE	GUIDANCE	PROPELLANT	WARHEAD	LAUNCH WEIGHT/ LENGTH	SPEED/ RANGE
SS-1 (Scud)	Surface-to-surface artillery missile	Inertial	Liquid	Nuclear	6300 kg/ 11.25 m	--/ 270 km
SS-12 (Scaleboard)	Surface-to-surface tactical missile	Inertial	Liquid	Nuclear	6800 kg+/ 11.25 m	--/ 800 km
SA-2 (Guideline)	Medium-range surface-to-air missile	Radio command	Solid booster /w/ liquid sustainer	HE	2300 kg/ 10.7 m	--/ 40-50 km
SA-3 (GOA)	Shipborne or land-based surface-to-air missile	Command /w/ homing	Solid		--/ 6.7 m	--/ 25-30 km
SA-4 (GANEF)	Land-mobile surface-to-air guided missile	Command /w/ radar homing	4 Solid Propellant Boosters; Ramjet sustainer		1800 kg/ 8.8 m	--/ 70 km
SA-6 (Gainful)	Surface-to-air guided missile	Ground command /w/ radar homing	Solid; integral rocket	HE	550 kg/ 6.2 m	--/ 60 km
SA-7 (GRAIL)	Man-portable anti-aircraft missile	Infra-red homing	Solid		15 kg/ 1.5 m	--/ 9-10 km
SA-8 (Gecko)	Surface-to-air missile air defense system	Command	--		--/ 3.2 m	Mach 2/ 16 km

	Description	Guidance	Propulsion	Warhead	Length	Range/Speed
SA-9 (Gaskin)	Short-range anti-aircraft missile					-- 16 km
AS-1 (Kennel)	Standoff air-to-surface weapon (Deployed on Tu16)	Radio command	Turbojet motor		8.44 m	Mach 0.9/ 90 km
AS-2 (Kipper)	Standoff air-to-surface missile (Deployed on Tu16)	Active terminal homing	Turbojet motor		10. m	-- 210 km
AS-3 (Kangaroo)	Standoff air-to-surface missile (Deployed on Tu-95)		Turbojet motor	possibly nuclear		-- several hundred km
AS-4 (Kitchen)	Air-to-surface cruise missile		Rocket motor liquid fuel	possibly nuclear	11.3 m	-- app. 500 km
AS-5 (Kelt)	Air-to-surface cruise missile		Rocket propulsion motor		8.59 m	-- app. 500 km
AS-6	Air-to-surface cruise missile (Deployed on Backfire)					-- high-altitude supersonic
AS-7 (Kerry)	New Missile Technology					
AS-8	New Missile Technology					

TABLE 10 (Cont.)

SYSTEM	ROLE	GUIDANCE	PROPELLANT	WARHEAD	LAUNCH WEIGHT/ LENGTH	SPEED/ RANGE
AA-1 (Alkali)	Air-to-air missile	Radar; passive homing	Solid		-- 188 cm	Mach 1.2/ 6-8 km
AA-2 (Atoll)	Air-to-air missile	Infra-red homing	Solid		-- 280 cm	
AA-3 (Anab)	Air-to-air missile	I-Radar version	Solid		-- 360 cm	
		II-Infra-red homing	Solid		-- 360 cm	
AA-5 (Ash)	Air-to-air missile	I-Radar	Solid		-- 330 cm	
		II-Infra-red homing	Solid		-- 330 cm	
AA-6 (Acrid)	Air-to-air missile	I-Radar	Solid	HE fragmentation	750 kg/ 6.29 m	Mach 2.2/ 40-50 km
		II-Infra-red homing	Solid		-- 5.8 m	-- 20 km
AA-7 (Apex)	Air-to-air missile	I-Radar	Solid		-- 4.3 m	-- 35 km
		II-Infra-red homing	Solid		300-350 kg/ shorter than radar version	-- 15 km
AA-8 (Aphid)	Air-to-air missile	I-Radar	Solid	HE	54 kg/ 2.1 m	-- 8 km +
		II-Infra-red homing	Solid		shorter than radar version	-- 8 km

TABLE 11

USSR STRATEGIC BOMBERS

SYSTEM	IN SERVICE	WING SPAN/ LENGTH	POWERPLANT	MAXIMUM SPEED AT ALTITUDE	RANGE/ WEIGHT	WEAPONS LOADING AND ARMAMENT
TU-95 (Bear) Heavy Bomber, Long Range	1956,	WS: 159 ft L: 155.10 ft	Four Kuznetsov NK-12MV Turbo-props, each rated at 14,795 lbs. thrust.	0.78 Mach	R: (Max. w/ 25,000 lbs payload) 6755 nm ; Wt.(Max T.O.) 340,000 lbs.	Normal-25000 lbs. Maximum-40000 lbs. Three pairs of 23 mm cannon in remotely-controlled dorsal and ventral barbettes, and manned tail gun turret.
Mya-4 (Bison A) Heavy Bomber, Long Range	1956	WS: 165.7½ ft L: 154.10 ft	Four Am-3D turbojets, each rated at 19,180 lbs. thrust	0.87 Mach	R: 5254 nm	Maximum-20000 lbs. Nuclear or conventional gravity bombs.
Backfire B Medium Bomber Intermediate Range	1974	WS: Fully swept-90 ft. Fully spread-113 ft. L: 139.4 ft	Two Kuznetsov NK-144 modified turbofans	2.0 Mach	R:(Unrefueled) 3500 nm Wt. GROSS T.O.- 286,000 lbs. EMPTY- 114,640 lbs.	Two As-6 air-to-ground missiles on wing stations or 15x500 kilogram bombs in the bomb bay (maximum 20000 lbs.) One 37 mm tail-mounted cannon

TABLE 12

USSR NUCLEAR-POWERED BALLISTIC MISSILE SUBMARINES

CLASS	IN SERVICE	DISPLACEMENT	LENGTH	MAIN PROPULSION MACHINERY	SPEED	MISSILE LAUNCHERS/ TYPE	TORPEDO TUBES/ SIZE/ LOCATION
Hotel II SSBN	1960	3700 tons/ surface; 4100 tons/ submerged	380 ft	Nuclear Reactor; steam turbine, 22500 shp.	20 knots submerged	3 tubes/ SS-N-5	6/21 inch/bow; 4/16/aft, (anti- submarine)
Yankee SSBN	1968	8000 tons/ surface; 9000 tons/ submerged	428 ft	Nuclear Reactor; steam turbines, 24000 shp.	25 knots	16 tubes/ SS-N-6	8/21 inch/?
Delta I/II SSBN's	I-1973 II-1976	8000+ tons/ surfaced/ 9000+ tons/ dived	450 ft for Delta I 500 ft for Delta II	Nuclear Reactors; steam turbines, 2 propellers; 24000 shp.	25 knots	12 tubes/ SS-N-8 in Delta I; 16 tubes/ SS-N-8 in Delta II	8/21 inch/?

TABLE 13

SOVIET/WARSAW PACT AIRCRAFT

AIRCRAFT SYSTEM	IN SERVICE	ROLE	POWERPLANT	SPEED/ RANGE	WEIGHT	WING SPAN/ LENGTH	ARMAMENT
Beriev M-12 (Mail)	1962	Ocean Reconnaissance/ Amphibious Support Aircraft	2-4190 hp Ivchenko AI-20D single-shaft turboprops	380 mph/ 2485 miles	66,140 lbs.	WS: 97.6 ft. L: 99.0 ft.	6600lb of sono buoys and AS bombs in internal weapons bay. 1-3 external hard points under each wing.
Ilyushin IL-28 (Beagle)	1950's	Bomber and Ground Attack Aircraft	2-5952 lb thrust Klimov Vk-1 single-shaft turbojets	559 mph/ 684 miles	46,297 lbs.	WS: 70.4 3/4 ft. L: 57.10 3/4 ft.	2-23mm NR-23 cannon fixed in nose and two NR-23 in powered tail turret. Internal bomb capacity, 2205 lbs.
Ilyushin IL-38 (May)	late 1950's early 1960's	Maritime Patrol and Anti-submarine aircraft	4-Ivchenko AI-20 Single-shaft turboprops, 5000 hp each	450 mph/ 4500 miles	180,000 lbs.	WS: 122.8½ ft. L: 129.10 ft.	Internal weapons bay; anti-submarine torpedos, bombs and mines.
Ilyushin IL-76 (Candid)	1973	Heavy Freight Transport	4-26,455 lb thrust Soloviev D-30KP two-shaft turbofans	560 mph/ 3100 miles	346,125 lbs.	WS: 165.8 ft. L: 152.10½ ft.	Rear turret
Kamov Ka-25 (Hormone)	1965	Ship-based ASW, search/ rescue and missile guidance helicopter	2-900hp Glushenkov GTD-3 free-turbine turboshafts	120 mph/ 400 miles	16,535 lbs.	WS:(Rotor Diameter) 51.8 ft. L:(Fuselage Length) 34 ft.	Internal weapons bay; One or two 400 mm AS torpedos, nuclear or conventional depth charges.

TABLE 13 (Cont.)

AIRCRAFT SYSTEM	IN SERVICE	ROLE	POWERPLANT	SPEED/ RANGE	WEIGHT	WING SPAN/ LENGTH	ARMAMENT
Mikoyan/ Gurevich MiG-15 (Fagot)	1948	Single-seat Fighter	1-5005 lb thrust RD-45F single shaft turbojet	668 mph/ 885 miles	12,566 lbs.	WS: 33.0 3/4 ft. L:36.3½ ft.	One-37 mm N-cannon with 40 rounds under right wing-2/23 mm NS cannon each with 80 rounds under left wing. Two under-wing hard-points for tanks and stores up to 1102 lbs.
Mikoyan/ Gurevich MiG-15 UTI (Midget)	1948	Dual-Control Trainer	1-5952 lb thrust VK-1 single shaft turbojet	630 mph/ 885 miles	11,905 lbs.	WS: 33.0 3/4 ft. L:32.11¼ ft.	One-23mm NS cannon with 80 rounds or 12.7 mm UBK-E with 150 rounds under left side. Additional under-wing options.
Aero L-29 Czech (Maya)	1963	Trainer	1-1960 lb thrust M-701 single-shaft turbojet	407 mph/ 397 miles	7804 lbs.	WS: 33.9 ft. L: 35.5½ ft.	2-7.62mm guns
Aero L-39 Czech (Albatros)	1973	Trainer	1-3792 lb thrust Walter Titan two-shaft turbofan	466 mph/ 565 miles (internal fuel)	10,141 lbs.	WS: 31.5 ft. L: 40.5 ft.	External load of tanks, bombs, rockets or 7.62 mm gun pods
Anotonov An-2 (Colt)	1948	STOL Aircraft	1-1000 hp WSK-Kalisz ASz-62IR	160 mph/ 560 miles	12,125 lbs.	WS: 59.8½ ft. L:41.9½ ft.	none

Aircraft	Year	Type	Engine	Performance	Weight	Dimensions	Armament
Anotonov An-12 (Cub)	1958	Transport	4-4000 hp Ivchenko AI-20K single-shaft turboprops	482 mph/ 2236 miles	121,475 lbs.	WS: 124.8 ft. L: 121.4½ ft.	Powered tail turret with 2-32mm NR-23 cannon
Anotonov An-22 (Cock)	1965	Heavy Transport	4-15000 hp Kuznetsov Nk-12MA single-shaft turboprops	422 mph (cruising)/ 3100 miles (/w/ max. fuel and payload)	176,350 lbs.	WS: 211.4 ft. L: 189.7 ft.	none
Anotonov An-26 (Curl)	1960's	Transport	2-AI-24T 2820 hp plus one RV-19-300 turbojet	267 mph/ 400 miles	24V-29, 320 lbs. 26-52, 911 lbs.	WS: 95.9½ ft. L: 24- 77.2½ ft. 26- 78.1 ft.	none
Anotonov An-24V (Coke)	early 1960's	Troop Transport	2-Ivchenko AI-24A single-shaft turboprops	267 mph (cruising)/ 341 miles	46,300 lbs.	WS: 95.9½ ft. L: 77.2½ ft.	none
Mikoyan/ Gurevich MiG-17 (Fresco)	1952	Single-seat Fighter	1-5952 lb. thrust Klimov UK-1 single-shaft turbojet (later version One-4732/7452 UK-1F /w/ afterburner.)	711 mph/ 913 miles	14,770 lbs.	WS: 31. ft. L: 36.3 ft.	1-37mm cannon and; 2-23mm NS-23 cannon; later versions: 3-23mm Nudelmann Rikter NR-23 cannon, one under right side of nose, two under left; four wing hardpoints for tanks, total or 1102 lb. of bombs, packs of 8-55mm air-to-air rockets or air-to-ground missiles.

TABLE 13 (Cont.)

AIRCRAFT SYSTEM	IN SERVICE	ROLE	POWERPLANT	SPEED/ RANGE	WEIGHT	WING SPAN/ LENGTH	ARMAMENT
Mikoyan/ Gurevich MiG-19 (Farmer)	1955	Single-seat fighter	2-6700 lb. thrust Mikulin AM-5 Single-shaft after-burning turbojets	920 mph/ ?	16-20,000 lbs.	WS: 29.6½ ft. L: 42.11½ ft.	See MiG 15, MiG 17.
Mikoyan/ Gurevich MiG-19SF	1956	Single-seat fighter	2-Klimov RD-9B after-burning turbojets, 7165 lb. thrust	920 mph/ 1,367 miles	19,180 lbs.	WS: 29.6½ ft. L: 42.11½ ft.	3-30mm NR-30 guns, one in each wing, one under right side of nose.
Mikoyan/ Gurevich MiG-21 (Fishbed)	1958	Single-seat fighter	1-Tumansky single-shaft turbojet with after-burner, 11-240 lb. thrust MiG-21MF-R-13-300 14,500 lb. thrust MiG-21 PFMA 1-R-11-G2S-300, 13668 lb. thrust	1285 mph/ 683 miles	18,740 lbs.	WS: 23.5½ ft. L: 46.11 ft.	2-30mm NR-30 cannons, fitted under fuselage. Left gun replaced to serve 2, K-13 'Atoll' missiles. PFMA multi-role version-4 pylons for 2-1100 lb. and 2-551 lb. bombs. Four S-24 missiles or tanks or K-13A missiles.
Mikoyan/ Gurevich MiG-23 (Flogger)	1971	Single-seat all-weather interceptor	1-Tumansky after-burning turbofan rated at 20,500 lb. thrust.	1520 mph/ combat radius 400 miles	33,000 lbs.	WS: 28.7 ft. L: 55.1½ ft.	One-23mm GSh-23 twin-barrel gun. Air-to-air missiles including two infra-red or radar-homing AA-7 or AA-8.

Name	Year	Type	Engine	Performance	Weight	Dimensions	Armament/Notes
Mikoyan/ Gurevich MiG-25 (Foxbat A)	1970	All-weather long-range interceptor	2-Tumansky R-266 after-burning turbojets 24,500 lb. thrust.	2100 mph/ high altitude combat radius without in-flight refueling, 700 miles	77,000 lbs.	WS: 46.0 ft. L: 73.2 ft.	Four wing pylons each carrying one AA-6 air-to-air missile.
Mikoyan/ Gurevich MiG-27 (Flogger)	early 1970's	Single-seat tactical aircraft	1-Tumansky after-burning turbofan 24,250 lb. thrust.	1055 mph/ 2000 miles combat radius, 600 miles.	see Mig 23	see Mig 23	One 23mm six-barrel Gatling gun. Seven external pylons carrying ordnance to include AS-7 guided missile and TNW to a total ordnance load of 4200 lbs.
Mil Mi-1 Poland (Hare)	1951	Utility helicopter	1-575 hp Ivchenko AI-26V seven cylinder radial	105 mph/ 360 miles	5,291 lbs.	Rotor diameter: 46.11 ft. L: 39.4 3/4 ft.	none
Mil Mi-2 Poland (Hoplite)	1961	Multi-role utility helicopter	2-WSK-Rzeszow GTD-350P turbo-shafts 431 hp. each	124 mph/ 105 miles	8,175 lbs.	Rotor diameter: 46.6 3/4 ft. L: 57.2 ft.	none
Mil Mi-4 (Hound)	1952	Transport and ASW helicopter	1-1700 hp Shevtsov ASh-82V 18 cylinder two-row radial.	cruising 99 mph/ 250 miles	17,200 lbs.	Rotor diameter: 68.11 ft. L: 55.1 ft.	None; for Army assault version: machine gun or cannon, optional pylons for rocket or gun pods. ASW radar.

TABLE 13. (Cont.)

AIRCRAFT SYSTEM	IN SERVICE	ROLE	POWERPLANT	SPEED/RANGE	WEIGHT	WING SPAN/LENGTH	ARMAMENT
Mil Mi-6 (Hook)	1959	Heavy transport helicopter	2-5500 hp Soloviev D-25V single-shaft free-turbine engines	186 mph/with full payload, 404 miles	93,700 lb.	(Rotor diameter): 114.10 ft. L: 136.11½ ft.	13.2 calibre gun
Mil Mi-8 (Hip, Haze)	mid-1960's	Utility helicopter for internal loads and externally mounted weapons; Haze; ASW.	2-1500 hp Isotov TV2-117A single-shaft free-turbine engines	161 mph/298 miles	26,455 lb.	(Rotor diameter): 69.10½ ft. L: 60.0 3/4 ft.	If fitted, external pylons for up to 8 pods of 57mm rockets or mix of gun pods and anti-tank missiles
Mil Mi-10 (Harke)	1962	Heavy-lift crane helicopter	2-5500 hp Soloviev D-25 V free-turbine engines	124 mph/with full load, 155 miles; without full load, 494 miles	96,340 lb.	(Rotor diameter): 114.10 ft. L: 137.5½ ft.	none
Mil Mi-12 (Homer)	late 1960's	Transport helicopter	4-6500 hp Soloviev D-25VF free-turbine engines mounted in 2 pairs	161 mph/with full load, 311 miles	231,000 lb.	(Rotor diameter): 114.10 ft. L: 130 ft.	none

| Mil Mi-24 (Hind) versions, A to D | early 1970's | Tactical multi-role helicopter D-version, gunship. | 2-1500 hp Isotov TV2-117A free-turbine turbo-shafts | 170 mph/ ? | 25,400 lbs. | Rotor diameter: 55.9 ft. L: 55.9 ft. | Hind A- 1-12.7mm nose gun; two stub wings for four guided anti-tank missiles and four additional stores. Hind D- 2 twin launchers for AT-2 'Swatter' anti-tank missiles; four UB-32 pods for 32- 57mm S-5 rockets. |
| Myasishchev M-4 (Bison A,B,C) | 1955 | (A) Heavy bomber (B) Strategic reconnaissance (C) Multi-role reconnaissance bomber | (A) 4-19,180 lb. Mikulin AM-3D single-shaft turbojets. (B) and (C) 4-28,660 lb. Soloviev D-15 two-shaft turbojets. | 560 mph/ 6835 miles with payload | (A) 352,740 lbs. (B) and (C) 375,000 lbs. | WS: (A) 165.7½ ft. L: (A) 154.10 ft. | (A) 10-23mm NR-23 cannons and 4 remotely controlled turrets (two guns in each turret) internal bomb bay for a minimum of 10,000 lb. weapon stores. (B) (C) 6-23mm cannons-internal bay for a minimum of 10,000 lb. stores. |

TABLE 13 (Cont.)

AIRCRAFT SYSTEM	IN SERVICE	ROLE	POWERPLANT	SPEED/ RANGE	WEIGHT	WING SPAN/ LENGTH	ARMAMENT
Sukhoi Su-7 (Fitter)	1959	Single-seat close support and inter- diction fighter	1-Lyulka AL- 7F turbojet 22,046 lb. thrust with maximum after- burner.	1055 mph/ 900 miles	30,000 lbs.	WS: 29.3½ ft. L: 57 ft.	2-30mm NR-30 cannon, each /w/ 70 rounds •4 wing pylons.
Sukhoi Su-9 (Fishpot B)	1959	Single-seat all-weather interceptor	1-Lyulka single- shaft turbojet with after- burner.	? ?	30,000 lbs.	WS: 27.8 ft. L: 54 ft.	4-AA-1 'Alkali' air-to-air missiles.
Sukhoi Su-11 (Fishpot C)	1967	Single-seat all-weather interceptor	1-AL-7 F-1, 22,046 lb. thrust	1190 mph/ 700 miles	30,000 lbs.	WS: 27.8 ft. L: 57 ft.	2-AA-3 'Anab' air-to-air missiles
Sukhoi Su-15 (Flagon) (Six ver- sions, A-F)	1967	All-weather interceptor	2-Lyulka AL-7F single-shaft turbojets, 22,046 lb. thrust	1520 mph/ combat radius, 450 miles •ferry range, 1400 miles	(D) 46,000 lbs.	WS: (A) 31.3 ft. (D) 36 ft. L: 70.6 ft.	2-underwing pylons carry one radar 'Anab' and one infra-red 'Anab' 2-fuselage pylons carry 23mm GSh-23 two barrel cannon between them.
Sukhoi Su-19 (Fencer)	early 1970's	Two-seat multi-role combat air- craft	2-Lyulka AL-21F3 24,500 lb. thrust after-burning turbofan engines	950 mph; at sea level, 1650 mph/ combat radius, 500 miles •ferry range 2500 miles	70,000 lbs.	WS: 56.3 ft. L: 69.10 ft.	1-23mm GSh-23 twin-barrel cannon 6 pylons on fuselage for stores including air-to-ground and air-to-air missiles.

Aircraft	Year	Type	Engine	Performance	Weight	Dimensions	Armament / Notes
Sukhoi Su-17 (Fitter)	1970	Single-seat attack and close support aircraft	1-Lyulka AL-21F-3 single-shaft turbojet, 17,200 lbs. thrust – 25,000 lb. max. afterburner	sea level, 798 mph; at optimum height, 1432 mph/combat radius, 391 miles	47,887 lbs.	WS: 45.11¼ ft. L: 61.6¾ ft.	2-30mm NR-30 cannon, each with 70 rounds. Eight pylons under fuselage and swing wings for maximum external load of 11,023 lbs.
Sukhoi Su-20 (Fitter)	1972–1973	Single-seat attack and close-support aircraft	1-AL-7F-1 22,046 lb. thrust	less than Su-17		WS: 45.11¼ ft. L: 61.6¾ ft.	See Su-17. This version includes six pylons.
Tupolev Tu-16 (Badger) Versions A to G	1954	Strategic bomber	2-Mikulin AM-3M single-shaft turbojets rated 20,950 lb. thrust	587 mph/3000 miles	150,000 lbs.	WS: 110 ft. L: 120 ft.	6-23mm NR-23 cannon in radar directed manned tail turret and remotely aimed upper dorsal and rear ventral barbettes. •internal weapons bay for 19,800 lb. weapons load.
Tupolev Tu-20 (Bear) Versions A to F	1956	Strategic bomber	4-14,795 hp. Kuznetsov Nk-12M single-shaft turbo-props	540 mph/with bomb load, 7800 miles	340,000 lbs.	WS: 159 ft. L: 155.10 ft.	6-23mm NS-23 cannons in radar directed manned tail turret and remote-aimed dorsal and ventral barbettes. •internal weapons bay for weapons load of 25,000 lb.

TABLE 13 (Cont.)

AIRCRAFT SYSTEM	IN SERVICE	ROLE	POWERPLANT	SPEED/ RANGE	WEIGHT	WING SPAN/ LENGTH	ARMAMENT
Tupolev Tu-22C (Blinder) Versions A to D C-Main Version	1963	Naval Air ECM/ESM surveillance, multi-sensor reconnaissance aircraft.	2-after-burning turbojets each with 27,000 lb. thrust	920 mph/ 1400 miles	185,200 lbs.	WS: 90.10½ ft. L: 132.11½ ft.	In versions other than Tu-22C, 1-23mm NS-23 cannon. Internal weapons bay for 20,000 lb. weapons load. C-version, limited weapons capability.
Tupolev Tu-26 (Backfire B)	1974	Reconnaissance bomber and missile platform	2-Kuznetsov Nk-144 after-burning turbofans, each with 48,500 lb. thrust	1520 mph/ combat radius (Internal fuel) 3570 miles	231,500 lbs.	WS: 113 ft. L: 132. ft.	Weapons bay for free fall bombs including the largest nuclear weapons. Can carry two AS-6 'Kingfish' missiles on external wing racks.
Tupolev Tu-28P (Fiddler)	1961	Long-range all-weather interceptor	2-large axial turbojets each with 27,000 lb. thrust	1150 mph/ 1800 miles (Internal Fuel)	100,000 lbs.	WS: 65 ft. L: 85 ft.	Carries infra-red homing and radar homing 'Ash' air-to-air guided missiles.
Tupolev Tu-126 (Moss)	mid-1960's	AWACS aircraft	4-Kuznetsov Nk-12MV (14,795 hp each) single-shaft turboprops	500 mph/ 6000 miles	375,000 lbs.	WS: 167.8 ft. L: 182.6 ft.	none
Yakovlev Yak-26 (Mangrove)	mid-1950's	Two-seat reconnaissance	2-Tumansky RD-9B with after-burner	686 mph/ 1675 miles	26,000 lbs.	WS: 38.6 ft. L: 62 ft.	1-30mm NR 30 cannon.

Yakovlev Yak-27P (Mangrove)	1957	Interceptor	2-Tumansky RD-9B with after-burner	686 mph/ 1000 miles	24,000 lbs.	WS: 38.6 ft. L: 55. ft.	cannons, rockets, two missile pylons
Yakovlev Yak? (Mandrake)	1957	Reconnaissance aircraft	2-RD-9 non-after-burning turbojets, 6000 lb. thrust each	735 mph/ 1200 - 1600 miles	30,000 lbs.	WS: 71.0 ft. L: 51 ft.	none
Yakovlev Yak-28 28P-Firebar 28R-Brewer 28U-Maestro	1962	(P) all-weather interceptor (R) multi-sensor reconnaissance (U) dual-control trainer	2-Tumansky RD-11 single-shaft after-burning turbojets, each 13,120 lb. thrust	735 mph/ 1200 - 1600 miles	(U) 30,000 lbs. all others, 35,000 to 41,000 lbs.	WS: 426 ft. L: 71.0½ ft. (P) 74 ft.	Attack aircraft 1-30mm NR-30 cannon •weapons bay for free-fall bombs, 4400 lb. maximum. •pylons between drop tanks (28U) weapons bay and gun (28P) 2 'Anab' air-to-air guided missiles. 2 ad-ditional pylons for 2-K-13A 'Atoll' missiles (28R) none
Yakovlev Yak-36 (Forger) A and B versions	1975	VTOL naval attack and reconnaissance aircraft. B version, trainer	1-lift-cruise turbo-jet/or fan 17,000 lb. thrust 2-lift jets, 5600 lb. thrust each	722 mph/ combat radius, internal fuel, 200 miles	22,050 lbs.	WS: 25 ft. L: (A) 49.3 ft. (B) 58 ft.	•4 pylons under non-folding wing carry gunpods, ECM payloads, bombs, missiles, tanks. B version, none.

TABLE 14

UNITED STATES
FOREIGN MILITARY SALES AGREEMENTS AND DELIVERIES
1950-1977

(Dollars in Thousands)

	Agreements	Deliveries
	FY 1950- FY 1977	FY 1950- FY 1977
Worldwide	71 021 983	31 841 274
East Asia & Pacific	6 191 170	2 987 203
Australia	1 942 437	1 061 636
Brunei	10	1
Burma	3 292	2 682
China (Taiwan)	1 221 652	689 177
Fiji	160	62
Indochina	8 542	8 542
Indonesia	62 376	35 921
Japan	536 198	398 584
Korea	1 620 292	424 338
Malaysia	65 093	53 318
New Zealand	134 603	116 538
Philippines	139 930	68 304
Singapore	164 179	36 949
Thailand	291 239	89 984
Vietnam	1 167	1 167
Near East & So Asia	42 364 264	15 034 865
Bahrain	117	15
Egypt	69 432	10 890
India	75 641	67 531
Iran	18 077 356	6 033 759
Iraq	13 152	13 152
Israel	6 419 594	4 297 036
Jordan	914 810	388 633
Kuwait	659 332	116 556
Lebanon	20 019	14 041
Libya	29 595	29 594
Morocco	481 160	86 091
Nepal	72	72
Oman	2 808	1 782
Pakistan	412 851	166 720
Saudi Arabia	14 993 500	3 774 494
Sri Lanka	4	4
Syria	1	1
Tunisia	51 374	7 246
United Arab Emirates	3 682	255
Yemen	139 764	26 993
Europe	18 824 846	11 115 579
Austria	110 755	92 379
Belgium	1 464 012	156 001
Denmark	760 960	160 760
Finland	353	13
France	382 888	353 613
Germany	6 278 416	5 547 840
Greece	1 320 614	790 182
Iceland	513	504
Ireland	586	523
Italy	770 854	663 659
Luxembourg	2 826	2 773
Netherlands	1 586 555	222 724
Norway	1 536 868	288 255
Portugal	19 795	12 500
Spain	861 296	461 960
Sweden	107 178	62 747
Switzerland	733 008	202 313
Turkey	573 321	265 062
United Kingdom	2 300 198	1 818 275
Yugoslavia	13 850	13 496

TABLE 14 (Cont.)

	Agreements	Deliveries
	FY 1950– FY 1977	FY 1950– FY 1977
Africa	414 484	140 586
Benin	*	0
Ethopia	171 681	89 266
Gabon	72 396	148
Ghana	394	251
Kenya	70 909	1 039
Liberia	3 541	3 384
Mali	154	154
Niger	8	8
Nigeria	21 857	11 632
Senegal	9	4
South Africa	3 149	3 149
Sudan	91 904	0[1]
Zaire	48 482	31 551
American Republics	2 625 238	2 158 077
Argentina	192 295	144 505
Bolivia	2 082	1 839
Brazil	277 717	226 247
Canada	1 373 667	1 192 180
Chile	195 017	155 390
Colombia	27 406	22 452
Costa Rica	1 180	1 169
Cuba	4 510	4 510
Dominican Republic	2 192	2 095
Ecuador	46 911	18 962
El Salvador	3 429	2 489
Guatemala	28 648	22 560
Haiti	1 237	658
Honduras	9 215	7 756
Jamaica	153	148
Mexico	19 495	18 559
Nicaragua	5 584	4 492
Panama	5 271	4 431
Paraguay	674	448
Peru	170 030	107 486
Surinam	1	0
Trinidad/Tobago	85	85
Uruguay	19 604	17 795
Venezuela	238 835	203 821
International Organizations	601 976	404 960

*Less than $500

1-Ordered Fiscal Year 1977

Source: Department of Defense, Security Assistance Agency. Foreign Military Sales and Military Assistance Facts. December, 1977.

TABLE 15

Status of Multilateral Arms Control Agreements as of February 1978

	Antarctic Treaty	Limited Test Ban Treaty	Outer Space Treaty	Treaty Prohibiting Nuclear Weapons in Latin America	Nuclear Nonprolif- eration Treaty	Seabeds Arms Control Treaty	Geneva Protocol	Biological Weapons Convention	Environmental Modification Convention
Agreement Opened for Signature	12/1/59	8/5/63	1/27/67	2/14/67	7/1/68	2/11/71	6/17/25	4/10/72	5/18/77
Agreement Entered Into Force	6/23/61	10/10/63	10/10/67	4/22/68	3/5/70	5/18/72	2/8/28	3/26/75	—
COUNTRY									
U.S.	P	P	P	P(1)	P	P	P	P	S
U.S.S.R.	P	P	P		P	P	P	P	S
U.K.	P	P	P	P(1)(2)	P	P	P	P	S
Afghanistan		P	S		P	P		P	S
Algeria		S							
Argentina	P	S	P	S		S	P	S	
Australia	P	P	P		P	P	P	P	
Austria		P	P		P	P	P	P	
The Bahamas		P	P	P	P		P		
Barbados		P	P		S		P	P	
Belgium	P	P	P		P	P	P	S	S
Benin		P			P	S		P	S
Bolivia		P	S	P	P	S		P	S
Botswana		P	S		P	P	P	S	
Brazil	P	P	P	S(3)		S	P	P	S
Bulgaria		P	P		P	P	P	P	S
Burma		P	P			S	P	S	
Burundi		S	S		P	S		S	
Cameroon		S	S		P	S			
Canada		P	P		P	P	P	P	S
Central African Republic		P	S		P	S	P	S	
Chad		P			P				
Chile	P	P	S	S(3)			P	S	
China (Republic of)		p	p		P	p	p	p	
China, People's Republic of				P(1)			P		
Colombia		S	S	P	S	S		S	
Costa Rica		P		P	P	S		P	
Cuba							P	S	S
Cyprus		P	P		P	P	P	P	S
Czechoslovakia	P	P	P		P	P	P	P	S
Denmark	P	P	P		P	P	P	P	S
Dominican Republic		P	P	P	P	P	P	P	
Ecuador		P	P	P	P		P	P	

P—Party
S—Signatory

(1) Additional Protocol II.
(2) Additional Protocol I.
(3) Also ratified subject to preconditions not yet met.

Status of Multilateral Arms Control Agreements as of February 1978 (Continued)

	Antarctic Treaty	Limited Test Ban Treaty	Outer Space Treaty	Treaty Prohibiting Nuclear Weapons in Latin America	Nuclear Nonprolif- eration Treaty	Seabeds Arms Control Treaty	Geneva Protocol	Biological Weapons Convention	Environmental Modification Convention
Agreement Opened for Signature	12/1/59	8/5/63	1/27/67	2/14/67	7/1/68	2/11/71	6/17/25	4/10/72	5/18/77
Agreement Entered Into Force	6/23/61	10/10/63	10/10/67	4/22/68	3/5/70	5/18/72	2/8/28	3/26/75	—
COUNTRY									
Egypt		P	P		S		P	S	
El Salvador		P	P	P	P		S	S	
Equatorial Guinea						S			
Ethiopia		S	S		P	P	P	P	S
Fiji		P	P		P		P	P	
Finland		P	P		P	P	P	P	S
France	P		P	P(1)			P		
Gabon		P			P			S	
Gambia		P	S		P	S	P	S	
German Democratic Republic	P	P	P		P	P	P	P	S
Germany, Federal Republic of		P	P		P	P	P	S	S
Ghana		P	S		P	P	P	P	
Greece		P	P		P	S	P	P	
Grenada				P	P		P		
Guatemala		P		P	P	S		P	
Guinea						S			
Guinea-Bissau						P			
Guyana			S				P	S	
Haiti		S	S	P	P			S	
Holy See			S		P		P		S
Honduras		P	S	P	P	S		S	
Hungary		P	P		P	P	P	P	S
Iceland		P	P		P	P	P	P	S
India		P	S			P	P	P	S
Indonesia		P	S		S		P	S	
Iran		P	S		P	P	P	P	S
Iraq		P	P		P	P	P	S	S
Ireland		P	P		P	P	P	P	S
Israel		P	P				P		
Italy		P	P		P	P	P	P	S
Ivory Coast		P			P	P	P	S	
Jamaica		S	P	P	P	S	P	P	
Japan	P	P	P		P	P	P	S	
Jordan		P	S		P	P	P		
Kenya		P			P		P		
Khmer Republic (Cambodia)					P	S		S	
Korea, Republic of		P	P		P	S		S	
Kuwait		P	P		S		P	P	
Laos		P	P		P	P	P	P	
Lebanon		P	P		P	S	P	P	S
Lesotho			S		P	P	P	S	
Liberia		P			P	S	P	S	S
Libya		P	P		P		P		
Luxembourg		P	S		P	S	P	P	S
Madagascar		P	P		P	S	P	S	

P—Party
S—Signatory

(1) Additional Protocol II.

TABLE 15 (Continued)

Status of Multilateral Arms Control Agreements as of February 1978

	Antarctic Treaty	Limited Test Ban Treaty	Outer Space Treaty	Treaty Prohibiting Nuclear Weapons in Latin America	Nuclear Nonproliferation Treaty	Seabeds Arms Control Treaty	Geneva Protocol	Biological Weapons Convention	Environmental Modification Convention
Agreement Opened for Signature	12/1/59	8/5/63	1/27/67	2/14/67	7/1/68	2/11/71	6/17/25	4/10/72	5/18/77
Agreement Entered Into Force	6/23/61	10/10/63	10/10/67	4/22/68	3/5/70	5/18/72	2/8/28	3/26/75	—
COUNTRY									
Malawi		P					P	S	
Malaysia		P	S		P	P	P	S	
Maldive Islands					P		P		
Mali		S	P		P	S		S	
Malta		P			P	P	P	P	
Mauritania		P							
Mauritius		P	P		P	P	P	P	
Mexico		P	P	P	P		P	P	
Monaco							P		
Mongolia		P	P		P	P	P	P	S
Morocco		P	P		P	P	P	S	S
Nepal		P	P		P	P	P	S	
Netherlands	P	P	P	P(2)	P	P	P	S	S
New Zealand	P	P	P		P	P	P	P	
Nicaragua		P	S	P	P	P	S	P	S
Niger		P	P			P	P	P	
Nigeria		P	P		P		P	P	
Norway	P	P	P		P	P	P	P	S
Pakistan		S	P				P	P	
Panama		P	S	P	P	P	P	P	
Papua New Guinea							P		
Paraguay		S		P	P	S	P	P	
Peru		P	S	P	P			S	
Philippines		P	S		P		P	P	
Poland	P	P	P		P	P	P	P	S
Portugal		S			P	P	P	P	S
Qatar						P	P	P	
Romania	P	P	P		P	P	P	S	S
Rwanda		P	S		P	P	P	P	
San Marino		P	P		P			P	
Saudi Arabia			P			P	P	P	
Senegal		P			P	S	P		
Seychelles						P			
Sierra Leone		P	P		P	S	P	P	
Singapore		P	P		P	P	P	P	
Somalia		S	S		P			S	
South Africa	P	P	P		P		P	P	
Spain		P	P				P	S	S
Sri Lanka (Ceylon)		P	S		S		P	S	S
Sudan		P			P	S			
Surinam				P	P		P		
Swaziland		P			P	P	P		
Sweden		P	P		P	P	P	P	
Switzerland		P	P		P	S	P	P	

P—Party
S—Signatory

(2) Additional Protocol I.

TABLE 15 (Continued)

Status of Multilateral Arms Control Agreements as of February 1978

	Antarctic Treaty	Limited Test Ban Treaty	Outer Space Treaty	Treaty Prohibiting Nuclear Weapons in Latin America	Nuclear Nonprolif- eration Treaty	Seabeds Arms Control Treaty	Geneva Protocol	Biological Weapons Convention	Environmental Modification Convention
Agreement Opened for Signature	12/1/59	8/5/63	1/27/67	2/14/67	7/1/68	2/11/71	6/17/25	4/10/72	5/18/77
Agreement Entered Into Force	6/23/61	10/10/63	10/10/67	4/22/68	3/5/70	5/18/72	2/8/28	3/26/75	—
COUNTRY									
Syrian Arab Republic		P	P		P		P	S	S
Tanzania		P					S	P	S
Thailand		P	P		P		P	P	
Togo		P	S		?	P	P	P	
Tonga		P	P		P		P		
Trinidad & Tobago		P	S	P	S		P		
Tunisia		P	P		P	P	P	P	
Turkey		P	P		S	P	P	P	S
Uganda	P						P		S
United Arab Emirates								S	S
Upper Volta	S	P			P		P		
Uruguay		P	P	P	P	S	S		
Venezuela		P	P	P	P		P	S	
Viet-Nam, Republic of	S	S			P	S		S	
Western Samoa	P				P				
Yemen (Aden)					S	S		S	S
Yemen (San'a)	S				S	S	P	S	
Yugoslavia		P	S		P	P	P	P	
Zaire		P	S		P			P	
Zambia		P	P			P	P		
Total (4)	19P	105P 16S	73P 34S	22P 3S	103P 9S	61P 34S	106P(5) 3S	70P 43S	(4) 45S

P—Party
S—Signatory
(4) Byelorussian S.S.R. and Ukrainian S.S.R., are excluded from totals.
(5) Latvia, Estonia, and Lithuania have also ratified.

Source: U.S. Arms Control and Disarmament Agency. Arms Control 1977. ACDA Publication 96, May 1978.

FIGURE 1

Total US and Soviet Defense Activities, 1966-1976

A Comparison of US Outlays and Estimated Dollar Costs
of the Soviet Activities if Duplicated in the US

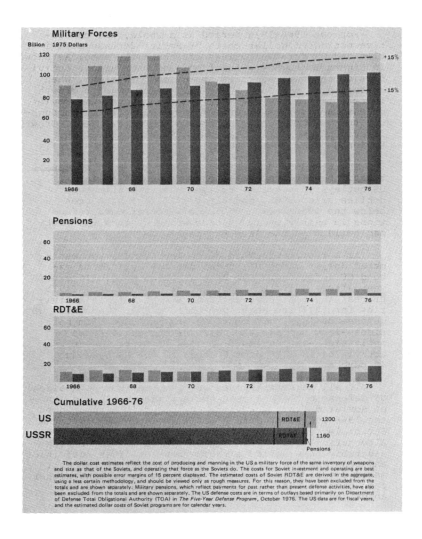

The dollar cost estimates reflect the cost of producing and manning in the US a military force of the same inventory of weapons and size as that of the Soviets, and operating that force as the Soviets do. The costs for Soviet investment and operating are best estimates, with possible error margins of 15 percent displayed. The estimated costs of Soviet RDT&E are derived in the aggregate, using a less certain methodology, and should be viewed only as rough measures. For this reason, they have been excluded from the totals and are shown separately. Military pensions, which reflect payments for past rather than present defense activities, have also been excluded from the totals and are shown separately. The US defense costs are in terms of outlays based primarily on Department of Defense Total Obligational Authority (TOA) in *The Five-Year Defense Program*, October 1976. The US data are for fiscal years, and the estimated dollar costs of Soviet programs are for calendar years.

Source: Central Intelligence Agency. *A Dollar Cost Comparison of Soviet and U.S. Defense Activities, 1966-1976.* Publication Number SR 77-100001U, January 1977.

FIGURE 2

US and Soviet Major Missions, 1966-1976
A Comparison of US Outlays and Estimated Dollar Costs
of the Soviet Activities if Duplicated in the US

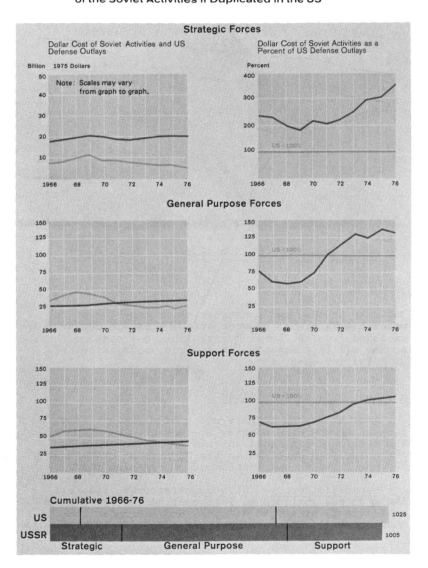

Source: Central Intelligence Agency. *A Dollar Cost Comparison of Soviet and U.S. Defense Activities, 1966-1976.* Publication Number SR 77-100001U, January 1977.

FIGURE 3

US and Soviet Forces for Strategic Offense, 1966-1976

A Comparison of US Outlays and Estimated Dollar Costs
of the Soviet Activities if Duplicated in the US.

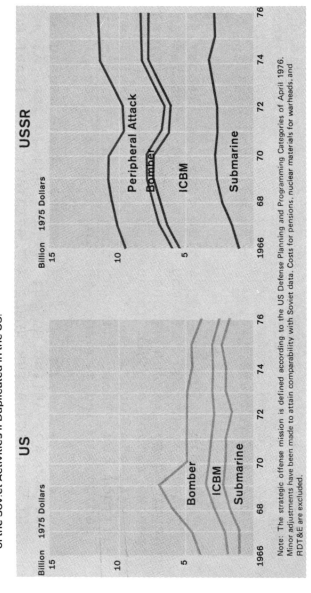

Note: The strategic offense mission is defined according to the US Defense Planning and Programming Categories of April 1976. Minor adjustments have been made to attain comparability with Soviet data. Costs for pensions, nuclear materials for warheads, and RDT&E are excluded.

Source: Central Intelligence Agency. *A Dollar Cost Comparison of Soviet and U.S. Defense Activities, 1966-1976.* Publication Number SR 77-100001U, January 1977.

FIGURE 4

US and Soviet Investment and Operating, 1966-1976
A Comparison of US Outlays and Estimated Dollar Costs of the Soviet Activities if Duplicated in the US

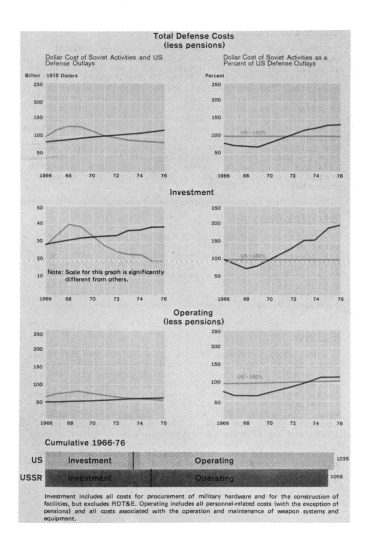

Investment includes all costs for procurement of military hardware and for the construction of facilities, but excludes RDT&E. Operating includes all personnel-related costs (with the exception of pensions) and all costs associated with the operation and maintenance of weapon systems and equipment.

Source: Central Intelligence Agency. *A Dollar Cost Comparison of Soviet and U.S. Defense Activities, 1966-1976.* Publication Number SR 77-10001U, January 1977.

FIGURE 5   Relative Burden of Military Expenditures

Military Expenditures as % of GNP	GNP Per Capita				
	Less than $200	$200–499	$500–999	$1000–3000	More than $3000
More than 10%		China (PRC) Egypt	Syria	Oman Iran Iraq	Israel Saudi Arabia Soviet Union Qatar
5–10%	Somalia Pakistan		Jordan Korea (ROK) Turkey Congo Peru	Bulgaria Singapore Poland Hungary South Africa Greece	Germany (GDR) Czechoslovakia United States United Kingdom
2–4.99%	Ethiopia Zaire Tanzania Mali India Chad Upper Volta Burma Burundi Bangladesh	Indonesia Mauritania Zambia Bolivia Mozambique Uganda Sudan Philippines Togo Thailand	So. Rhodesia Malaysia Morocco Argentina Ecuador Nicaragua	Romania Portugal Spain Bahrain Uruguay Cyprus	France Germany (FRG) Norway Australia Sweden Kuwait Belgium Italy Denmark Canada Switzerland
1–1.99%	Afghanistan Benin Rwanda Malawi Haiti	Madagascar Cent. Afr. Rep. Honduras Senegal Kenya Ghana El Salvador	Chile Guyana Tunisia Dom. Rep. Paraguay Guatemala Ivory Coast	Venezuela Ireland Brazil	New Zealand Finland Libya Luxembourg Austria
Less than 1%	Niger Nepal Sri Lanka Gambia	Sierra Leone Liberia Guinea-Bissau Nigeria Botswana	Columbia Jamaica Mauritius Costa Rica	Malta Mexico Panama Swaziland Barbados Trinidad & Tobago Surinam	Japan Iceland

Source: U.S. Arms Control and Disarmament Agency. Arms Control 1977. ACDA Publication 96, May 1978.

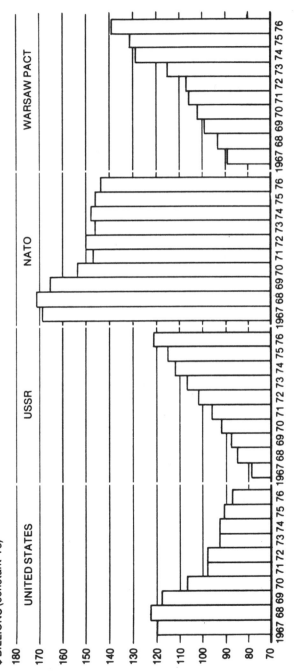

FIGURE 6   Military Expenditures—U.S., USSR, NATO
and Warsaw Pact

Source: U.S. Arms Control and Disarmament Agency. *Arms Control 1977.*

ACDA Publication 96, May 1978.

References

Primary Sources

NATO, Military Agency for Standardization (MAS), Defense Documentation Center, Defense Logistics Agency, *NATO Glossary of Military Terms and Definitions in English and French* [Short Title, AAP-6 (h)], 1 January 1969.

U.S., Air Force. *Dictionary of Basic Military Terms: A Soviet View*, 1976.

U.S., Arms Control and Disarmament Agency, *Arms Control and Disarmament Agreements—Texts and History of Negotiations*, 1977.

U.S., Arms Control and Disarmament Agency, *Verification: The Critical Element of Arms Control*, 1976.

U.S., Arms Control and Disarmament Agency, *World Military Expenditures and Arms Transfers, 1966-1975*, 1976.

U.S., Arms Control and Disarmament Agency, *Worldwide Effects of Nuclear Weapons . . . Some Perspectives*, 1975.

U.S., Atlantic Council Nuclear Fuels Policy Working Group, *Nuclear Power and Nuclear Weapons Proliferation*, Vol. I, 1978.

U.S., Atomic Energy Commission, Division of Technical Information, *Nuclear Terms: A Brief Glossary*, Understanding the Atom Series, 1967.

U.S., Central Intelligence Agency, *A Dollar Cost Comparison of Soviet and U.S. Defense Activities, 1966-1976*, 1977.

U.S., Congress, Budget Office, *Counterforce Issues for the U.S. Strategic Nuclear Forces*, Background Paper, January 1978.

U.S., Congress, Budget Office, *Assessing the NATO/Warsaw Pact Military Balance,* Budget Issue Paper for Fiscal Year 1979, December 1977.

U.S., Congress, Budget Office, *U.S. Strategic Nuclear Forces: Deterrence Policies and Procurement Issues,* Budget Issue Paper, April 1977.

U.S., Congress, Budget Office, *Planning U.S. General Purpose Forces: The Tactical Air Forces,* Budget Issue Paper, January 1977.

U.S., Congress, Budget Office, *Planning U.S. General Purpose Forces: The Theater Nuclear Forces,* Budget Issue Paper, January 1977.

U.S., Congress, Budget Office, *Planning U.S. General Purpose Forces: Overview,* Budget Issue Paper, January 1977.

U.S., Congress, Budget Office, *Planning U.S. General Purpose Forces: The Navy,* Budget Issue Paper, December 1976.

U.S., Congress, Budget Office, *U.S. Army Force Design: Alternatives for Fiscal Years 1977-1981,* Staff Working Paper, 16 July 1976.

U.S., Congress, Budget Office, *SALT and the U.S. Strategic Forces Budget,* Background Paper No. 8, 23 June 1976.

U.S., Congress, Budget Office, *Foreign Military Sales and U.S. Weapons Costs,* Staff Working Paper, 5 May 1976.

U.S., Congress, Budget Office, *U.S. Tactical Air Forces: Overview and Alternative Forces, Fiscal Years 1976-1981,* Staff Working Paper, 14 April 1976.

U.S., Congress, House Committee on Appropriations, *Department of Defense Appropriations for 1978*: 95th Cong. 1st Sess., 1978.

U.S., Department of Defense, Security Assistance Agency, *Foreign Military Sales and Military Assistance Facts,* December 1977.

U.S., Joint Chiefs of Staff, *Department of Defense Dictionary of Military and Associated Terms* (Short Title: JCS Publication 1), September 1974.

U.S., Library of Congress, Research Service, *Projected Strategic Offensive Weapons Inventories of the U.S. and USSR. An Unclassified Estimate,* 24 March 1977.

U.S., Library of Congress, Research Service, *U.S. Naval Expansion Program: An Analysis of the Cost of Expanding the Navy from 500 to 600 Ships*, 7 April 1976.

U.S., Library of Congress, Research Service, *United States/Soviet Military Balance: A Frame of Reference for Congress*, January 1976.

U.S., Library of Congress, Research Service, *U.S. Policy on the Use of Nuclear Weapons, 1945-1975*, 14 August 1975.

U.S., Library of Congress, Research Service, *Counterforce and Countervalue Options Compared: A Military Analysis Related to Nuclear Deterrence, 1972*, 1972.

U.S., Library of Congress, Research Service, *The Impact of SALT I on U.S. Nuclear Deterrence: A Military Assessment*, 1972.

U.S., Senate, Select Committee to Study Governmental Operations with Respect to Intelligence Activities, *Foreign and Military Intelligence*, no. 94-755, 94th Cong. 2d Sess., 1976.

Further Lexicographic and Conceptual References

Bode, John R. *Indices of Effectiveness in General Purpose Force Analysis*. Washington, D.C.: Braddock, Dunn and McDonald, Inc., 1974.

Douglass, Joseph Dean D., Jr. *The Soviet Theater Nuclear Offensive*. Washington, D.C.: Government Printing Office, 1976.

Federal Republic of Germany, Press and Information Office, *The Security of the FRG and the Development of the Federal Armed Forces*, White Paper 1975-1976, January 20, 1976.

Fischer, Robert Lucus. *Defending the Central Front: The Balance of Forces*. Adelphi Paper No. 127, London: International Institute for Strategic Studies, 1976.

Hoeber, Francis P. *Slow to Take Offense: Bombers, Cruise Missiles and Prudent Deterrence*. Washington, D.C.: Center for Strategic and International Studies, Georgetown University, 1977.

International Institute for Strategic Studies. *The Military Balance: 1977-1978*. Boulder, Colorado: Westview Press, 1977.

Lomov, N. A., trans. *Scientific-Technical Progress and the Revolution in Military Affairs, A Soviet View*. U.S. Air Force, Washington, D.C.: U.S. Government Printing Office, 1974.

Moore, John E., ed. *Jane's Fighting Ships, 1976-1977*. New York: McGraw-Hill, 1976.

Quanbeck, Alton H. and Wood, Archie L. *Modernizing the Strategic Bomber Force*. Washington, D.C.: The Brookings Institution, 1976.

Royal United Services Institute for Defense Studies, ed. *R.U.S.I. and Brassey's Defence Yearbook 1977-1978*. Boulder, Colorado: Westview Press, 1977.

Savkin, Y. Ye., trans. *The Basic Principles of Operational Art and Tactics. A Soviet View*. U.S. Air Force. Washington, D.C.: Government Printing Office, 1974.

Schlesinger, James R. *The Theater Nuclear Force Posture in Europe*. A Report to the Congress in Compliance with Public Law 93-365. Washington, D.C.: U.S. Government Printing Office, April 1, 1975.

Scott, Harriet Fast and Scott, William F. *The Armed Forces of the USSR*. Boulder, Colorado: Westview Press, 1978.

Sidorenko, A. A., trans. *The Offensive: A Soviet View*. U.S. Air Force. Washington, D.C.

Stockholm International Peace Research Institute. *Chemical Disarmament: New Weapons for Old*. Stockholm: SIPRI, 1974.

Stockholm International Peace Research Institute. *Incendiary Weapons*. Stockholm: SIPRI, 1975.

Stockholm International Peace Research Institute. *Tactical and Strategic Antisubmarine Warfare*. Stockholm: SIPRI, 1974.

Stockholm International Peace Research Institute. *World Armaments and Disarmament: SIPRI Yearbook 1977*. Cambridge: MIT Press, 1977.

Taylor, John W. R., ed. *Jane's All the World's Aircraft, 1976-1977*. New York: McGraw-Hill, 1977.

U.S. Army Command and General Staff College. *Conventional-Nuclear Operations*. Reference Book 100-30, Vol. 1, 6 August 1976.

U.S. Army Field Manual 100-5: Operations. Washington, D.C.: Department of the Army, 1976.

U.S., Central Intelligence Agency, *Handbook of Economic Statistics, 1977*. Research Aid Er-77-10537, September 1977.

U.S., Library of Congress, Research Service, *Some Perspectives on the NATO-Warsaw Pact Balance*, 76-83F, April 2, 1976.

U.S. Senate Committee on Foreign Relations. *Nuclear Weapons and Foreign Policy: Hearings,* Subcommittee on U.S. Security Agreements Abroad, Subcommittee on Arms Control, International Law, and Organization, 93rd Cong. 1st Sess., 2 December 1973.

U.S. Senate, Committee on Foreign Relations, *U.S. Security Issues in Europe: Burden Sharing and Offset, MBFR and Nuclear Weapons,* Staff Report for the Subcommittee on U.S. Security Agreements and Commitments Abroad, 93rd Cong. 1st Sess., 2 December 1973.

Wolfe, Thomas W. *Soviet Power and Europe (1945-1970).* Baltimore: Johns Hopkins Press, 1970.

WITHDRAWAL